Political Metaphor Analysis

ALSO AVAILABLE FROM BLOOMSBURY

Contagious Metaphor, Peta Mitchell
Contemporary Critical Discourse Studies,
edited by Christopher Hart and Piotr Cap
Language across Boundaries, edited by Anne Ife and Janet Cotterill
Metaphor and Intercultural Communication, edited by Andreas Musolff,
Fiona MacArthur and Giulio Pagani
Politeness in Historical and Contemporary Chinese, Yuling Pan and
Daniel Z. Kadar

Political Metaphor Analysis

Discourse and Scenarios

ANDREAS MUSOLFF

Bloomsbury Academic
An imprint of Bloomsbury Publishing Plc

B L O O M S B U R Y
LONDON · OXFORD · NEW YORK · NEW DELHI · SYDNEY

Bloomsbury Academic

An imprint of Bloomsbury Publishing Plc

50 Bedford Square
London
WC1B 3DP
UK

1385 Broadway
New York
NY 10018
USA

www.bloomsbury.com

BLOOMSBURY and the Diana logo are trademarks of Bloomsbury Publishing Plc

First published 2016

British Library Cataloguing-in-Publication Data
A catalogue record for this book is available from the British Library.

ISBN: HB: 978-1-4411-9817-4
PB: 978-1-4411-6066-9
ePDF: 978-1-4411-9700-9
ePub: 978-1-4411-0985-9

Library of Congress Cataloging-in-Publication Data
A catalog record for this book is available from the Library of Congress.

Cover image: Shutterstock

Typeset by Deanta Global Publishing Services, Chennai, India

Contents

Acknowledgements

This book owes its content and style to a decade of discussions with a multitude of colleagues and students at the Universities of East Anglia, Aston and Durham and other universities in Britain and abroad. Special thanks are due to Josephine Tudor who read the whole manuscript and provided detailed and invariably constructive criticism. Various chapters and parts had feedback from Jenny Arendholz, John Barnden, Birte Bös, Wolfram Bublitz, Rosario Caballero, Piotr Cap, Flavia Cavaliere, Jonathan Charteris-Black, Alan Cienki, Eliecer Crespo-Fernandez, Marta Degani, Alice Deignan, René Dirven, Lettie Dorst, Stanley Dubinsky, Gosia Fabiszak, Anita Fetzer, Luna Filipović, Alan Finlayson, Eugen Fischer, Charles Forceville, Dalia Gavriely-Nuri, Rainer Guldin, Chris Hart, Jack Hawkins, Albert Hijazo-Gascón, Sylvia Jakworska, Bertie Kaal, Zohar Kampf, Monika Kirner, Sonja Kleinke, Monika Kopytowska, Vassiliki Koutrakou, Zoltán Kövecses, Tina Krennmayr, Juyuan Li, David Lilley, Jeannette Littlemore, Graham Low, Zouheir Maalej, Fiona MacArthur, Stefan Manz, Mariana Neagu, Giulio Pagani, Klaus-Uwe Panther, Gill Philip, Stephen Pihlaja, Frank Polzenhagen, Fabio Poppi, Gabrina Pounds, Orsolya Putz, Günter Radden, Felicity Rash, Gudrun Reijnierse, Kim Ridealgh, Francisco Ruiz de Mendoza, Ljiljana Šarić, Christina Schäffner, Angela Schrott, Constanze Spieß, Harvey Starr, Gerard Steen, John Turnpenny, Andreja Vezovnik, Michael White, Alain Wolf, Ruth Wodak and Jörg Zinken. Without the patience and continuing support from the editors at Bloomsbury Publishers, the publication would not have been possible.

1

Introduction

During the 2012 presidential election campaign in the United States of America, rock musician T. Nugent tried to rally support for the Republican candidate at a National Rifle Association meeting in St. Louis by announcing a vigorous campaign against the incumbent President B. Obama: 'We need to ride into that battlefield and chop their heads off in November.' If, however, Obama was re-elected, he himself would be 'dead or in jail by this time next year' (Huffington Post 2012). The remark earned Nugent a meeting with two US Secret Service agents who came to establish that he had not meant to 'threaten anyone's life or advocate violence'. After the meeting, the Secret Service spokesman B. Leary declared that the issue had been 'resolved'; Nugent, on his part, defended his rhetoric by claiming that 'metaphors needn't be explained to educated people' (Huffington Post 2012). Events appear to have proved him right: three years later, in 2015, Obama is still president and Nugent still lives and is at liberty. So, might we conclude that all 'educated people' understood that he did not *really, literally* want to kill Obama, even if some, like the Secret Service, needed further clarification? Are metaphors really that easy to understand rightly, that is, as mere 'figurative talk' that has no bearing on reality?

Maybe Nugent was just lucky to meet not only educated but also reasonable Secret agents and well-behaved audiences. Historically, some notorious figurative political appeals have turned into literal reality. In spring 1967, for instance, members of the 'Kommune 1' in West Berlin, who were part of the student protest movement, agitated against the Vietnam War by distributing a pamphlet in which they asked, ironically, when the Berlin shopping malls 'would burn, to give their customers that sizzling Vietnam experience'.[1] Two 'Kommune 1' members, R. Langhans and F. Teufel, were less lucky than Nugent and were charged with incitement to arson. In their trial in March 1968, however, they were acquitted on account of the 'obvious' figurativeness of their proposal (Musolff 1996: 153). The acquittal turned out to be timely, for a month later, an even more radical group did in fact firebomb a shopping mall in Frankfurt, as a 'protest against the indifference with which people watch[ed] the genocide in Vietnam' (1996: 154). Had the pamphlet trial still been in process when this arson attack took place, its defendants might well have been convicted. The arsonists, two of whom went on to found the terrorist 'Red Army Faction', had read the pamphlet and had taken its figurative appeal literally. Legally, of course, they were responsible for their own actions (and duly sentenced later), and the pamphlet could not be proven to have *caused* those actions, but a degree of moral responsibility on the part of its authors can hardly be denied.

In another terrorist's message, the link between political metaphor and terrorist action is even more evident. In 2001, O. Bin Laden addressed his followers after the '9/11' mass murder of almost 3,000 people by his terrorist organization al-Qaeda: 'Here is America struck by God Almighty in one of its vital organs' (Bin Laden 2001).[2] Literally, it is not true that God himself had 'struck' the United States, nor is it true that the Twin Towers in New York and the Pentagon in Washington DC were 'organs' of a biological entity called *America*. Even if we assume that Bin Laden and his followers genuinely believed themselves to be acting on behalf of God and viewed America as a kind of monster organism, their depiction of mass murder as a kind of body blow in a boxing match cannot be viewed as a 'literal' statement. If we categorize it instead as 'figurative' or 'metaphorical', what do we imply about the relationship between such language use and its social and political consequences? What communicative function does metaphor fulfil in political discourse?

This book aims to formulate answers to these questions by using insights from Conceptual Metaphor Theory (CMT) and Critical Discourse Analysis (CDA) as its starting point. CMT was first outlined by G. Lakoff and M. Johnson in their 1980 book *Metaphors We Live By*. They proposed that metaphor is not just a merely ornamental feature that is typical of only a few specialized forms of speech; as a means of expressing beliefs, values and attitudes, it is also essential to human communication and is of high social, ethical and political significance. According to Lakoff and Johnson,

> Metaphors may create realities for us. ... A metaphor may thus be a guide for future action. Such actions will, of course, fit the metaphor. This will, in turn, reinforce the power of the metaphor to make experience coherent. In this sense metaphors can be self-fulfilling prophecies. (Lakoff and Johnson 1980/2003: 156)

Since the publication of *Metaphors We Live By*, there has been a boom of publications on metaphor and other non-literal uses of language. They have moved metaphor into the centre of theories of meaning (i.e. semantics and pragmatics) and of applied linguistics, which deals with the acquisition, use and impact of metaphor in all kinds of social contexts. Within the field of applied metaphor studies, a further secondary boom has occurred for analyses of the use of metaphor in public political discourse, which has generated hundreds of dedicated monographs and editions and over a thousand articles and book chapters over the past twenty-five years.[3] P. Twardzisz, a critic of this development,[4] has diagnosed 'the politicization of metaphor research' (Twardzisz 2013: 50) in the wake of CMT's rise and on account of its cooperation with *Critical Discourse Analysis* (CDA), a branch of applied linguistics that studies the relationship between language, ideology and power relationships.[5] In the words of one of CDA's founders, N. Fairclough, metaphors are of interest in CDA because 'different metaphors have different ideological attachments' (Fairclough 2001: 119). Metaphors are seen in this perspective as providing a direct access to conceptual, including ideological, structures, which CDA aims to uncover. By exposing and explaining them, CDA-inspired 'Critical Metaphor Analysis' (Charteris-Black 2004) aims to render political metaphors less dangerous for politicians, journalists and members of the public who use and 'receive' them without, it is assumed, realizing their ideological bias and manipulative effect.[6]

This scholarly occupation with metaphor as an object of criticism has its counterpart in popular discourse in the form of journalists' and politicians' complaints about the 'power' of the metaphor as used by political adversaries, for example, the use of war metaphors for sports (Culf 1996; Hamilton 2012) or non-military conflicts, for example, *war on drugs, war on poverty and business as war* (Jones 2013; Simons 2015), illness therapy and nature metaphors for social and political problems or confrontations (Bakewell 2013; Sontag 1978), or journey metaphors for contentious political processes (such as European integration and German unification).[7] The use of metaphors, similes or comparisons of topical mass killings/deaths with the Jewish Holocaust by the Nazis has achieved such notoriety that they are publicly and legally censured (Shachar 2014; Musolff 2015b).

However, as the introductory cases showed, the ideological bias of metaphors does not always determine their popular impact. Appeals to *ride into a battlefield and chop opponents' heads off, burn down warehouses* or *striking a blow against a state organ for God* are all potentially dangerous utterances but whether or not that potential is realized depends on their relationship to the social and political circumstances of their use. Their real consequences (or lack thereof) are visible only in hindsight and are dependent on the uptake by their audiences. For a metaphor to have far-reaching impact, the receiving audience need not just to understand it in terms of its figurative meaning structure and identify its target referent as intended by the speaker, but also to accept and believe it as a plausible and persuasive interpretation of their social reality. Any study of metaphor that is committed to, or at least interested in, a critical investigation of how metaphors can serve to convey ideologies and negotiate power relationships, therefore, needs to focus on their *multi*functionality in situations of actual use.

According to R. Jakobson's famous model of language functions, any proper analysis of speech events has to conceptualize them as fulfilling several purposes at the same time, that is, *referring* to aspects of the context, *expressing* the speaker's attitudes, *influencing* the hearer's actions, as well as exhibiting *poetic, reflexive* (metalingual) and *phatic* (basic social relationship-establishing) aspects (Jakobson 1960). The particular ordering and terminology of this model, which built upon earlier functionalist concepts of language and was superseded by more elaborate ones, such as, *inter alia*, D. Hymes's 'Ethnography of Speaking' (1968) and M. A. K. Halliday's 'Systemic-Functional linguistics' (1978), is today mainly of historical interest. But three of the functionalists' principal insights remain of importance for the study of meaning and, specifically, metaphor, that is, (a) that every communicative language use is *multifunctional*, (b) that it includes reflexive and meta-linguistic dimensions and (c) that the referential function is *not* necessarily the primary one.

Especially in politics, metaphors are not only used to denote specific target concepts; they always have pragmatic 'added value', for example, to express an evaluation of the topic, to make an emotional and persuasive appeal, and/ or to reassure the public that a perceived threat or problem fits into familiar experience patterns and can be dealt with by familiar problem-solving strategies. Metaphors in political discourse also lend themselves, as we shall see in more detail later (Chapter 4), to reflexive uses that allude to preceding figurative utterances and modify them. Reflexive and 'echoic' metaphor uses convey the speakers' interpretations of preceding utterances as well as their own (second-order) stance on the target topics, which recipients are invited to share. For this reflexivity to be recognized, however, we must assume some kind of discourse-historical awareness on the part of the recipients, that is, knowledge of the historicity of the metaphorical formulations they encounter. In the course of this book we will present evidence of such historical awareness being explicitly articulated and referred to. In methodological and theoretical terms, this dimension of metaphor use can perhaps best be handled by the 'discourse-historical approach' (DHA) pioneered by R. Wodak, which aims at an integration of linguistic, social and historical methods, so as to arrive at an in-depth 'triangulation' of language use in its full sociohistorical context (Wodak 2001b; Reisigl and Wodak 2009). While being closely related to the CDA approach in general (Wodak 2001a, 2007; Fairclough 1995, 2005), DHA's main emphasis lies on a context-driven analysis of intertextual and interactional meanings rather than on the discovery of 'ideologies' as biased collective knowledge structures.

It is this discourse-historical interest that informs the discussion of political metaphor in this book. It pursues a data-driven approach that starts from documented usage examples and focuses on interpreting their sociopolitical 'situatedness' and effects. Theoretical models will be introduced, discussed and assessed in relation to these interpretations and the challenges they pose, rather than from an abstract meta-theoretical perspective. The following chapters are ordered by four major political metaphors that have been much debated publicly, that is, the depiction of politics and political entities in terms of WAR, FAMILY, BODY and PERSON. In discussing these metaphors, we will also touch on general issues of how figurative language is conceptually organized and how it is actually interpreted by real-life users (rather than by introspectively 'intuiting' linguists or by informants in artificially concocted and controlled experiments). These issues will be considered not for their own sake, but for shedding light on political metaphor as an object of study for a critical linguistic enquiry that aims to understand real discourses as they are conducted, not as they should be according to a special theoretical or ideological framework. It is up to readers to judge whether that aim has been achieved and what, if any, practical applications they may wish to derive from it.

2

Political conflict as *war*

2.1 Metaphors and concepts

On 27 June 2014, the British daily newspaper the *Daily Telegraph* reported the outcome of negotiations about the presidency of the new European Union (EU) Commission, in which the conservative British prime minister David Cameron had in vain opposed the election of the former prime minister of Luxembourg, Jean-Claude Juncker. The newspaper's assessment was that

(1) Britain has moved a step closer to leaving the European Union after David Cameron declared 'war' on Brussels,

on the basis of an explicit quotation attributed to Cameron:

(2) This is going to be a long, tough fight. And frankly sometimes you have to be ready to lose a battle in order to win a war (*The Daily Telegraph*, 27 June 2014).

As Cameron's 'war' did not entail sending 'real' troops to the European continent, the terms *war, fight* and *battle* in this text can be viewed as instances of an exaggerating non-literal language use to characterize the diplomatic conflict between the British government and other national governments in the European Union. Specifically, they may be called 'metaphorical' because they make the readers think of the topic (peaceful if tough negotiations) on the basis of assumptions about a thematic field, which they know it does not belong to (i.e. war as a type of violent conflict in which typically large numbers of people die and get wounded, etc.). Metaphor thus brings together different areas of experience and knowledge so that a particular topic is cognitively and communicatively presented in terms of another topic. In addition, as we can see in example (2), metaphor can serve the speaker to develop a specific argumentative conclusion. By distinguishing between the (whole) *war* and a (single) *battle*, Cameron argues that his defeat in the choice of the commission president does not mean he has given up his attempts to effect major structural and political changes in the Union: those *battles* still have to be *fought* and may be *won*. Cameron here uses the strategic logic of real military confrontations, as invoked on earlier occasions by war leaders like General De Gaulle after the Fall of France in 1940 (Lukacs 1990: 147), to present his political position as not being as hopeless as it might seem.

These representations of a diplomatic conflict as war can serve us as an introductory example of one main type of metaphor that CMT as part of cognitive linguistics has focused on: that is, conventional 'structural' metaphors that are 'grounded in systematic correlations within our experience' and that 'allow us … to use one highly structured and clearly delineated concept to structure another' (Lakoff and Johnson 1980/2003: 61).[1] CMT views such uses as evidence of a 'mapping' between a 'source domain' of related concepts, that is, in our example, that of war, and the 'target domain' of the actual topic, that is, here, the conflict between the British and other EU member state governments over the EU Commission. Domains are understood as sets of non-expert, 'encyclopedic' knowledge and experiences that competent members of a discourse community have about any given topic. This knowledge is typically organized around some basic, 'prototypical' concepts at the centre and includes associated sets of less well-defined concepts at the periphery.[2]

The organization of encyclopedic knowledge in domains also underlies a further non-literal type of language use, that is, metonymy: the referential relationship between an expression and a target concept that it is conceptually closely related to but not congruent with. In example (1), for instance, the place name *Brussels* stands for the governing institution of the 'European Union', on account of the Union's Commission headquarters being based in the Belgian capital. In the classic CMT approach, metaphor and metonymy are differentiated by one main criterion, that is, the fact that in the latter, the mapping is within one domain, whereas metaphor always involves at least two different domains (Kövecses 2002: 146–9; Lakoff and Johnson 1980/2003: 33–40). The metonymy in (1) can thus be classified as a PLACE FOR INSTITUTION mapping (*Brussels* stands for seat of the EU Commission).[3]

The seemingly neat intra- v. inter-domain mapping distinction has been questioned and refined to allow for the inclusion of a variety of intermediate cases and also combinations. This research has shown that it is more plausible to assume a 'continuum' between metonymy and metaphor (Dirven 2003) and mutual 'interactive' motivation and combination, that is, deriving metaphor from metonymy and vice versa (Barcelona 2003; Panther and Radden 1999;

Radden 2003; Benczes et al. 2011) to the point of their merger (integrative or cumulative) in 'metaphtonymy' (Goossens 2003). Furthermore, the 'intrusion' of pragmatic and real-life knowledge into metonymy construction, which goes far beyond mere referential function and encompasses all functional aspects of communication, has been recognized more fully (Bierwiaczonek 2013; Littlemore 2015; Rice 2012). In sociopolitical contexts, for instance, it has been shown to be instrumental in discriminatory discourse, for example, by way of reducing human beings to their body parts. Even a seemingly innocuous PLACE FOR INSTITUTION metonymy such as *Brussels* for European Union betrays a subtle political bias in reducing the complex entity of EU Commission (and perhaps the whole of the European Union) to one city reference outside Britain, which in combination with the NEGOTIATION AS WAR metaphor suggests that once this target has been 'conquered', D. Cameron will have won his 'victory', without further regard to other political elements of the European Union. We will return to the role of metonymy in 'aiding and abetting' the political function of metaphor later in the book but for now only note that CMT claims to subsume both in its domain-based approach to concept building.

Lakoff and Johnson have claimed a distinct primacy of the *conceptual* aspect over the *linguistic* level for both metaphor and metonymy, but have emphasized it most strongly for metaphor, insisting that metaphor and its analysis concern not 'mere talk' or 'mere language' (Lakoff and Johnson 1980/2003: 4–5, 1999: 123, 2003: 244) but fundamental principles of thought and reasoning. This 'promotion' of metaphor to a central category of human cognition has attracted substantial criticism, especially for inflating metaphor's theoretical status and alleged pervasiveness in language which leads to categorizing almost all linguistic meaning as 'figurative', thus undermining the analytical usefulness of the literal/figurative distinction and ad hoc assumptions about cognitive architecture.[4] CMT's apparently dismissive view of 'mere' language seems indeed an odd stance to take, for even if interpreted as only highlighting the conceptual aspect of metaphor, it still betrays a methodological naivety inasmuch as the only empirically testable evidence for the conceptual structures that CMT can find are linguistic or other semiotic data (e.g. pictorial, gestural, symbolic signs) used in and for communication. CMT's hypotheses about conceptual metaphors, thus, have to rely on discourse data of some sort: dismissing discourse as secondary puts CMT's core evidence in question and, in the worst case, leads to a circular argument. If the linguistic (or other semiotic) data are seen as mere reflections of concepts but the latter are in fact only abstracted from the data, is there any independent evidence of the posited conceptual structures?

In response, Lakoff and some of his collaborators have attempted to reinforce their argument with reference to neurophysiological research that links the conceptual operation of cross-domain mapping (and thus metaphor) to unconscious simulation processes in the brain, to establish a 'neural' theory of metaphor.[5] Specifically, the discovery of 'mirror-neurons', first observed in monkeys' grasping actions, has been used to interpret the existence of neurophysiological circuits that are formed by repeated motor-sensory experiences as evidence for 'basic' mappings; the latter are viewed as the building blocks for all complex concept formation in human thought, communication and behaviour. While this theory construct is impressive in its breadth, ranging as it does from physiological to socio-psychological/cognitive and semantic hypotheses, its empirical underpinning is thin and highly contested.[6] Most importantly for our purposes, mirror neuron activity is so far removed from complex meaning construction, including figurative language use, in political discourse that it is irrelevant for its analysis and therefore will not be discussed in this book.

Instead we shall base our exploration of political metaphor analysis on the less grandiose but more plausible argument that Lakoff and Johnson had initially put forward, that is, that on account of their systematic relatedness 'we can use metaphorical linguistic expressions to study the nature of metaphorical concepts and … gain an understanding of the metaphorical nature of our activities' (Lakoff and Johnson 1980/2003: 7). This perspective, which makes no 'chicken-or-egg' assumptions about concepts and expressions, is sufficient to analyse examples such as (1) and (2) as uses of lexical and argumentative elements of the thematic field of concepts related to war. Lexical elements are words and phrases such as *battle, declare/lose/ win war*; the argumentative element in question consists of the commonplace conclusion that 'if a battle has been lost, it does not mean the whole war has been lost' (which is mapped by Cameron in (2) onto the EU negotiations). This lexical and inferential systematicity of conceptual metaphor seems to be a crucial insight that is worth exploring further.

2.2 Inferences from metaphors in relation to conceptual domains

Having rejected a neurophysiological underpinning for the systematic relationship between expressions and concepts, we need to clarify the assumptions underlying the general cognitive hypothesis before we can proceed further. We can take as our starting point Lakoff and Johnson's own discussion of war metaphor in *Metaphors we live by*, which preceded their 'neural turn' and is comparable to our initial examples, that is, a statement by the former US president J. Carter from the 1970s that the then hotly debated 'energy crisis' was 'the moral equivalent of war'. Lakoff and Johnson described what we called the 'argumentative function' as a 'network of entailments' that 'highlighted certain realities and hid others: ... there was an external, foreign, hostile enemy (pictured by cartoonists in Arab headdress); energy needed to be given top priorities; the populace would have to make sacrifices; if we didn't meet the threat, we would not survive' (1980/2003: 156).

While rightly highlighting the argumentative effect of metaphor, Lakoff and Johnson's use of the term 'entailment' for the implied inferences could be misleading if it were read as suggesting a particular type of logical implication, that is, that of descriptors in two propositions sharing essential meaning aspects so that one cannot be true if the other is false,[7] that is, a definition based on truth values of logically formed statements. Such a definition has little to do with Lakoff and Johnson's 'entailment network' concept, which is more akin to the 'prototype' theory of categorization (Lakoff 1987: 91–114; Taylor 1995: 40–75). To avoid such confusion, we will use here the more general term 'inference' to capture all types of argumentative conclusions drawn from metaphors.

The cognitive focus on mappings and inferences as essential features of metaphors has important ramifications for the rhetorical category of simile, that is, formulations of the type *X is like Y* (Aristotle 1991: 224–8; Black 1962: 35–7). Insofar as metaphors and similes both involve mappings and lead to argumentative conclusions, they are subsumed in CMT in one general category, metaphor. In both metaphors (*X is Y*) and similes (*X is like Y*), non-expert knowledge about a familiar area of experience, the source domain, is inferentially transferred onto a less familiar topic in a different domain. The primary evidence for the domain transferal is the 'clash' of terminology in a piece of text or discourse, that is, the contrast between the topical application (e.g. political negotiations, energy crisis) of particular terms, for example, *war, battle, strategy,* and the 'semantic' or 'lexical field' that they normally belong to, that is, VIOLENT CONFLICT (small capitals here and later on indicate conceptual status in distinction to linguistic expressions, which are either in italics when given as generic examples, or in quotation marks when relating to explicit quotations).

The semantic field is the lexical manifestation of a conceptual domain, but the latter transcends it because in addition to lexical information it also includes commonly held beliefs, folk theories and 'encyclopedic' knowledge about the source topic.[8] Its main function is not to accurately describe or categorize but to integrate the target topic into a set of familiar concepts and assumptions and structure it from a particular viewpoint (Fillmore 1975; Croft and Cruse 2004: 7–39). This integration, or 'framing' (see also below, 2.4) of a contentious issue in an utterance or a stretch of discourse through metaphor can narrow the range of assumptions that are usually associated with the topic, present a coherent interpretation and suggest a seemingly promising course of action, which thus 'confirms' the metaphor and makes it into a 'self-fulfilling prophecy' (Lakoff and Johnson 1980/2003: 156).

A relatively recent example of such a metaphor-based prophecy has been the US-led 'war-against-terror', which US president G. W. Bush announced in the aftermath of the 2001 '9/11' terrorist attack by al-Qaida and which has figured prominently in international debates about 'Islamicist' terrorism.[9] As quoted in the Introduction, al-Qaida's leader, bin Laden, had claimed that the attack was part of a 'holy war' against the United States, and Bush accepted this 'war declaration' by announcing the commitment of the United States to 'waging a war on terror' (Bush 2001). This 'war' did become military reality through invasions of two foreign nation states (Afghanistan and Iraq) that were suspected of supporting the terrorists, and subsequent military operations that lasted for more than a decade. One can hardly think of more real consequences of a metaphor frame being imposed on an event, which, alternatively (and at least equally legitimately) could have been framed as the act of a criminal terrorist gang or religious fanatics. The consequences of the metaphorical conceptualization of an issue in terms of war may not always be as momentous as in the case of the 'war on terror' but they are never negligible. The 1970s 'energy crisis-as-war' metaphor was no innocent reconceptualization either; it served specific political purposes by simplifying a complex and politically contentious topic into a 'campaign' that had to be won, and it gave preference to a perspective on the environment that prioritized the use of 'hard', non-renewable energy sources over 'soft' energy supply options (Lakoff and Johnson 1980/2003: 157, 242).

2.3 Conceptual domains and metaphor corpora

War-based metaphors are not restricted to the topics of energy crisis, diplomacy or terrorism; in fact, they can be shown to be represented across most fields of public political debate,[10] as well as in medical research and treatment and public health policy, for example, therapy as *warfare against illnesses* (e.g. *cancer, AIDS, Ebola, obesity*) and the *war against drugs*, in sports news, and in business-related discourse.[11] Some researchers have interpreted these predominantly English-sourced findings as proof of the ubiquity of war metaphors and, hence, of 'male militaristic values' in Western culture, whereas in non-Western cultures 'non-adversarial conflict resolution is quite normal' (Goatly 2007: 81; see also Rigney 2001: 63–80). However, the evidence provided for this latter contention is anecdotal at best, so the alleged 'typicality' of war metaphors in Western cultures cannot be regarded as having been empirically demonstrated.

Another problem with claims about the ubiquity of war metaphors is that even the evidence from English data quoted in the cognitive research literature seems sketchy when investigated in detail. Older CMT literature often relied mainly on idioms that could be assumed to be well established ('entrenched') in the lexicon of a language or discourse community. This is, for instance, the list of expressions that Lakoff and Johnson cite as evidence for the conceptual metaphor ARGUMENT IS WAR as being 'reflected in our everyday language':

Your arguments are *indefensible*.
He *attacked every weak point* in my argument.
His criticism were *right on target*.
I *demolished* his argument.
I've never *won* an argument with him.
You disagree? Okay, *shoot!*
If you use that *strategy*, he'll *wipe you out*.
He *shot down* all of my arguments. (Lakoff and Johnson 1980/2003: 4)

In the immediately following text, Lakoff and Johnson provide a few more examples in paraphrases that are similar to those in their comment on the ENERGY CRISIS AS WAR metaphor. However, most of these expressions, for example, *attack, strategy, win* have arguably more to do with fighting or conflict in general than specifically with war. Even *shoot* is not necessarily rooted in the WAR domain but can just as easily be associated with dueling. Only two expressions in the list, that is, *shoot down* and *wipe out*, would be most plausible in a typical war that is larger than a fight between individuals or small groups, but one, *demolish,* is only very loosely connected, as it belongs more plausibly to a conceptual domain such as CONSTRUCTION. Systematic demolitions, for example, of houses, bridges and fortresses, may be part of a war but so can a myriad of other things that we would not associate primarily with the WAR domain. Even if we allow for 'fuzzy' conceptual boundaries of the domains and for maximum variation in non-expert knowledge and experience, the choice of this particular set of expressions as evidence that 'the ARGUMENT IS WAR metaphor is one that we live by in this culture' (Lakoff and Johnson 1980/2003: 4) is quite arbitrary. We might, of course, go to a higher level of abstraction and reformulate the supposed metaphor ARGUMENT IS WAR as ARGUMENT IS FIGHTING. But who determines which level of abstraction is the right one? Logically, there is no reason to stop at any specific level of abstraction until we reach an extremely high level such as ADVERSARIAL ACTIVITY OF ANY KIND IS FIGHTING,[12] but at this degree of generality the posited conceptual metaphor turns into an almost tautological proposition that tells us very little about conceptual structures, let alone about culture-specific world views.

This issue raises further problems for the cognitive approach as a method to gain insights into conceptual structures. CMT's main claim of theoretical innovation was to reveal hitherto unnoticed systematic conceptual structures on the basis of observable data (mainly linguistic, but in multimodal analysis, also gestures, artefacts, etc.). If the data are 'found' by selecting a handful of dictionary items in order to fit more or less the preconceived conceptual structures, without checking for or even considering alternative descriptions, any 'discoveries' of domains and mappings become circular. There is, however, an obvious remedy to this problem nowadays, that is, to test any metaphorical cross-domain mappings against empirically documented, naturally occurring language use. Over the past decades, cognitive metaphor analysis has been adapted and hugely refined by incorporating corpus linguistic as well as socio- and psycholinguistic approaches (which will be referenced in the following chapters). Present-day studies of real-world metaphor use are unthinkable without researchers specifying the construction of their own corpora, their search procedures and, in quantitative analyses, their statistical methods.

We shall follow the same method here by relying in our discussion on two metaphor-specific research corpora, which have been compiled over the course of the last two decades, in addition to other researchers' corpus-based metaphor studies. The first of these metaphor corpora is EUROMETA, a bilingual sample of metaphors used in the press coverage of European politics, which was started in the 1990s as part of a collaborative project on British and German discourses about EU politics and has since been further augmented by data from two general computer-based corpora, that is, the 'Bank of English' at the University of Birmingham and 'COSMAS' at the Institute for German Language in Mannheim, as well as from internet searches, to yield an overall bilingual corpus of currently more than 494.000 words.[13] The second corpus consists of contemporary and historical data of the uses and interpretations of body-based metaphors in sociopolitical contexts (BODYPOL) sourced from public media and political treatises, across eight languages, that is, Dutch, English, French, German, Greek, Italian, Russian, Spanish and Swedish. This corpus is still under construction and so far includes texts amounting to 610.000 words.[14] Together, the two corpora include well over a million words but on account of heterogeneous sampling, they are unsuitable for statistical, 'corpus-driven' analysis.[15] Instead we shall use them for the main purpose of supplying us with a corpus-based evidence of real-world metaphor data: any findings regarding frequency and distribution patterns presented here can thus only be regarded as tentative (i.e. not statistically corroborated).

In the first place, these text samples had to be identified as containing metaphors. In this field, too, metaphor analysis has come a long way over the past decades, thanks to the work of two (overlapping) groups of researchers, one called PRAGGLEJAZ named after the first name initials of its members,[16] the other one headed by one of the PRAGGLEJAZ founders, G. Steen. They developed a four-, later, five-step 'Metaphor Identification Procedure' ('MIP', later 'MIP-VU') of finding, specifying and confirming the use of lexical units in other than their basic ('literal') senses within a given textual-pragmatic context. MIP(-VU)'s advantages over 'intuitive' identification methods are obvious: it provides an ordered set of questions and operations that can be applied to any text and leads from (a) an initial notice of a semantic incongruity through (b) successive hypotheses regarding plausible source and target domain assignations, (c) their connection in a proposition, (d) their comparison aspect and its underlying analogy to (e) the determination of the metaphorical mapping. It can and has been tested intersubjectively by separate researchers identifying metaphors in the same texts.[17]

2.4 Discursive frames in metaphor corpora

While the examples from the EUROMETA and BOPDYPOL corpora which we will shortly discuss in detail have not been elicited through the MIP(-VU) method, they are fully testable against it. For EUROMETA, the application of MIP-VU criteria shows that expressions from about 10–12 source domains, of which WAR-FIGHTing is one, are applied to three main target topics: EU-internal and -external diplomatic conflicts and negotiations, the creation of the single currency 'euro' and other shared policies, and British-vs.-EU disagreements.[18] How do we group expressions into one domain rather than in another (or into several domains) in a corpus while avoiding the 'arbitrariness' problem indicated above in the ARGUMENT IS WAR example? While the prototypical core vocabulary of a domain (e.g. *battle, war, shoot down*) is relatively uncontroversial, the more 'outlying' conceptual items can be categorized on the basis of their repeated co-occurrence, or 'collocation', in individual texts and in the whole sample. The following example shows, for instance, that it makes good sense to group WAR- and FIGHTING-related expressions together although the two domains are not absolutely identical:

(3) Last night's emerging *truce* between the European Commission and the big parties of the European Parliament is likely to open the Union's only directly-elected institution to fresh charges of crying wolf. ... The Euro-assembly has *marched its troops up the hill* several times to face the Commission and governments, only to shuffle away from *battle*. Its *onslaught* two years ago against the Commission over its handling of Britain's BSE crisis came to nothing. ... The *fight* over

the Commission has *battle-lines* that cut across the two main political blocs. ... Wilfried Martens [= the leader of the center-right 'European People's Party'], opposes the '*nuclear*' *option* of censure, which would oust the whole Commission. However, many of the German Christian Democrats ... are on the *warpath* against the Commission. ... The likely outcome will be a deal in which the two main blocs *hold their fire* in return for concessions. (*The Times,* 12 January 1999, italics here and in all further quoted examples by AM)

When analysing such a passage we find that it combines general fighting vocabulary with specific war lexemes that include traditional and even obsolete war terminology (*warpath*) on the one hand, twentieth- and twenty-first-century military jargon (*nuclear option*) on the other, and with proverbial phraseology (*march troops up the hill*, which alludes to the nursery rhyme about 'The Grand Old Duke of York' who 'had ten thousand men, He marched them up to the top of the hill, And he marched them down again', see Opie and Opie 1997: 442–3). This combination of lexemes and idioms forming a loose ensemble of interconnected concepts is expected by the authors to be understood without much difficulty by their readers and to give the text a distinctive figurative character.

Not all articles in the corpus go to such great length of painting a detailed picture of warfare between (EU)-political opponents: often, we find only one-off uses of a term that can be linked to the source domain of war in a headline or quotation, such as the following ones:

(4) From Google to Amazon: EU *goes to war* against power of US digital giants. (*The Observer,* 06 July 2014)

(5) Summit *battle* over EU budget. (*The Daily Telegraph,* 26 March 1999)

(6) The route into *Fortress* Europe. (*The Observer,* 25 June 2000; topic: immigration into the EU)

In these and similar cases, we are not dealing so much with either an argumentative use, as in example (2), or a colourful and entertaining depiction of a conflict, as in (3), as with a kind of shorthand reference to EU-related conflicts by way of exaggeration ('hyperbole'). In the genre of newspaper headlines, such hyperbolic rhetoric is quite routine[19]: it has the function of catching the readers' attention rather than invoking a whole conceptual frame. At most, the war-related headline expressions can be said to set up a potential war frame, which may or may not be elaborated further in the remainder of the respective article. 'Frame' in this sense is a discursively constituted configuration of culture-based conventionalized knowledge (Taylor 1995: 89), which becomes visible in the lexical and argumentative convergence of diverse expressions from the same semantic field.[20]

The strongest evidence of conceptual framing emerges from the corpus sample in the form of whole debates being shaped by a metaphor. Emphatic framing through war-related metaphors occurred, for instance, in the British discussion about EU politics in the summer of 1996, when a conflict arose between the United Kingdom government under Prime Minister John Major and the European Union over British beef exports (which were banned by the European Union due to public health risks from BSE-infected meat) and which coincided with a strengthening of its Eurosceptic wing of Major's Conservative Party. This crisis narrowed his room for compromise in the negotiations with the commission and, as a result, his government pursued a 'non-cooperation policy' against the EU Commission, which lasted until the Union's European Council summit meeting in Florence on 21–22 June 1996 (Major 2000: 648–58). It so happened that in addition to these political developments a European Football Championship tournament was held in England in late June triggered in the tabloid press the use of the Second World War-related puns regarding British–German relations, such as the *Daily Mirror's* title 'Achtung Surrender – For you, Fritz, ze Euro 96 is over', the *Sun's* headline 'Let's Blitz Fritz', and the *Daily Star's* 'Herr we go – bring on the Krauts' (Press Complaints Commission 1996; *Who ate all the goals?* 2012). While the tabloids' linkage of football and the Second World War-name calling were officially criticized as being xenophobic and 'poorly judged' (Culf 1996), the quality press's treatment of the political conflict 'Britain vs. EU' as a war escaped censure but was arguably even more intensive and influential. Across the political spectrum from the left to the right, newspapers commented on the conflict as if it were an escalating military operation, which in parts followed the narrative of historical wars in Europe (metaphorical lexis highlighted by italics):

Phase 1: War declaration

(7) Major *goes to war* with Europe. John Major provoked the biggest crisis in Anglo-European relationships since Britain joined the European Union in 1973 by declaring yesterday a policy of non-co-operation with her partners *in retaliation* at their refusal to lift the ban on British beef exports. (*The Guardian*, 22 May 1996).

(8) *Cry havoc and let slip the cows of war.* The vexations that Mr Major proposes to visit on Brussels are more than justified. … The risk is that as time drags by they will simply excite the hopes of the Tory Right that the Government will go further, and *reach for some*

nuclear button: withholding payments, leaving an empty chair, even threatening to withdraw from the Community. (*The Daily Telegraph*, 22 May 1996)

(9) *But will it be over by Christmas?* The tone of John Major's statement invoked echoes of an earlier declaration of hostilities with the Continent. One could hear the grave intonations of a silver-haired prime minister: '*I have to tell you now that no such undertaking has been received and that consequently this country is now at war with Germany.*' It was not, of course, quite so momentous. And yet … there was a catch in Mr Major's voice which suggested that a Rubicon had been crossed. (*The Daily Telegraph*, 22 May 1996)

Phase 2: Fight/battle

(10) *For beef, Major and St George.* Conservative supporters want the Prime Minister to disrupt European Union business and to *retaliate* against Germany, according to an NOP poll. … If John Major heeds their message he could be driven to escalate the '*beef war*', which would risk his Commons majority. (*The Independent*, 28 May 1996)

(11) Santer leads *assault* on Britain. Britain's relations with Brussels reached a low point last night after Jacques Santer, the European Commission president, condemned the Government …. (*The Daily Telegraph*, 30 May 1996)

(12) Europe gangs up on Major. Germany last night dramatically *raised the stakes in the beef war* when it unilaterally declared it would continue the ban on beef derivatives which the European Commission had agreed to lift after sustained pressure from the British government. (*The Guardian*, 1 June 1996)

Phase 3: Outcome/aftermath

(13) Beef deal is hours away, says Major. …To loud Labour cheers, Tony Blair [= leader of the Labour Party opposition] added: 'Mr Major is now so desperate to extricate himself from the mess that he will settle for anything. There is humiliation in this deal. There is ignominy in this deal. In fact, it is no deal at all – it is a *rout*.' (*The Daily Telegraph*, 21 June 1996)

(14) Who *blinked first?* (*The Sunday Times*, 23 June 1996)

(15) *How the beef war was lost* ... Word had reached [Roger] Freeman
[= the Minister handling the British beef cull] that the evening bulletins
... were running stories of a final British *capitulation* in Brussels. (*The
Observer*, 23 June 1996)

These examples are representative of most of the quality press's coverage of
EU–British relations during May to June 1996. Both the politicians' statements
and the journalists' paraphrases, summaries and comments contain general
fighting lexis as well as old and modern military terminology, but also
allusions to war-related Shakespearean phrases, for example, 'For ..., ... and
St. George' (from *Henry V*) and 'Cry havoc!, and let slip the dogs of War' (from
Julius Caesar), First-World-War-related slogans ('over by Christmas'), and
reminiscences to historic quotations, such as the Second World War prime
minister Neville Chamberlain's declaration of war ('the grave intonations of a
silver-haired prime minister').

The integration of such allusions into word plays and puns (e.g. 'cows
of war', in place of *dogs of War*) and in hedging statements ('It was not, of
course, quite so momentous. And yet ...') indicate that they were intended to
be read as tongue in cheek. Nevertheless, the high frequency and intensity
of war-related terminology, slogans, quotations and associated puns in the
coverage of one topic over six to eight weeks succeeded to establish the WAR
'frame' being so firmly in the public consciousness that the British-European
'beef war' became an object of historical comment in its own right.[21]

We may characterize it even more specifically as a *dynamic frame* or
'script' in the sense introduced by R. C. Schank and R. P. Abelson (1977:
36–68) with respect to a canonical sequence of default events. Major's 'beef-
war' became a narrative in which (from the British viewpoint) Britain had been
attacked by a hostile European coalition and was entitled to declare and enter
a war. All political parties, as well as all media across the whole (EU-)political
spectrum shared this WAR script, which favoured a 'clear-cut' outcome, that
is, victory or defeat, over any compromise deal (e.g. of the EU lifting the ban
in exchange for enhanced controls), even though this was the most likely and
also the actual outcome. In terms of the government's debate management,
it proved to be a major mistake insofar as its own initial acceptance of the WAR
script (see examples 7 and 8) furnished the opposition with ample material
of combative rhetoric to declare the outcome an unambiguous defeat, that
is, a *rout* or *capitulation*, due to Major *blinking*, that is, losing his nerve, *first*
(examples 13–15).

All in all, the English EUROMETA sample contains 152 texts with 127
distinct lexical or phrasal items that can be linked to a basic meaning of FIGHT
or ARMED CONFLICT but refer to non-violent political conflicts and can therefore,
in line with MIP-VU rules, be said to be metaphorical. The following tables give

an overview of all items: Table 2.1 focuses on generic fight/war vocabulary and Table 2.2 on allusive metaphorical usage that applies references to historical or literary war-related concepts and formulations.

The expressions listed in Table 2.2 indicate 'fuzzy' areas at the domain boundaries, where popular aspects of cultural and historical knowledge are

Table 2.1 War-Fighting metaphors in EUROMETA

Fighting – general	back down, blink (first), duel, fight (v.)/(n.), go in ('We're goin' in'), lose, march, move or perish, win
war: general	battle, battle lines, battleground, campaign, hostilities, skirmish, treason, war, warpath
war – offensive strategy	ambush, attack (+ counter-attack), assault, charge, escalate, foray, invasion, onslaught, offensive, outflank, retaliate/retaliation
war – defensive strategy	beleaguered, barricaded, defence, hold fire, last stand, retreat, stand (firm)
war – strategic outcome	capitulation, defeat, rout, surrender, truce, victory, white flag
war – fighting action	bombard, bomber, fire broadsides, shoot (down), shot, pound (v.), sink (v.t.)
war – destructive effect	casualties, cut to pieces, lie in flames, mown down
parties to war	allies, combatants, enemy, foe, patriot, warring party, warrior, mutineers
military topography	front, headquarters, ring of steel, terrain, territory
armed forces	army, battalion, expeditionary force, paras, troops
military ranks	Colonel, conscripts, general
weapon systems/war technology	chariot wheels, battlements, bulwark, drawbridge, fortress, missile, nuclear button/option, tank, torpedo (v.), weapon
war emotions	bravado, belligerent, gung-ho
war communication/ symbolism	Britannia, colours, raise standard, sabre rattling, throw down gauntlet

Table 2.2 Historical/Literary war allusions in EUROMETA

	Falkland War	WW2	WW1	Napoleonic wars	Other
General reference	Falklands, Falklandise				
military units/ strategies/ actions	task force	Blitz/Blitzkrieg, dambusters, Kamikaze mission, panzers, phoney war, loose talk, Cattle of Britain (punning allusion to the (1940) *Battle of Britain*)		Waterloo	crusade
enemy side		Third Reich, Hitler, Nazi, axis, Krauts, jackboots, Gauleiter, Fatherland	Hun	Napoleon	
war-related policies		appeasement, appeaser (for British opposition leader), collaborators, Quisling	entente cordiale, Brest-Litovsk		
war slogans			over by Christmas		by jingo
allusions to war-related quotations		... fight ... on the beaches, ... will ... never surrender, ... I have to tell you that no such undertaking has been received .... A Treaty too far	All quiet on ..... front		
Shakespearean allusions (*Henry V, Julius Caesar*)	'For ...., England and St. George', 'Cry havoc' ....., 'Cows of War' (pun on 'Dogs of War')				
Homeric allusions	Trojan Horse				
Nursery rhyme allusions	march .... up the hill				

associated more or less loosely with the core concepts of WAR and FIGHTING. Insofar as they are applied to a non-violent political conflict (the BSE-related negotiations about the EU ban on British beef) war allusions such as *We'll fight them on the beaches, British expeditionary force in Brussels, appeaser, taskforce* and puns (e.g. *cows of war, Cattle of Britain*) are as metaphoric as the more prototypical expressions *war, battle, rout* and *warpath*. Unlike the latter, however, the allusive metaphors situate the relevant referents at a second-order level of popular historical memory that functions as a specialized source script. The effect is a kind of 'double interpretation': readers need have a (vague) awareness of the *Battle of Britain* and famous war speeches as part of real historical wars (with a known outcome) in order to understand the allusions in *Cattle of Britain* or Churchillian phraseology before they can apply them – often with an ironic twist – to stages in the 'Beef War'.

In the case of more mythical wars, such as Homer's 'Trojan War' or Shakespeare's versions of the fifteenth-century 'Wars of the Roses', the popular knowledge frames accessed are most probably less precise but are still presumed to exist at a vague awareness level. The respective readers are of course not expected to have detailed knowledge of the plots of *Henry V, Julius Caesar* or the *Iliad* but only an approximate concept of the gist of a *Trojan Horse* concept or the rousing effect of the 'Cry God for Harry, England, and Saint George!' and 'Cry Havoc!' slogans in order to understand the figurative passages.

2.5 Summary

The outcome of our first foray into CMT and its application to FIGHTING/WAR metaphors shows that a corpus-based version of CMT can indeed help reveal systematicity in the use of metaphor. It shows that the theoretical assumption of conceptual source domains is borne out by documenting thematically related sets of lexical and phrasal items in a corpus, which form coherent collocation patterns. It also provides a basis for analysing the emergence of coherent frames through highly frequent and systematic usage that allow the public to interpret a target topic in terms of narratives, such as the 1996 'Beef War' script, which shape the political dynamic by entrenching a particular perspective and evaluation of it. In this sense, Lakoff and Johnson's statement that metaphors can become 'self-fulfilling prophecies', quoted in the Introduction,[22] is justified.

However, rather than overstretching the notion of 'framing' to include any use of lexical items, including the passing reference to belligerent-*sounding* background imagery (see examples 4–6), it seems to us more plausible to reserve it for texts and discourses that form thematically, lexically and argumentatively coherent ensembles at both literal and figurative levels. As examples (1)–(3) and (7)–(15) show, metaphorical frame-building emerges in the discursive process rather than 'underlying' it *a priori* but once started, it can develop a dynamic of its own.[23]

If metaphorical frames dominate whole discourse communities (ranging as they may from relatively small groupings to national and international public political cultures)[24], they can indeed assume the dimensions of a full-blown 'world view' and its manifestation in social reality. The most horrific and far-reaching case of a metaphor 'becoming reality' in this sense was perhaps the reconceptualization of Jewish people from a group defined by religion to a 'parasite race' in German Nazi discourse before and during the Holocaust (Bein 1965; Chilton 2005; Musolff 2010a). Building on the growth of racism in the nineteenth century, the JEWS AS PARASITE metaphor was further developed into a self-corroborating ideological framework by Hitler and other racist ideologues and became official state policy in Nazi Germany after 1933, which was proclaimed incessantly through all controlled media, education establishments and government statements to 'predict' the genocide of millions of European Jewish people and many more millions of alleged co-'parasites'.

However, in this historical case and in other instances of metaphor use in political discourses under authoritarian and totalitarian regimes, we have to bear in mind that the near-absolute dominance of specific frames in the public sphere of Nazi Germany was not owed so much to their persuasive or convincing structure or content but to the ability of the regime to control all utterances made in public and to denounce and penalize any deviation from the official 'party line' as an act of treason. Under such circumstances, it is no surprise that any discursive variation seems to have vanished from public discourse. Hence, the entrenchment of metaphors in such a discourse community has to be judged cautiously. On the other hand, it stands to reason that the metaphors in question must have already enjoyed a high degree of popularity and prominence in public usage, and of success in ideological competition, before the regime had established full control over the public domain, that is, that even if they were contested by opponents these metaphors sounded convincing enough to be believed by large parts of the community. We will return to the issue of historically mediated entrenchment again later (Chapters 5 and 6), but first we will explore further the relationship between the everyday 'background' usage of metaphor and its intensive application as a dominant frame in a discourse community so that it shapes active politics. In order to elucidate this relationship, we need to probe further into the category of 'conceptual domain', which lies at the centre of the CMT approach.

3

Metaphors, cognitive models and scenarios

3.1 Political metaphor and FAMILY models

If WAR-/DUEL-based metaphors provide an antagonistic perspective on sociopolitical relationships, what domain could be better suited to counter them than that of the FAMILY, which, we might assume, highlights relationships of love, harmony or at least solidarity among its members? A 'prototypical' FAMILY concept, we might assume, is centred on 'good' exemplars of family life that are connected to culture-specific, folk-theoretical beliefs; in Western cultural traditions for instance, these are expressed in traditional sayings, such as the Biblical Commandment to 'Honour your Father and your mother' (Exod. 20.12), the praise of marriage in Proverbs (18:22), 'He who finds a wife finds a good thing and obtains favour from the LORD', and the parable of the 'Prodigal Son' in the New Testament (Lk. 15.11-32).[1]

Being a member of a family, and being acknowledged as such, is usually considered a good thing. This view is also reflected in the use of FAMILY metaphors in British public debates about European politics. When ten Eastern European countries joined the European Union in spring 2004, British media across the political spectrum hailed their accession as the long-overdue return into the European *family of nations*. The conservative *Daily Telegraph*, for instance, greeted them with the headline 'Welcome back to the free family of Europe' and the left/liberal-leaning *Guardian* praised the enlargement for remedying historical discrimination of central and Eastern European countries as Western Europe's 'poor relatives' (*The Daily Telegraph*, 1 May 2004; *The Guardian*, 29 April 2004). This positive bias of the family concept is confirmed by the fact that the option of leaving the European Union, which has recently become highly topical in Britain, is discussed by its proponents in terms of metaphors such as those of a *withdrawal* or *retreat* from an elitist or dysfunctional *club* and of *fighting its corner*, but not as *leaving the European family*.[2]

The family-based metaphors used to depict the European Union might, however, be seen as an exceptional case, because they concern inter-state relationships. In a more traditional sense, the political family metaphor pertains, as Lakoff (1996: 155) has highlighted, to the relationship of the nation and its citizens: it 'allows us to reason about the nation on the basis of what we know about the family ... just as a parent functions to protect his or her children, so the government functions to protect the citizens'. Lakoff proceeds to analyse the divide between conservative and liberal ideologies in the United States as that of two versions of the NATION AS FAMILY metaphor, that is, the 'Strict Father' and the 'Nurturant Parent' family models, which are 'culturally elaborated variants of traditional male and female models', rooted in long cultural experience' and each 'induc[ing] a set of moral priorities', which in turn are further structured metaphorically, for example, as an ACCOUNTING operation (1996: 43, 44–64, 155). The 'Strict Father' model is based on the notion of a 'traditional nuclear family', with the father having primary authority to set and enforce strict rules for the children's behaviour, whereas in the 'Nurturant Parent' family model, love, empathy and nurturance are primary, and children become responsible, self-disciplined and 'self-reliant through being cared for, respected, and caring for others, both in their family and in their community' (1996: 33–34). These ideologies are not thought of as deriving from the metaphor; instead, the latter only 'projects' them onto the sphere of politics and sanctions the formulation and decision-taking of political parties and institutions (1996: 154). In a series of publications, Lakoff has used this theory of two FAMILY models to explain US government initiatives of the last twenty-five years, from health care and gun law policies through the post-Cold War reordering of world politics to the recent US-led wars in the Middle East (Lakoff 1992, 1996, 2001, 2003, 2004a, b, 2006, 2013). In this chapter we will first explore Lakoff's hypotheses and their underlying theoretical assumptions critically and then attempt to develop an approach that modifies some of them so as to account for corpus-based evidence of real-life uses of FAMILY-based metaphors in politics.

3.2 Two metaphor models – one domain?

As the various aspects of the FAMILY source domain are assumed to be differentially used in manifold applications, the prototype notion of FAMILY that informs them needs to be highly idealized, in the sense of an 'idealized cognitive model' (ICM), that is, not a summary of all empirical manifestations of families but a relationship between prototypical core notion and its main aspects which forms a 'complex structured whole' (Lakoff 1987: 68) that leaves peripheral details only vaguely defined, thus allowing for all kinds of non-typical FAMILY constellations. The two principal FAMILY models are 'built into our unconscious conceptual systems', as Lakoff emphasizes time and again (Lakoff 1996: 28, 37, 38, 154, 155).

This 'unconsciousness' claim has a practical significance that goes beyond CMT's 'neural theory' version, which we mentioned in the preceding chapter. In his 1996, 2004 and 2006 books on *Moral Politics, Don't Think of an Elephant: Know your values and frame the debate,* and *Thinking Points,* Lakoff alleges that conservatives in the United States have developed 'an elaborate language of their moral politics' from the STRICT FATHER model, which gives coherence to their views on issues as diverse as social programmes and taxes, crime, death penalty, environment and abortion. Liberals on the other hand lack a similarly powerful conceptual framework according to Lakoff because they 'assume that metaphors are just matters of words and rhetoric', which puts them at a disadvantage in any public discourse' (1996: 386–7).

Lakoff openly advertises his application of CMT to the family metaphor in politics as a therapeutic, enlightening engagement for the liberal side in US politics to redress the alleged disadvantage in party-political struggles that exposes conceptual structures, which the users themselves may not be aware of. This utilization of his metaphor theory to support specific political causes and Lakoff's concomitant self-positioning as a metalinguistic counsellor, ready to expose a hidden, unconscious conceptual framework which can only be revealed by his theory, has generated both enthusiastic approval and sceptical accusations of taking a patronizing view of the public as being in need of 'therapy' and of 'politicizing' linguistics.[3] In Lakoff's defence, it could be argued that the 'politicization' accusation seems superficial, given that his cited books are about politics and political discourse. Furthermore, Lakoff himself highlights the dividing line between conceptual analysis and political-ideological criticism in his books (1996: 23, 335–7; 2004: xv), which is only to be commended as an instance of explicit reflection on his commitments as researcher and political activist. However, the 'therapeutic' stance taken up by Lakoff and some representatives of CMT/CMA still seems patronizing towards the ordinary language users and it also raises issues that have a direct bearing on CMT's foundations, because it seems contradictory that ideologies that are supposedly based on 'unconscious', conceptual metaphors (e.g. the NATION AS FAMILY metaphor) can be known and used by one side (conservatives) better than by the other (liberals), so that the latter are in need of remedial therapy by 'Critical' Cognitive Linguists. Such a therapy might perhaps enable them to reflect on the metaphoricity of their language use, but what has that got to do with its political impact? If conceptual metaphor is so deeply 'entrenched' that its users are unaware of its existence, how was it acquired? And lastly, what empirical *linguistic* evidence is there for a *politically* based distinction of 'liberal' and 'conservative' FAMILY ICMs?

These questions point to a lack of clarification of the relationship between the moral 'models' (Strict Father vs. Nurturant Parent versions) vis-à-vis the NATION AS FAMILY metaphor. According to Lakoff's theory they are two versions/models of one and the same underlying metaphor, and by implication, its source domain. But how can one and the same source domain be the basis for contradictory target inferences? In defence of Lakoff's interpretation it could be argued that the inferences for the prominent domain elements (e.g. FATHER, MOTHER, CHILD) are mutually exclusive across the STRICT FATHER and NURTURANT PARENT versions and that every recipient automatically selects the fitting version (and deselects all non-fitting ones) depending on the respective target topic. However, such an interpretation would in fact presuppose the existence of two 'parallel' source domain versions in addition to the moral models 'derived' from them. This construction would contradict the one-domain analysis and would be psychologically implausible.

Furthermore, the empirical linguistic evidence Lakoff presents for his two-model theory in *Moral Politics* is very small. It is almost completely listed in one paragraph that refers to idioms, sayings and a couple of historically prominent arguments:

> We talk about our founding *fathers*. George Washington was called 'the father of his country', partly because he was the metaphorical 'progenitor' who brought it into being and partly because he was seen as the ultimate legitimate head of state, which according to this metaphor is the head of the family, the father. The U.S. government has long been referred to as '*Uncle* Sam'. George Orwell's nightmare head of state in 1984 was called 'Big *Brother*'. ... When our country goes to war, it sends its *sons* (and now its *daughters*) into battle. A *patriot* (from the Latin *pater*, 'father') loves his *fatherland*. We ask God in song to 'crown thy good (i.e., the good of the nation) with brotherhood'. The metaphor even comes up in legislative argument. Senator Robert Dole, in arguing for the balanced-budget amendment, chided liberals as thinking that 'Washington knows best', a slogan based on the cliché 'Father knows best', which has also been the title of a popular TV show. (Lakoff 1996: 153–4)

This 'evidence' of about a dozen examples (which has since been amplified in later publications to about 40, see Lakoff 2002, 2004a: 38–41) is underspecifying the political applications that it is supposed to demonstrate, even if we take Lakoff's dismissive attitude to 'mere' discourse data into consideration. What is conspicuous is the almost complete absence of expressions that are typical for the NURTURANT PARENT version: it figures more as a desideratum in Lakoff's political value system than in the data. A number of attempts have been made to verify or at least exemplify the family metaphor's ubiquity in studies of US parliamentary debates, presidential speeches as well as elections and actual policies (Ahrens 2011; Ahrens and Lee 2009; Cienki 2004, 2005, 2008; Degani 2015; Goatly 2007: 386–8). They confirm the occurrence of the NATION AS FAMILY metaphor, especially in the STRICT FATHER version, in documented corpora, but the significance of this evidence for a cognitive theory of political discourse is still under debate.

One problem in applying the two-models account of the NATION AS FAMILY metaphor to contemporary data is the uneven balance in the frequency of and internal cohesion of the two competing models, which, as mentioned before, Lakoff attributes to an allegedly better organized conservative policy of framing all political issues according to their values through the 'STRICT FATHER' model (Lakoff 2004: 3–32). For Lakoff, even the discourse of 'liberal' (by US standards) leaders such as the Democrat presidents Clinton and Obama seems to be either a smokescreen 'to mollify people who have Nurturant values, while the real policies are strict father policies' (in Clinton's case) or an application of STRICT FATHER punishment strategies against the 'bad children' in the WORLD COMMUNITY AS FAMILY, which Obama used in his war rhetoric against Syria, even though 'his instincts are liberal' (Lakoff 2004: 21; 2013). One might suspect that *any* official speech by national or international leaders, would qualify as being STRICT FATHER oriented for Lakoff, on account of its speaker assuming executive authority. This politically motivated ascription of the STRICT FATHER model to all presidents, however, makes the model distinction useless for analytical purposes.

From a diachronic perspective, it should come as no surprise that current political discourses are strongly slanted in favour of the STRICT FATHER version, given the male-oriented gender bias of the NATION AS FAMILY metaphor in its millennia-long history. The Latin etymology of Lakoff's own examples, that is, English *patriot, patriotism, fatherland,* which can be replicated for many other European languages, shows that the Western tradition of this model goes back at least to Roman Antiquity where the *paterfamilias* was almost the 'owner' of the whole family (Johnson 2007; McDonnell 2006). The STRICT FATHER model has an historical advantage of at least two thousand years of development and refinement, so it is little wonder that it still shows a higher degree of coherence and is more frequently used than the NURTURANT PARENT model. Viewed in this light, hypothesizing about liberals' naivety or inability to construe their FAMILY metaphors efficiently in political debates seems highly speculative.

Ultimately, the problems of finding evidence for Lakoff's hypothesized STRICT FATHER vs. NURTURANT PARENT split in the NATION AS FAMILY (or WORLD COMMUNITY AS FAMILY) metaphor go back to his definition of the 'domain' category. Lakoff understands the NATION AS FAMILY metaphor as a conceptual domain based on a universal ICM, which forces him to also assume such universality for the two competing sub-'models', which then have to be laboriously linked to supposedly independently given moral value/ideology systems.[4]

Instead, the evidence of a bias in favour of a STRICT FATHER authority-centred family in Western discourses can much more easily be explained as reflecting culture-specific sociohistorical developments. *Cognitively*, the NURTURANT PARENT alternative is and has always been available; however, in terms of political influence, the STRICT FATHER model has been dominant until relatively recently. Even its present-day critics have to contend with the fact that their views conflict with a formidable, age-old opposition. Therefore, instead of clinging to the universalist 'one domain-two models' set-up, we can redefine the source aspect of the NATION AS FAMILY metaphor as a *discourse*-based conceptual structure that incorporates evaluative bias elements, which make it useful for argumentative exploitation. This discourse-based, culturally and historically mediated version of a source domain is what has been referred to as a 'metaphor scenario'.[5] It is closely related to the theory of semantic 'frames' (Fillmore 1975; Taylor 1995: 87–90) as 'schematic' conceptual ensembles that include a selection of domain elements and an action 'script', which help the receiver to integrate new linguistic or other semiotic input into a context that makes it meaningful. 'Scenarios' are a less schematic subtype of frame insofar as they include specific narrative and evaluative perspectives, which make them attractive for drawing strong inferences in political discourses as well as in policy planning.[6]

Unlike Lakoff's 'entailments', inferences from scenarios are not assumed to be cognitively or logically binding but are contestable and depend for their success on their discursive plausibility. A scenario is a set of assumptions made by competent members of a discourse community about the prototypical elements of a concept, that is, participants, 'dramatic' story lines and default outcomes, as well as ethical evaluations of these elements, which are connected to the social attitudes and emotional stances that are prevalent in the respective discourse community. Viewed in this perspective, the STRICT FATHER model is the default scenario of Western FAMILY concepts that is routinely invoked as source when linguistic instances of the FAMILY metaphor are used. Likewise, the POLITICAL CONFLICT AS WAR metaphor, which we identified in the previous chapter, shows clear traces of narrative and argumentative bias. Its dynamic scenario version includes a *war declaration* between two or more *enemies*, the start of *hostilities* and various *battles* up to a final outcome which is assessed as a *victory* or *defeat/rout.* This scenario is more than a random selection of conceptual elements from the general WAR domain, but rather a particular set of presuppositions that are chosen for specific argumentative purposes (e.g. with the aim of *declaring victory*). The emphatic 'framing' effect that metaphors can achieve (in the sense of Lakoff/Johnson's 'self-fulfilling prophecy' realization) is attained when a discourse community decides to settle on a particular scenario as their dominant (or even exclusive) perspective on reality.

3.3 Family scenarios

The 'scenario' category is not posited *a priori* for theoretical purposes but is chiefly motivated by data, specifically, the frequency, distribution and collocation clusters of MIP-VU criteria-compatible lexical and phraseological items. This evidence makes it, for instance, plausible to group the source concepts of two conceptual domains in EUROMETA, that is, LOVE MARRIAGE and FAMILY, together, because *parents* in the EU *family* are most often also presented as a *couple* who experience the ups and downs *of married life*:

> FAMILY (MEMBERS), as exemplified by the lexical items: *baby, child(ren), cousins across the channel, custody, family, (founding) father(s), foundling, godparents, mother, mama, mummy, 'Mutti', orphan, parents, poor relations*;

> LOVE/MARRIAGE RELATIONSHIP, lexical items: *(great) catch, couple, courting, courtship, divorce, flirting, engagement, get into bed with, honeymoon, joint account, love (v.), love (n.), love-in, love affair, love at first sight, love rat, marry, (shotgun) marriage, marriage of convenience, ménage à trois, nuptials, partnership, pre-nuptial dances, promiscuous, romance, separation, sleep with, (pushy) suitor, tie the knot, (love) triangle, wedding, (marriage) vows, woo.*

In various combinations, the respective concepts build up to three mini-narratives, which seem to resemble drama or soap opera plots:

a PARENT–CHILD relationships that relate to themes of SOLIDARITY and HIERARCHY-AUTHORITY (i.e. *EU as a whole – member states – accession candidates*; or *EU – euro currency*; or *EU state(s) – euro currency*);

b MARRIED LIFE of the EU *couple* (i.e. France and Germany, with Britain often seen as a third partner in an potential *ménage à trois*); these include all manner of MARRIAGE PROBLEMS from ADULTERY, SEPARATION, DIVORCE, to MARRIAGE OF CONVENIENCE and RENEWED NUPTIALS;

c   LOVE/MARRIAGE relationship (and problems) between Britain and the European Union and its institutions.

These conceptual clusters, which account for all metaphorically used FAMILY/ LOVE lexemes in the corpus, provide the narrative and evaluative scenarios for debating EU political issues in British print- and online media. The actual, positive or negative evaluations of participant relations in the individual texts vary of course in relation to party- and euro-political leanings of the respective authors and media, but these evaluations take place within the framework of the above-listed three scenarios.

In the first scenario, the EU *family* appears to have an egalitarian structure, with all member states being presented as *marriage partners* or *children with equal rights and mutual obligations*. This model is used mainly when *new family members* are to be welcomed or transgressions against the *family discipline* by one member state are sanctioned (for examples, see Musolff 2009a: 536–7). The second scenario of Europe is that of a *hierarchical family* structure, either with the Franco-German *couple* dominating the rest of the European Union (and challenged only to some degree by Britain as potential *lover*) or with the EU Commission as a power centre that can grant or withhold benefits from *suitors* or *family members*. Britain plays a contradictory role in the latter scenario: in some cases, it is portrayed as a potential partner in the privileged elite group (i.e. extending the *couple* to a *triangle*); on other occasions, it is depicted as the *supplicant/hopeful or spurned lover*, in a similar way as some of the nations that have only recently joined the European Union or have not even yet been included. This hierarchical FAMILY model underlies most of the British press's MARRIAGE/FAMILY-based depiction of the European Union, and it contradicts the 'official' egalitarian community model, in which all EU members are equal *family members* (Musolff 2009a: 537–8). The third scenario is also hierarchical but views the European Union as a homogeneous entity with which Britain is engaged in a bilateral but asymmetric love/ marriage relationship (or in its breakdown). Within this configuration, the EU Commission and some countries (most often, again, France or Germany) and their politicians are foregrounded as personifications of the EU entity as a whole, which thus appears as the significant Other in relation to which Britain has to define and/or (re-)assert herself (Musolff 2009a: 538–40).

None of these scenarios can plausibly be said to be grounded in experiential or folk-theoretical domain knowledge. Can a family that regularly recognizes new (adult?) children as returning into its bosom, or a married couple whose partners alternately are looking for a *ménage a trois* (with always the same third partner!) or a marriage relationship that is continuously threatened by divorce (in some cases even before a wedding has taken place) credibly be derived from the prototypical core concept of FAMILY? Evidently, dysfunctional families can be and are experienced in reality but that does not make them source concepts for metaphorical mappings. Dysfunctional families may be part of the experience-grounded ICM of FAMILY, but most probably only in the outer margins of the prototype where it becomes questionable if these types of relationships still qualify for FAMILY status. The 'grounding' of metaphorical mappings in users' own life experiences is a necessary but not sufficient condition for the validity of inferences. It must be complemented by a 'focusing' effect (Black 1962) that makes it possible to access knowledge/experience frames which can be creatively applied to the target topic in question. If the target is, for instance, a currency union with eleven members, then the respective FAMILY metaphor formulation allows for eleven fathers and one child. This 'focusing' effect takes place not at the general level of domains but at the level of scenarios as they emerge in discourse.

3.4 Further scenario functions

Scenarios can be exploited also for 'meta-representational effects' (Sperber 2000) through allusion to previous uses and their narrative and often hyperbolic or humorous reinterpretation. The EU *family* scenes of *marital rows, divorce* and *adultery* provide ample material for 'echoic' humorous or polemical stance-taking in the EU debate, as examples from recent discussions about a potential British exit ('Brexit') from the European Union illustrate:

(1) In a sign of increasing impatience with Britain in Brussels, French MEP Joseph Daul, … responding to an attack from UKIP leader Nigel Farage, said *he would accept an 'amicable divorce' of Britain and the EU – but he wanted 'custody of all the children'.* Some took that as a reference to an independent Scotland. (*Daily Mail*, 7 November 2012)

(2) Ms Merkel [German Chancellor] *dismissed a suggestion from the Ukip [= UK Independence Party] leader Nigel Farage that Britain should have a 'simple amicable divorce'* from Brussels. (*The Independent*, 8 November 2012)

(3) Britain and Europe are *like a couple in a difficult marriage. One day they have a blazing row; the next they want to kiss and make up.* (*The Economist*, 5 July 2014)

(4) John Major is to warn that Britain is in danger of *stumbling out of the EU in a divorce that would be 'final'.* (*The Guardian*, 13 November 2014)

(5) Jean-Claude Juncker has compared British membership of the EU
to a *doomed romance* and suggested it is time for Britain *to get a
divorce* from Europe. It is the first time the president of the European
Commission has publicly contemplated a British exit and he reinforced
his message by insisting *he would not get down on his knees to beg
Britain to stay.* (*The Daily Telegraph,* 18 January 2015)

Similar to the British depiction of the Franco-German *love affair/marriage,*[7] but
with a strong increase in recent years, the British–European relationship is
predominantly depicted as being a *troubled marriage* that is threatened by
separation or *divorce.* In at least one third of all texts, however, the respective
text passages are not authored by journalists but are quotations from politicians,
which in some cases (see examples 1 and 2 above) contain secondary
citations in reference to other politicians' words. In further cases, the core
story is amplified into a 'blow-by-blow' account of 'scenes from a marriage'
melodrama (3, 4) and may include a meta-communicative commentary, (1, 5).
Apart from building strong argumentative stances through their narrative and
evaluative contents, scenarios such as that of the UK–EU MARRIAGE THREATENED BY
DIVORCE also establish intertextual relationships among the texts in which they
appear.

One further characteristic is the strong figure-background effect that
scenarios can create in cases where the default version of one or several
scenario elements is abandoned and even contradicted by loading it with
an opposite evaluation or bias. This applies to the FOUNDING FATHER and MOTHER
scenarios. Presumably coined in analogy with the model of the US 'Founding
Fathers' (signers and framers of the US Constitution), the European Union's
founding fathers are predominantly understood to have been post-war
politicians of the originally six European countries (Belgium, France, Italy,
Luxembourg, the Netherlands and West Germany) who decided to integrate
their economies since the 1950s. Most references to these *founding fathers*
in the corpus are reverential and positively slanted, which confirms traditional
beliefs about FATHERHOOD as conferring authority and responsibility, as in the
following quotations:

(6) The EU was designed to bind a continent together in peace. ... If they
were still among us, Robert Schuman, Jean Monnet, Altiero Spinelli,
founding fathers all of the EU, might be wondering: 'How did Europe
lose its way?' (*The Observer,* 10 May 2014)

(7) 'Such a divided European Union was not what the *founding fathers*
had in mind. We will all need to give much greater consideration to its
implications than has, until now been conceded', Mr Rifkind [British

foreign secretary] will say in an address to mark the 50th anniversary of Winston Churchill's famous 'United States of Europe' speech (*The Guardian*, 18 September 1996).

(8) Last week's theatrical call from Bonn and Paris to match a European economic and monetary union with a political union, ... has rekindled old British passions concerning the whole idea of European unification. What do they mean by 'political union'? The words imply the merging of states ... into some form of a single federated state. That was *the great dream of the founding fathers of the original European communities* – a United States of Europe. In practice, Messrs Kohl and Mitterrand [German and French political leaders at the time] mean something much more mundane. (*The Independent*, 24 April 1990)

In these texts, topical Euro-political developments are unfavourably compared with presumed stances held by the *founding fathers*. In example (6), the journalist puts his own doubts anachronistically ('if they were still among us') in their mouth. In (7), the then British foreign minister, faced with attempts by the 'Franco-German couple' to impose its agenda on the whole of the European Union, uses the *founding fathers'* (presumed) political ethics as an argument against a perceived dangerous development. Such a move only makes sense of the basis of the assumption that the *founding fathers* reference conveys some of their authority on his own position. In (8), the alleged Franco-German *founding fathers'* 'dream' of a 'federated state' is invoked, which the commentator does not necessarily agree with; still, it is compared positively with the 'mundane' plans of the present-day politicians, on account of its genuinely visionary qualities.

In the wake of a recent strengthening of 'Eurosceptic' tendencies in Britain in the run-up to a referendum on its EU membership, however, *(founding) father* figures no longer automatically hold such kudos. The *Daily Express*, for instance, portrayed them as inimical to British interests and historically superseded by later events:

(9) Of the ... driving convictions of the *founding fathers* of the EU we agree with not a single one. So why stay? (*Daily Express*, 9 August 2014)

(10) Days before restrictions on Romanian and Bulgarian migrants are lifted ... [PM David Cameron], said: 'The EU's founding fathers simply did not envisage that the accession of new countries would trigger mass population movements across Europe.' (*Daily Mail*, 21 December 2013)

Even where the *founding fathers* are invoked in warnings against present-day EU political dangers, they are treated without much reverence and more as the target of anti-EU jokes:

(11) The dislike European citizens have expressed in elections for federalism – and the contempt for their voters which national leaders have now indicated by choosing arch-federalist Juncker – *might even have made Europhobes out of the EU's founding fathers.* (*Daily Mail,* 30 June 2014)

In contrast to FATHER concepts, MOTHERHOOD appeared to be almost absent from EU debates as a source for metaphors for a long time. It was only occasionally used to depict France as the female partner of the Euro *couple* that *begat* the euro currency *child,* or the EU Commission as an (over-?)generous, nurturing parent:

(12) France, the *mother of EMU* [Economic and monetary union], is locked in a bind of … savage proportion. (*The Guardian,* 18 January 1996)

(13) In *Europe family* the Commission played the *role of mama, the great dispenser of favours.* (*The Times,* 17 March 1999)

Since the repeated electoral successes of Angela Merkel as German chancellor and her ensuing emergence as the main power broker in the European Union due to her country's relatively strong performance during the financial crisis of 2008–13, however, her German nickname 'Mutti' ('mummy') has caught on and is exploited for punning and polemical purposes by British columnists. It seems to have turned the gender roles of the Franco-German *couple* around (example 14) due to their leading politicians' sex and, more importantly, has begun to put the esteem for the EU *mother's* nurturing qualities in question (16–18):

(14) Greece has been shirking its workload, spending on tomfoolery, disobeying its over-indulgent parents. *Father France, after personal indiscretions of his own at the City's roulette tables,* has rather retired from *paternal duties, leaving poor Mother Merkel, and wealthy young Germany, to keep the naughty ward in order. A single parenting job from hell.* (*The Independent,* 18 June 2012)

(15) On Sunday Angela Merkel attempts to win a third term. … With much of Europe facing economic turmoil, the *continent is looking to 'Mutti' – mother – to lead it through the crisis.* (*Channel 4,* 20 September 2013)

(16) [David Cameron] has pledged to start 'renegotiating' our terms of membership. … But if … the polls show we are going to vote to leave, then you will see that *Mutti Merkel is not so mumsy after all.* (*Daily Express,* 23 September 2013)

(17) Merkel will be even more inclined than she is already to run the European show by pragmatic inter-governmental deal-making. ... But ... she does not have a strategic partner in either of the EU's other two leading powers. ... Britain could, but won't; France would, but can't. *That leaves Merkel as Europe's single Mutti.* (*The Guardian,* 25 September 2013)

(18) The Chancellor, *whom Germans nickname 'Mutti' ('Mum'), stands for old-fashioned bourgeois virtues.* .... She [now] bestrides the Continent: no colossus, to be sure, *but an astute, stern and occasionally ruthless matron.* (*The Daily Telegraph,* 11 May 2012)

Merkel's metaphorical *Mutti* role is highlighted in these examples with regard not just to Germany but to the whole European Union as that of a *single parent,* or disciplinarian *matron.* This SINGLE PARENT/MOTHER concept violates traditional assumptions about motherhood, which used to underwrite the mapping between the concepts of the CARING MOTHER MARRIED TO STRICT FATHER and a NURTURANT NATIONAL LEADER. The new applications of MOTHER concepts again underline the role of the STRICT FATHER scenario as a *default* narrative, which does not determine every single instance of metaphorical conceptualization but rather serves as a background against which the diverse uses of THE MOTHER concept become meaningful, either as confirmation (see examples 15, and to some extent, 17), as an emphatic negation (14 and 16) or as a transformation into *matron* (18).

3.5 Summary

In this chapter we have discussed in detail the application of CMT's 'domain' concept to the NATION(S) AS FAMILY metaphor and shown that it is too broad and at the same time too rigid to provide a sufficient grounding for metaphors. Organized as they are around prototypical core concepts that shade into less typical examples, domains may underwrite abstract image schemas, but they do not provide sufficiently specific conceptual material to motivate the collocation patterns and clusters that can be found in the corpus data. The problem is not that domains are only ever partially represented in utterances or debates: this fact has been acknowledged by Lakoff and Johnson themselves (1980/2003: 52–5). But what CMT on its own cannot account for is the evidence of repeated use of a small set of recurring narrative-evaluative patterns (e.g. FAMILIAL SOLIDARITY/HIERACHY, MARRIAGE PROBLEMS, PARENT–CHILDREN

RELATIONSHIP). This finding points to a salient characteristic of metaphor use in political discourse, that is, a highly economical use of source domain material. On the one hand source concepts can be bent and shaped in any way, such as MARRIAGE or PARENTHOOD of eleven countries with one euro CHILD, or multiple FATHERHOOD and SINGLE MOTHERHOOD for a FAMILY of by now twenty-eight nations, and ever more nations as PRODIGAL CHILDREN lining up to return into the family. On the other hand, these source concepts form a small set of scenarios that is limited to a few mini-melodramas that are rehearsed again and again, whereas other parts of the source domain effectively *never* get mentioned. CMT's view of metaphor as a cross-domain mapping does little to explain these choices. The following chapters will therefore look in detail at the emergence and successive development of metaphor scenarios in discourse, first at a micro-historical level, that is, regarding relatively short time spans, and then in a longer-term perspective.

4

The life and times of a metaphor scenario:

Britain at the heart of Europe

4.1 Memories of a metaphor

In October 2014, the British prime minister D. Cameron promised that if re-elected in the following year (which he was), his government would hold a referendum on whether Britain should leave the European Union. Cameron's initiative was politically risky: he maintained that he wanted the United Kingdom to stay in the European Union after having negotiated reforms to suit British national interests, but there was still a chance that the referendum might lead to a British exit ('Brexit') from the Union. A *Financial Times* blog made fun of his ambivalent stance by publishing a fictitious dialogue between him and the newly appointed EU Commission president, J.-C. Juncker:

(1) JCJ: So just to clarify. Aside from not joining the euro, you want to limit the free movement of people, cut the power of the European Court and the European Parliament…

DC: And since we are opting out of so much, we should pay less too.

JCJ: This is quite a list of demands, David. What do we get in return?

DC: *A Britain at the heart of Europe, of course.* (Shrimsley 2014, italics here and in the following examples: AM)

This mock dialogue portrays Cameron as limiting the British commitment to the European Union to bare membership (i.e. non-exit) while refusing to engage with any of the EU common policies. A seemingly paradoxical effect is achieved through the contrast between his minimalist engagement with the (conventionally) metaphorical meaning of the idiom *at the heart of* as designating a location at 'a central part, a vital or essential part' of something.[1] Cameron is presented here as trying to promote a maximally distanced and loose relationship of the United Kingdom with the European Union as an equivalent of *being at its heart*. To *Financial Times* readers, his (imaginary) response to Juncker's query comes across as either grotesquely inadequate or disingenuous, which is reinforced by the tagged-on phrase *of course*, suggesting a brazen attempt of reinterpreting reality.

The use of the phrase *of course* here can, however, also be seen as an allusion to the discourse history of the slogan *Britain at the heart of Europe* in public debates.[2] EUROMETA contains 221 instances of this slogan; they go back to 1991, when the then incumbent (Conservative) prime minister J. Major launched it in a high-profile speech in Germany. In his speech Major indicated a break with the EU-critical stance of his predecessor, M. Thatcher. From now on, he announced, Britain would

(2) work 'at the very heart of Europe' with its partners in forging an integrated European community. (quoted in *The Guardian*, 12 March 1991)

This optimistic-sounding promise had, according to Major's own interpretation in his autobiography, which was published nine years later, 'an unexceptional objective', that is, to express the 'self-evident' wish of his government to 'improve our profile in Europe' and 'protect our own interests' by 'not letting others dominate the debate' (Major 2000: 268–9). With the benefit of hindsight, he conceded that his metaphorical formulation created 'havoc' in his party and was 'misrepresented' as expressing acceptance of EU 'federalism', that is, in British political jargon, centralized government from the EU centre (Major 2000: 269–70).

This case of a well-prepared, prominent metaphor use, which, as the speaker himself admits, was subsequently misunderstood and misrepresented, confronts us with two significant issues that will be pursued throughout this book:

a) How to account for the possibility of a fundamental discrepancy between the speaker's intended meaning of a metaphor use and its actual uptake and interpretation in public discourse and

b) The apparent paradox of a metaphor gaining in popularity and becoming entrenched by being disputed and contested rather than by approval and widespread acceptance.

According to the 'classic' CMT account, conventional metaphors are understood automatically due to their grounding in 'embodied' experience. Furthermore, this automatic comprehension is conceived of as favouring uncritical acceptance of the metaphor's 'entailments' by the great majority of recipients, which only the intrepid therapeutic work of the critical linguist may be able to rectify (see Lakoff's 'exposure' of the STRICT FATHER model, as discussed in the preceding chapter). However, it is arguably better for a political metaphor to be hotly debated and criticized than to be simply uncritically accepted: the more it is disputed and reinterpreted, the more salient will it become in the public sphere and the longer will it stay 'alive' in it. In our EUROMETA data we find sufficiently many examples of the Britain *at the heart of Europe* slogan to follow in detail the micro-history of this metaphor. A total of 147 of the 221 relevant texts, that is, more than 66 per cent, quote or explicitly allude to preceding speakers' utterances, and many of these quotations also include explicit interpretations and evaluations of the preceding uses. We can thus study in detail how the seemingly innocuous metaphor CENTRAL EU AUTHORITY AS HEART OF EUROPE was established in British public political discourse, how it was expanded, modified and entrenched and how it has maintained its 'framing' power, and which role the 'scenario' aspect plays in this history. In particular, I will argue that the notion of BRITAIN BEING AT/CLOSE TO THE HEART OF EUROPE amounted to an embryonic scenario that was further developed through strong intertextual referencing into a fully fledged narrative-evaluative pattern which has provided a template for EU political statements to this day. The 2014–15 'Brexit' debates have already supplied a number of new instantiations[3]; more can be expected to follow.

4.2 The emergence of a metaphor scenario

From a cognitive viewpoint, the 'positive bias' of the concept *being close to* or *at the heart* of something, which is evident in Major's initial use (example (2)), is not hard to understand. The heart as an organ is not just anatomically close to the centre of our bodies; it is one of its absolutely essential organs, whose activity we are aware of as being necessary for our survival. A living human body is inconceivable without a functioning heart; we feel our heartbeat and know how to listen to it and measure it. Heart injuries and diseases as well as their therapies are, for obvious reasons of self-preservation, among the most frequently and extensively discussed health issues. Furthermore, we experientially associate strong feelings, such as love, anger and fear, with changes in the heartbeat that we can feel ourselves, and these perceived correlations are corroborated by physiological and medical measurements.

It is little wonder then that the conceptual link EMOTION–HEARTBEAT–HEART has led to a host of lexicalized idioms, proverbs and stories in various languages that portray the heart as the SEAT OF FEELINGS and also depict the lack of certain feelings, for example, love, compassion and courage, as HEARTLESSNESS.[4] For English, S. Niemeier (2000) has shown that the conceptualization of the heart as a location of emotions is based on a complex of metonymies and metaphors (rather than only the latter, as in the classic CMT account). It incorporates a number of folk-theoretical models that range from the basic metonymy HEART FOR PERSON over HEART AS A LIVING ORGANISM and HEART AS AN OBJECT OF VALUE reifications to more elaborate models of HEART AS A CONTAINER FOR EMOTIONS (Niemeyer 2000: 190–208). Most idioms that include the phrase *at the heart of X* imply that its prepositional object is something valuable, desirable and/or essential and that therefore *being at the heart* or *being close to the heart of X* is also desirable.

It was in this positively biased sense that the phrase was used first by Major in 1991 but, given the ubiquity of *heart*-based idioms, including *X at the heart of Y*, it is not probable that he or his speechwriter 'invented' the *Britain at heart of Europe* phrase from nothing. EUROMETA, which goes back to 1990, has four occurrences of *at the heart of Europe* that precede Major's 1991 use,[5] and doubtless more could be found if we looked further back in the history of Euro-political discourses. Major not so much created the metaphor but rather 'picked up' a readily available idiom and employed it to signal a shift of his government's policy towards a more EU-friendly stance. As a politician's metaphor, his slogan had a degree of vagueness built into it and left open exactly what Major was planning to do in order to be *at the heart* of EU politics. The left-leaning newspaper, The *Guardian,* assessed it as an astute political sound bite precisely for meaning different things to different people: it had 'delighted' Major's German audience but also gave both sides of the British public – including the EU sceptics – cause to hope that the prime minister 'had signalled a political "shift in their direction"' (*The Guardian*, 12 and 13 March 1991).

This ambiguity was exposed by the leaders of the parliamentary opposition to Major's government later that year when they commented on his negotiations with the EU partner governments at Maastricht about a new EU treaty that promised 'ever closer union' but allowed Britain to 'opt out' of two of the two main treaty initiatives (i.e. monetary union, which would lead to the creation of the 'euro' currency, and the so-called 'social chapter', a drive to partly harmonize social policies). Citing Major's metaphor, the Labour Party leader of the opposition, N. Kinnock asked, in the House of Commons,

    (3) how the Prime Minister [could] claim to be at the heart of Europe
       when, because of his actions, our country [was] not even part

of the key decisions that [would] shape the Europe of the future
(Hansard 1991)

and the leader of the smaller opposition party, the Liberal Democrats,
P. Ashdown, concluded that Major who had 'wanted to be at the heart of the
process [of European integration],' had in reality

(4) condemned this country to be semi-detached from it. (Hansard 1991)

Major's announcement and Kinnock's and Ashdown's statements all
presupposed that *being at the heart of Europe* was a good thing; what the
opposition parties' leaders criticized was thus not the promise but the prime
minister's alleged inability to fulfil it. The British electorate, however, apparently
endorsed his policies, including the outcome of the Maastricht Treaty
negotiations, and returned him to power in the April 1992 general election.
For much of the period 1991–2, EUROMETA records similar quotations of his
slogan by the media and fellow politicians that either endorse his commitment
to work *at the heart of Europe* or remind him of the duty to fulfil that promise
in the face of growing EU scepticism within his own party.

In September 1992, however, Major's government was forced by
speculation in the financial markets to withdraw the Pound Sterling from the
Exchange Rate Mechanism (ERM) of the European Union, a system that fixed
member states' currencies within certain bands and effectively foreshadowed
the subsequent currency union.[6] The magazine the *Economist* immediately
analysed in detail Major's commitment to a 'Britain "at the heart of Europe"'
as being threatened by a 'coronary in Europe's new heart' (*The Economist* 26
September 1992). In this vivid reuse-cum-reinterpretation of the metaphor,
the criticism was no longer directed at Major's (in-)consistency in fulfilling his
commitment but it targeted the apparently failing vitality of the 'new heart'
of Europe, that is, the ERM. Clearly, a heart that has suffered a 'coronary'
attack is not as valuable or desirable as a healthy heart; hence, *being close to
it* in the sense of being involved in its workings is not (any more) an attractive
prospect. The positive bias of the BRITAIN AT THE HEART OF EUROPE scenario was
thus reversed. Instead of assuming CLOSENESS to it to be a good thing, the
assumption was now that such proximity was dangerous and should be
avoided. As in the case of the STATE AS FAMILY metaphor, the metaphor scenario
was 'countered' by an opposite version.

While never matching the frequency of uses and quotations of the slogan
based on the HEALTHY HEART scenario, the opposite SICK HEART scenario version did
resurface regularly in high-profile interventions in the public debate in Britain
over the following years. In 1994, for instance, the publication of French and
German proposals for EU reforms, which favoured the creation of a politically

integrated *inner circle* of member states, from which less committed states such as Britain would be excluded for the time being,[7] threatened to expose Major's vision of *Britain at the heart of Europe* as empty rhetoric. The prime minister responded within days in a speech in Leiden (Netherlands) in which he rejected the proposals. This adversarial stance, however, did not help to strengthen the idea of his government being close to the European Union's political centre and the press did not wait long to point this out and exploited Major's metaphor by polemical punning, for example, by stating that in his attempts to put Britain 'at the heart of Europe' he often 'found himself alone at the end of a limb', or suggesting that if Major still 'wanted to be at the heart of Europe, it was, presumably, as a blood clot' (*The Independent,* 8 and 11 September 1994). Over the following months, a semantic-political battle ensued, in which the prime minister and loyal members of his cabinet insisted on Britain staying *at the heart of Europe* while EU sceptics opposed the phrase, and the press queried its earnestness and precise meaning (Musolff 2004a: 105–8).

In 1995, the former head of the EU Commission's unit for the EU's monetary policies, B. Connolly, published a book under the title *The Rotten Heart of Europe,* in which he blew the whistle on severe management and corruption problems in the Commission and pointed out risks for the planned European Monetary Union (Connolly 1995). The book's catchy title immediately drew attention and soon provided a rallying cry for British EU sceptics, with the attribute *rotten* adding a further drastic version to the SICK HEART scenario. It was followed by variations on the same theme, for example, identifying a 'hole in the heart of Europe' (*The Independent,* 10 December 1995), or a 'diseased heart' (N. Lamont, former Chancellor of the Exchequer, quoted in *The Guardian,* 10 October 1996), or scenes of Britain 'blocking' the European heart's 'arteries' (E. Heath, former prime minister, quoted in *The Daily Telegraph,* 21 June 1996), and of 'smiling silence at the heart of Europe' (*The Independent,* 1 December 1997), as well as the damning verdict: 'Britain can't be at Europe's heart. It doesn't have one' (*The Sun,* 6 May 1998).

With the change of government from Conservative to Labour in 1997, assessment of the EUROPEAN HEART'S HEALTH split along party-political lines. While the assumption of a HEALTHY HEART informed renewed positively slanted uses in Tony Blair and other Labour politicians' rhetoric, the growth of the EU-sceptic faction among the Tories expressed itself in further pathological imagery, especially after a renewed boost in publicity for Connolly's book in early 1999 when a scandal of multiple nepotism cases in the EU Commission under J. Santer forced the whole EU Commission to resign. EU-sceptic press media and politicians had a field day, speaking as they did of irreparable 'rot' and 'corruption' at the EU's *heart,* which would 'never be cleaned out' (e.g. *The Times,* 17, 21 March, *Daily Mail,* 17 March, *The Sun,* 17 March 1999). But the pejorative use of the heart imagery was not restricted to them. Even the EU-friendly *Guardian* and *Independent* now spoke of a *vacuum* or *hole at the heart of Europe* (*The Guardian*, 17 March 1999; *The Independent,* 21 March 1999), and *The Economist* (20 March 1999) sarcastically commented that just when Blair was about 'to lodge Britain at its rightful place in the heart of Europe ... abruptly, the heart of Europe got sick'.

Statements in favour of *Britain at the heart of Europe* now ceased to be linked to the possibility of Britain joining the 'Eurozone' of common currency countries, which had come into being at the start of 1999.[8] Deprived of the reference to the most important topical EU-political project, the slogan became for Tony Blair's and, later, Gordon Brown's Labour governments what it had been in the last phase of Major's term of office, that is, a formula that served EU-friendly politicians as a vague commitment,[9] and their opponents to diagnose its *ills*, such as a *split* at the heart (*The Guardian*, 30 June 2000, 16 December 2003), the *smell of a rotting heart* (*Daily Mail*, 2 August 2002) or a *missing* heart (Kremer 2004). Other, even more polemical uses linked the *heart of Europe* phrase to grotesque physiological allusions, for example, to the infection danger caused by the 2001 'foot and mouth' cattle epidemic in Britain, which would make an upcoming EU meeting receive Blair with 'his promise to be "at the heart of Europe"' only after having 'wiped his feet in a trough of disinfectant' (*The Guardian*, 4 April 2001), or to the European Union responding to Blair's commitment to being close to its heart by 'showing us its backside' (*The Sun,* 3 September 2001).

Here we can see how the metaphor's scenario structure is used to achieve pragmatic and rhetorical effects that go beyond simply criticizing the optimistic bias of the default version, that is, the commitment *to be at the heart of Europe.*

Pragmatically, each use that quotes, mentions or alludes to a preceding use of the slogan *Britain at the heart of Europe* is a 'metarepresentation' in the sense that a 'higher-order' utterance has a 'lower-order' utterance embedded inside it (Wilson 2000: 414). In the above-cited cases, the higher-order representation includes a reference to the SICK HEART scenario, which, through juxtaposition with the preceding HEALTHY HEART version, also serves to implicitly denounce and ridicule the latter and thus achieves an 'echoic', that is, ironic or even sarcastic effect.[10] The notions of HEART DISEASE/ROT/DEATH, BACKSIDE or FOOT AND MOUTH EPIDEMIC do not add to the semantic understanding of the phrase *Britain at the heart of Europe,* but mock the implicit optimism of its default version by invoking BODY-/SICKNESS-related concepts that are scary and/or disgusting and serve to dissuade the readers from sharing the cited speaker's optimism. The positively slanted HEALTHY HEART default scenario thus serves as the ground against which the new polemical counter-version of the SICK HEART or DISGUSTING BODY-PART versions can be highlighted as more plausible in view of specific political context condition, such as an EU political scandal or conflict. The more far-fetched and grotesque the new counter-scenario is, the stronger is its ironical or sarcastic effect in contradicting the benign or optimistic view of the HEART OF EUROPE. The readers' acceptance or rejection of the counter-scenario is of course in principle indeterminate and depends on their own political views, but the ironical effect is achieved once they recognize the allusion to the preceding use of *Britain at the heart of Europe* and its (supposed) implicit refutation by the counter-scenario.

4.3 Scenario development

One might speculate that the ironical and sarcastic reinterpretations, which the *heart of Europe* phrase has been subjected to through allusions to pathological conditions or other associations with offensive BODY imagery, would have a lasting pejorative effect on its positive default slant, but that seems not to be the case. When in May 2010, a new Conservative-led government under D. Cameron came to power, the commitment to 'put Britain back at the heart of Europe' was still part of governmental 'Eurospeak', as programmatic statements from the Conservative foreign secretary Hague and the Liberal deputy prime minister Clegg show (*The Scotsman*, 1 July 2010; *The Guardian*, 16 December 2011). Since the 2010 election, another fifty-three uses of the phrase *(at the) heart of Europe* are recorded in EUROMETA: they include historical references to previous uses and new applications such as an international spat over an article in the *Economist* that criticized France for being the 'time-bomb at the heart of Europe' on account of its economic weakness, (*The Economist*, 15 December 2012).[11] Since 2014, however, the dominant context for uses of the *Britain at the heart of Europe* slogan have been the debates about a referendum on Britain's continued EU membership, which have become official UK government policy in the wake of the Conservative election victory in 2015. In these debates, *Britain at the heart of Europe* has become a synonym for Britain remaining an EU member state; hence, calls by politicians for Britain to stay in the European Union are often reported as advice *to stay at the heart of Europe*, even if the phrase was not included in the passages from the respective interviews or speeches quoted in the respective articles.[12] The spoof quotation from the *Financial Times'* fictitious conversation between D. Cameron and J. C. Juncker in example (1) fits perfectly with this trend: even though the current UK government stands aloof from almost all shared EU policies, such as the common currency, social harmonization, immigration policy and other commitments, it still officially claims to keep Britain *at the EU's heart* by preventing a 'Brexit' (at least for the time being, i.e. until the referendum has been held). The use of the slogan in today's debates seems to serve the main purpose of upholding the claim that the UK under Cameron enjoys and exercises EU membership, without any further policy specification. A notable exception to this anodyne usage was an explicitly critical statement by the former EU Commission president, José Manuel Barroso, who was quoted as alleging that the UK was no longer 'at the heart of decisions ... because of anti-EU sentiment within the Conservative party' (*The Guardian,* 29 December 2014). Significantly, Barroso made this statement only after having retired from the Commission, that is, in an unofficial capacity. It seems that any explicit negation of CLOSENESS TO THE HEART OF EUROPE has acquired almost taboo status for active politicians, on account of being interpretable as denying or querying membership status to its referent.

Summarizing our sketch of the metaphor's 'discourse career' so far, we note that it is characterized by an enduring, positively loaded default HEALTHY-HEART scenario of the *Britain at the heart of Europe* slogan and the occasional occurrence of prominent but short-lived counter versions that negate it by using scary or disgusting BODY/HEALTH-related concepts. In its default use, the background assumptions of the phrase *at the heart of Europe* (HEALTHINESS and CENTRALITY, which make CLOSENESS worthwhile) are not highlighted, but they are activated *ex negativo* once a discourse participant finds it advantageous to use them to criticize its target topic (CENTRAL EU INSTITUTIONS OR POLICIES) emphatically.

In terms of frequency patterns, the positively slanted (i.e. endorsing, promising or reassuring) scenario uses outweigh the negative ones (i.e. mocking or detracting) by about 5:1 (within EUROMETA). This pattern suggests that the basic evaluation of the HEART OF EUROPE metaphor is 'positive' in the sense that being close to the centre of the European Union is at the very least assumed to be preferable to being remote from it. By comparison, uses in which the HEART OF EUROPE is diagnosed as being DISEASED are relatively rare but they are highly prominent when they occur and often generate a burst of polemical requotations and reinterpretations. Such high-profile denunciation and debunking of the positive default scenario version, however, bolsters its frequency (on account of its repeated quotations by all sides during a topical debate) both in the short and medium term, which goes some way to explain its longevity over a quarter of a century. In order for even the most polemical attacks on the HEART OF EUROPE to 'work', its default optimistic version must be presupposed in the shared memory of the public. In addition, the sample provides evidence for the press issuing from time to time 'reminders' of prominent uses: in the case of *Britain at the heart of Europe*, for instance, its initial formulation in J. Major's 1991 speech has continued to be referenced for more than two decades: twenty-three years after giving his speech, he was still 'the man who said that Britain's place was at the heart of Europe' (BBC, 13 November 2014).

The development of metaphor scenarios thus seems to be bound up with the public memory of a shared discourse history within a given speech community: this memory provides the background against which every new use gains its communicative and political significance. In a few cases, speakers or writers comment explicitly on this discourse history. The slogan *Britain at the heart of Europe* has provoked several such metacommunicative comments, which not only highlight an alleged discrepancy between its default promise and actual policy but also reflect on the whole course of the debate:

(5) One British metaphor, at least, *has ceased to beat*. John Major said
     in Bonn in March 1991, that he wanted to put Britain '*where we
     belong, at the very heart of Europe*'. ... He was saying, in words that
     he knew could not be mistaken by his hosts, *that he spoke their
     language, metaphorically if not literally. The heart is the symbol of the
     CDU*, the party of Helmut Kohl, and the main force behind integration.
     Like many pro-Europeans, *Major was using an organic metaphor,
     one that compared Europe to a living thing. ... Neither Mr Major nor,
     increasingly, others in Europe, have been speaking in quite this way
     for the past three years*. (*The Independent*, 11 September 1994)

(6) The *litany passes from government to government. A Britain at the
     heart of Europe. We'll hear the chant 1,000 times again this month*. ...
     But *hold the stethoscope and listen carefully, for the heart has some
     curious murmurs*. Two days in Euro-town, hearing the officialdom of
     Brussels talk to itself and the world passing through, opens the mind
     as well as *that wretched old heart*. Who says there are no debates
     where bureaucrats rule? Here are a few of them: ... There are many
     more in a similar vein – and one thing binds them together. *They bear
     no relationship to the British 'debate', hearts, livers, gall bladders and
     all*. (*The Guardian*, 1 December 1997)

In these comments, the respective authors use the HEART metaphor at three levels: (a) as a reference to Major's and/or Blair's *Britain at the heart of Europe* promises, (b) as a motif for their own stance on these promises and (c) for commentaries on the whole course of the British–EU political debate. In (5), the metaphor and its optimistic promise is first quoted, then associated with the factually unrelated, but figuratively close political symbolism of the German political party CDU that provided Major's immediate audience, and, lastly, assessed (prematurely, as we know from the corpus data) as having disappeared from public debate. This disappearance could be further interpreted as the *death* of the metaphor of Europe 'as a living thing'. In (6), the metaphor is recycled into a second-order narration of what can be heard if 'you', that is, the reader, as invited by the writer, truly listens to the actual *heartbeat* of debates in Brussels. These debates are contrasted with a sarcastic caricature of the British *heart of Europe* debate as a jumbled-up mix of irrelevant pseudo topics: *hearts, livers, gall bladders* etc.

Such elaborately construed reformulations of the HEART OF EU metaphor, which use the basic scenario as a platform for a second-order metaphorization, show the full cognitive potential of the scenario structure, as well as the inadequacy of approaches that do not take the historicity of metaphor into account. With regard to the *Britain at the heart of Europe* data in particular, the discourse-historical approach (see Chapter 1) has the advantage of being able to account for the dialectical relationship between stable default usage patterns over an extended period on the one hand, and, on the other hand, occasional high-profile deviations from those patterns. To speak of a *diseased heart of Europe* of course only makes sense in a context, in which the negative evaluation of European policy is topical. But its ironical/polemical value as part of a contra-EU argumentation, presupposes knowledge of a default version that is positively loaded (the HEALTHY HEART) so that notions of the SICK/MISSING/ROTTEN HEART OF EUROPE can achieve a surprising, ironical or sarcastic effect. The topicality of such a high-profile scenario reinterpretation is often only short-lived and then the background default scenario 'resurfaces'. It provides a readily available reservoir, as it were, of evaluative-narrative discourse material that can be reactivated whenever needed.

4.4 Scenarios and blends

Before we conclude this chapter, we need to consider an alternative explanation for the micro-history of the slogan *Britain at the heart of Europe* that might help to elucidate further some of the implications of the scenario approach to metaphor. Conceivably, it could be argued that the phrase *at the heart of X* is not metaphorical, or only in a historical sense, that is, in that it was coined and taken up by the English-speaking community hundreds of years ago, only to have faded by now into a 'dead' metaphor which adult speakers of today do not connect with body-related concepts and only associate with notions of centrality and essentiality.[13] From a cognitive viewpoint, however, the idiom could be considered to be a 'live' metaphor in the sense of being based on an embodied mapping from the physiological domain to some abstract domain (Gibbs 2005: 182–7). Any variants of the HEART-source concept such as those that we encountered in the corpus, for example, of the type DISEASED HEART, BLOCKED ARTERIES, ROTTEN HEART etc., could then be interpreted as instances of a cognitive 'elaboration' process that revives or resuscitates the 'dead' or 'half-dead' original mapping (Lakoff and Turner 1989: 67–70).

However, this interpretation would only again confuse the 'scenario' category with that of the 'domain', as it is only the latter that can be viewed as a 'semantic field'-like space around the prototypical organic concept of HEART. The lexical 'fading-and-resuscitation' perspective only relates to such a domain-based theory framework. The scenario aspect, on the other hand, applies to the socio pragmatically situated default meaning of the whole phrase *at the heart of X,* that is, something along the lines of 'positively valued closeness to the centre of X'. Its connection with the HEART AS BODY ORGAN prototype is in fact quite tenuous because physical closeness to that body organ is not necessarily a desirable thing. One could more plausibly construe the positive notion of such closeness from the emotional bond between persons who listen to each other's heartbeat, but then we are in the realm of HEART AS SEAT OF EMOTIONS metaphors rather than in that of HEART AS CENTRE concepts, in which abstract entities are envisaged to be close to the centre of a 'virtual' two- or three-dimensional space. This opens up the question of multiple source concepts that underlie the phrase *at the heart of X,* that is, the organic physiological domain and an (imaginary) space domain.

While the original CMT framework did not consider in detail multiple source domain assignations, a related theoretical development, that is, 'Conceptual Integration Theory' (CIT) or 'Blending Theory', developed by G. Fauconnier and M. Turner, has explicitly focused on the integration of several 'mental spaces' (Fauconnier 1994) into conceptual networks of varying complexity.[14] Concept-integrating networks consist of several input spaces, which are viewed as being combined into a 'generic' space and then condensed into a 'blended' space, which is in an epistemological sense 'more' than the sum of the generic space elements. CMT's 'conventional source-target metaphors' are re-explained in this framework as instances of 'single-scope networks' that incorporate 'two input spaces with different organizing frames, one of which is projected to organize the blend' (Fauconnier and Turner 2002: 126). At a further stage, 'double-scope networks' have more than two 'inputs with different (and often clashing) organizing frames as well as an organizing frame for the blend that includes parts of each of those frames and has emergent structure of its own' (2002: 131). Examples for such blends are humorous counterfactual constructions, for example, the depiction of an angry person as a figure that has smoke coming out of his ears, or the ironical characterization of US president W. Clinton's ability to survive political scandal by way of a hypothetical comparison with a fictitious passenger liner *Titanic* that sinks the iceberg (instead of being sunk by the iceberg herself (2002: 221–2). The hyperbolic effect derives not just from the incongruity of complex inputs, but from the absurdity of the initial generic space, which necessitates additional inferences to construe an analogical conclusion that makes sense.

The juxtapositions of the phrase *at the heart of Europe* with diagnoses of *rottenness, illness* or *death*, which we quoted above, come close to but do not quite reach the same level of a counterfactual merger of mental spaces, insofar as they still maintain some source domain coherence (coming as they do from the broad semantic field of BODY/HEALTH-related concepts), but some variations on the *heart of EU* motif as used on the occasion of 2014 elections to the EU parliament exhibit scenario combinations that lend themselves to a CIT-style analysis as cases of blending:

(7) This Thursday's European elections could prove a resounding success for Nigel Farage and for populist anti-EU parties across Europe, *wheeling a Trojan horse directly into the heart of Brussels.* (*The Observer*, 18 May 2014)

(8) How *Brussels elite was stunned by a flurry of right (and left) hooks* from disgruntled Europeans [:] There has never been a night like it. Early on Sunday evening, even before the last polls had closed, *the first tremors were shaking the pillars of European power.* Then came the *full force of the earthquake.* And by the time *the dust had settled,* it was clear that something had fundamentally changed *at the heart of Europe's body politic.* (*Daily Mail*, 27 May 2014)

In both quotations we have multiple source input spaces, that is, besides the positioning concept AT THE HEART OF EU, the notions of WHEELING IN A TROJAN HORSE in example (7), and of BOXING MATCH and EARTHQUAKE in (8). These additional source concepts provide further input spaces to characterize the target input referent, that is, the election outcome, as a momentous change at the centre of European politics. By referencing the legendary confidence trick from the Trojan War as told by Virgil in the *Aeneid*,[15] example (7) highlights the European Union's partly self-inflicted problem of having to cope with an increased presence of EU-sceptical parties in its own parliament, which evokes the vision/spectre of the EU-'capital' Brussels *as a new Troy that is doomed to be destroyed by clever invaders.* In (8) readers witness a fast evolving crisis that proceeds from a *boxing fight* through the *tremors and aftermath of an earthquake* to a vision of fundamental change affecting the *heart* of the Union. The source input spaces involved in these 'blended' scenarios are not congruent; on the contrary, the rhetorical persuasiveness of the texts in which they appear depends on the clash of partly incongruous inputs. Such conceptual clashes are not absolutely irreconcilable (or else they would prevent any meaningful inference) but require the readers to go beyond reconstructing default scenarios of established source domain elements and instead construct new blends. The *heart of Europe* allusion in (7) and (8) plays the role of a background element among the input spaces, which is referenced rather than actively used in the foreground.

Scenario theory is thus compatible with CIT and confirms CIT's general claim that conceptual integration is pervasive and begins at the level of embryonic scenarios such as at the HEART OF X. Further integrations (e.g. metonymies, conventional and unconventional metaphors, reflexive, ironical or counterfactual constructions) differ from those simpler networks in their higher degree of network complexity rather than in essence (Fauconnier and Turner 2002: 119–37). Separating 'dead' from 'live' metaphors makes little sense in this perspective; what matters more is their combination into meaningful scenario configurations. From a scenario-theoretical viewpoint, as from a CIT perspective, even a minimal integration network/scenario configuration is not 'dead', because it implies narrative-evaluative elements *in nuce,* which provide background material for further pragmatic and rhetorical elaboration. In the case of incongruous inputs being combined, more complex blendings produce new, non-default scenarios that achieve special narrative, evaluative and stylistic effects. Scenario analysis can account for the whole range of conceptual integration networks by formulating, on the basis of distribution and collocation patterns and intertextual referencing in a corpus sample, empirically testable hypotheses about the meanings of metaphorical utterances in their respective contexts of use. These contexts include socially shared discourse-historical knowledge, such as the awareness about famous precedent formulations.

4.5 Summary

In this chapter we have applied the scenario-oriented approach of metaphor analysis to corpus data that document the development of a prominent slogan, that is, *Britain at the heart of Europe,* from its prominent coinage (which is not the same as 'invention') through several stages of uptake in the British public. As with WAR-based metaphors (see Chapter 3), we noted that the metaphor usage varies between background usage, that is, brief mentioning of some source-lexical material without further elaboration to extended and intertextually productive scenario formulations that expressed a strong evaluative bias, narrative structure and also had programmatic functions (e.g. as political promises or commitments). In addition we observed a high degree of intertextual referencing (quotation and comment), a small part of which consisted of special reformulations of the source image or combinations with further source input so as to achieve complex blending effects, which provided rich material for rhetorical exploitation, that is, polemical reversal, irony, punning, etc.

The initial scenario version of *Britain at the heart of Europe* (ascribed first to Major, then Blair) provided – and was explicitly invoked – as a reference point to reformulate the political assessment of Britain's relationship with the European Union in terms of its positive default bias. Such explicit reminders serve as a kind of discourse-historical reset button, which, when pressed, reinstates the initial bias (of CLOSENESS TO HEART being desirable) and overrides the semantic decline that may have occurred through repeated uses in a pejorative or ironical sense. Despite occasional discourse-historical obituaries (see example 5 above), the scenario can survive as an evaluative-narrative discourse unit in the medium term. It might, however, still be argued that the 'life span' of twenty-five years for the *Britain at the heart of Europe* slogan is not substantial enough to base on it any conclusions regarding the significance of metaphors' historicity and of their users' awareness of this historicity. In the following chapter we will therefore consider diachronic metaphor development as a 'phenomenon of long duration' in a case that spans not a few decades but more than two millennia.

5

The belly and the *body politic*

5.1 Memories of a fable

One metaphor scenario that has gained considerable historical and literary fame in Western cultures is the 'Fable of the Belly'. Its history can serve us as a case study to a look at the long-term development of metaphors. The fable dates back to early collections attributed to Aesop and was handed down through the ages by historians and philosophers as a lesson on the futility of rebellion.[1] It tells of a 'revolt' of the body 'members' against the belly, that is, the stomach, which takes all the nourishment without moving while the other parts of the body have to do the 'work'. The rebellion is doomed because without the belly first receiving, then digesting and redistributing all the nourishment, the other members will also starve. In the classic Aesopian fable, the members learn their lesson before it is too late because the belly has 'convinced' them of the error of their revolt (Aesop 2002: 35).

The fable was well known in Antiquity and used by Roman historians, most famously Livy and Plutarch, as a set piece of political rhetoric in the mouth of a senator of the Roman Republic, Menenius Agrippa, who quells a plebeian revolt by applying the story to them (as the body members) and the senate as the belly/stomach in order to justify the latter's rule (Livy 1998: 322–5 (= *Ab Urbe Condita*, II: 32–3); Plutarch 2001: 294–5 (= passage in the *Life of Coriolanus*). The fable remained in currency throughout the lifespan of the Roman Empire, again became popular in the medieval *Mirror for Princes* tradition and reached the height of its fame during the Renaissance when, on the basis of new translations of Plutarch's and Livy's writings, it was retold and reinterpreted many times (Harvey 2007: 23–37; Patterson 1991: 118–25), most famously in English literature in Shakespeare's drama *Coriolanus* (Shakespeare 1976).

Shakespeare's version of Menenius' metaphorical argument with the plebeians is set at the beginning of the drama (Act I, Scene 1, 101–69) and at first follows Livy's and Plutarch's template of the senator voicing the members' complaints against the belly, intimating that he empathizes with the rebels to a degree (to prepare his subsequent counterargument):

(1) There was a time when all the body's members

Rebell'd against the belly, thus accused it:

That only like a gulf it did remain

I' th' midst o' th' body, idle and unactive,

Still cupboarding the viand, never bearing

Like labour with the rest.

(*Coriolanus*, I, 1, 95–100)

The leader of the rebellious plebeians, 'First Citizen', who has previously announced that he is not prepared to be 'fobbed off with a tale' (I, 1: 93), interrupts the senator and impatiently asks for 'the belly's answer', inverting in the process, Menenius' scenario version:

(2) What! The kingly-crowned head, the vigilant eye,

The counsellor heart, the arm our soldier,

Our steed the leg, the tongue our trumpeter.

With other muniments and petty helps

In this our fabric, if that they – ...

Should by the cormorant belly be restrain'd,

Who is the sink o' the body,–

The former agents, if they did complain,

What could the belly answer? (*Coriolanus*, I, 1, 121–30)

Here, the First Citizen introduces a whole hierarchy of political *body parts* that starts from the top ('the kingly crowned head') through the *heart* ('counsellor') down to the *arms* and *legs*, that is, soldiers and cavalry and allocates the 'cormorant [i.e. gluttonous] belly' the ignominious status of the *sink of the body*. This counter-scenario presents a direct challenge to Menenius' version because it negates the role of the *belly* as the central, most important organ in the political body. In response to this interruption, the senator has to muster all his rhetorical skills to revalidate the belly's function as 'the store-house and the shop Of the whole body', including 'the court, the heart, ... the seat o' the brain; And [all] the cranks and offices of man', even to 'strongest nerves and small inferior veins' (*Coriolanus*, I, 1, 137–4).

As often in Shakespeare's works, the metaphor is further exploited in word play and ends with Menenius allocating the status of 'the great toe' to his Citizen-opponent (I, 1, 160–3).[2] The most important aspect for our present purpose is, however, the implicit appeal by both sides to different metaphor scenario versions of the STATE AS BODY metaphor in order to buttress and justify their alternative conclusions, which are contradicting each other no less than Lakoff's STRICT FATHER and NURTURANT PARENT models of the NATION AS FAMILY metaphor, as discussed in Chapter 3. There we argued that the NATION AS FAMILY metaphor was based on only one scenario that had a default version (the traditional STRICT FATHER model) and that its alternative was a specialized version that derived its semantic and political relevance from its deviation from the default scenario. A similar argument can be made for the First Citizen's use of the traditional hierarchical evaluation of political *body parts* in the Fable of the Belly: his head-dominated version derives its argumentative import from the opposition to Menenius' fable version which assumes the belly's supremacy.

However, we may ask whether this relationship between default and marked version is confirmed by an analysis of the relationship between scenarios and conceptual metaphors in larger historical and linguistic contexts. Is the argumentative splitting of a metaphor into two scenario versions only an ephemeral, emergent discourse phenomenon that can be explained with reference to a particular context of political argument and polemic, or can we trace it as a pattern in long-term discourse developments and across different languages? These are the questions we shall try to elucidate in this chapter.

5.2 The *body politic* tradition

Historical overviews of the conceptualization of the NATION (STATE) AS A BODY locate the origins of this tradition in Western thought in pre-Socratic Greek philosophy and highlight a first flourishing in the writings of Plato and Aristotle, with *The Republic* and *Timaios*, *Politics* and *De motu animalium* as the respective key texts. They highlight two main scenarios that have informed debates about the nation state since then: (1) its functional-anatomical hierarchy as a political *body* from the top, the *head,* down to the *feet* (which is easily recognizable in the First Citizen's protest in *Coriolanus*) and (2) its *state of health*. These 'foundation scenarios' were developed further in the course of Western political philosophy,[3] by Greek, Hellenistic and Roman historians as well as Stoic, Neo-Platonist philosophers and merged with Christian theological traditions, especially St. Paul's *Epistles to the Romans and Corinthians,* which also incorporated motifs from Old Testament texts in which the chosen people appeared as the *Lord's body.*

Via the 'Church Fathers', especially St. Augustine (*The City of God*), this complexion of concepts was transmitted as 'blueprint' for metaphor scenarios to political thinkers of the Middle Ages. Its central significance in medieval thinking about society, state and nation can be gauged from the treatise *Policraticus* (c. 1159), written by the cleric John of Salisbury (c. 1115–1180) and dedicated to his friend Thomas Becket. In the treatise, John, who survived his friend's 'murder in the cathedral' and later became Bishop of Chartres, analysed the Christian medieval polity systematically through the analogy with the human body, combining as he did a hierarchical perspective from the head down to the feet with a strong emphasis on the church's role as the soul that rules the whole organism including the head (the prince), and on the mutual duty of care among all body parts (John of Salisbury 1990: 66–7).[4] The feet, which owe the rest of the body obedience, have a right to be cared for by the other body members: 'Remove from the fittest body the aid of the feet; it does not proceed under its own power, but either crawls shamefully, uselessly and offensively on its hands or else is moved with the assistance of brute animals' (John of Salisbury 1990: 67).[5] The (head's) duty of care for all body members is matched by the duty to remedy any 'illness and blemishes', even by way of amputation of any afflicted members, on the authority of the New Testament passage (Mt. 18.9): 'If your eye or your foot offend you, root it out and cast it away from you,' which John extends even further: 'Indeed, neither the ears nor the tongue nor whatever else subsists within the body of the republic is safe if it revolts against the soul for whose sake the eyes themselves are gouged out' (John of Salisbury 1990: 63, 140–1).

This 'radical cure' approach to the 'outcome' of the ILLNESS THERAPY scenario, which John borrows from the Bible, is representative of his overall discussion of diseases in the body politic. John utters dire warnings as regards infections or injuries in various body parts, for example, *heart, hands, feet* (1990: 84, 105, 126), but, of course, a disease of or injury to the *head* is the most serious. John asserts that 'a blow to the head ... is carried back to all the members and a wound unjustly afflicted upon any member whomsoever tends to the injury of the head' and quotes Plato as having warned of an oppressive magistrate being equal to a 'swollen head' that makes it 'impossible for the members of the body to endure it either at all or without difficulty' and even leads them to suicide, for 'if the affliction would be incurable, it is more miserable to live than to die' (1990: 63, 137).[6]

If the application of radical therapy to *all* members of the Christian state, including the *head,* could be considered a subversive maxim when applied to the prince as the *head of state* (Nederman 1988), its application to the church was even trickier: its supreme *head,* as Christ's representative on earth, was the pope: Could he also fall ill, as *head of the Christian body*? John treated this question by way of 'reporting' a conversation he had during a visit to the Vatican with the reigning (English) Pope Hadrian IV, in which he informed the Pontiff about complaints about corruption and simony in the church: 'If you are father, therefore, why do you accept presents and payments from your children?' According to John, the pope responded by telling the Fable of the Belly and deducing from it the church's right to receive, and allocate, the nourishment to the Christian body according to merit and utility (John of Salisbury 1990: 135–6).

By integrating the Fable of the Belly as a (pseudo-)quotation from the pope into a treatise based on the head-to-feet analogy between body and state, John combined two incongruent scenarios of the STATE AS BODY metaphor – not, however, by putting them 'into the mouths' of adversaries in an argument (as Shakespeare was to do in *Coriolanus*). Both scenarios have a common ground in being essentially hierarchical, but the problems of applying both at the same time shine through if we consider the depiction of the church as the *soul that rules the head* in John's initial exposition of the metaphor (1990: 66). Taken to its logical conclusion, the pope is presented as the belly (= ruler) of a body (= church), which is the soul that rules the head (= ruler) of the worldly state. This scenario conflict would play out over the next few centuries in the political reality of continuous competition between the pope and princes, kings and emperors for supreme authority over medieval Christendom or 'national' parts of it, such as the nascent European nation states (Kempshall 1999; Nederman 1992; Nederman and Forhan 1993; Wilks 1963). Towards the end of the Middle Ages, however, the target notions of state and church authority over society or state as a *body* changed radically. One crucial element that was added was a distinction between a mortal and vulnerable physical body and the holy, 'mystical' and eternal body of the sovereign, which had been initially developed theologically to distinguish between the physical and spiritual bodies of Christ (and, by extension, of the church). In the long process of the secularization of theological into political concepts, this distinction was crucial in the formation of early modern political thought and informed the notion of the 'King's two bodies'.[7]

This distinction was still implicit in the multiple loan translations from late medieval Latin, *corpus mysticum/corpus politicum*, into European vernacular languages over the course of the sixteenth century, which included the English coinage *body politic* and its cognates, for example, French, *corps politique*; German, *politischer Körper*; Italian, *corpo politico*; Dutch, *politiek lichaam*; Russian, *политическое тело*; Greek, *Πολιτική Σώματος*; etc. (Charbonnel 2010: 91–110). However, in the emergent political theories of the Renaissance and early Enlightenment, the 'natural-virtual' distinction was backgrounded by a new focus on the relationship between the sovereign and the nation as his *body politic*, of which he could be seen as the *head* or the *physician* or the (domineering) *husband* (Hale 1971: 48–117; Musolff 2010a: 99–106). As a result, the modern meaning of *body politic* has changed into denoting to the whole of a nation state or society, whereas morphologically the phrase has kept the Latinate pattern, 'noun + post-positioned adjective' which is now archaic (Hughes 1988: 186; Görlach 1999: 477). In present-day English usage, it is of also possible to speak of a *political body*, but this phrase is not a synonym of *body politic*: it refers to specific institutional entities ('bodies'), for example, parliament, government, parties, that are parts of the whole, not the whole itself. Besides the lexicalized phrase *body politic*, a few political *body* aspects have also become lexically entrenched as idiomatic phrasal items, for example, *head of state, head of government, (long) arm of the law, organ (of a party)* (Deignan 1995: 2; *Shorter Oxford English Dictionary* 2002, vol. 1: 258).

At the time of Shakespeare's use of political body imagery in *Coriolanus*, *body politic* had already been established for almost three generations. In speeches to his parliament, King James I (1566–1625) depicted himself as head of his nation's body (Hale 1971: 111–17), and body-related anatomical, organic, medical and alchemistic terminology had been in continuous use as source for political metaphors in European languages, due to the pervasive influence of neo-Platonic Renaissance notions of the (human) body as the 'interface' of micro- and macrocosm.[8] Against this background, Shakespeare's use of the Fable of the Belly in *Coriolanus* must be seen as the invocation of a commonplace motif, which gained its specific political, historical and aesthetic significance through the echo effect of multiple traditions: Menenius voiced the classical belly-centred version, whereas the First Citizen articulated the no less venerable head-to-feet version, which reappeared in various forms in many of Shakespeare's historical dramas and tragedies (Diede 2008; Dobski and Gish 2013). The *body politic* metaphor and its different scenarios (top-down and belly fable) thus formed part of a broader intellectual context, a 'discourse' in the Foucauldian sense of a large set of sociocultural dispositions taken for granted by whole communities and eras (Foucault 1982, 2002).[9]

In Shakespeare's time, the classic literary, philosophical and historical traditions were still understood by sufficiently many educated people for them to be recycled, alluded to and reformulated in an abundance of intertextual resonances and allusions. Such a dense, overdetermined discourse framework cannot be assumed to hold for other eras; it would be absurd, for instance, to assume it for present-day English culture. But does this mean that there is no conceptual and discursive continuity at all? Is this at all an empirically testable question? It is here that the second metaphor corpus mentioned in the Introduction will be referred to: a multilingual sample of uses of the BODY-NATION metaphor across various languages BODYPOL, which currently includes just over half a million words. From BODYPOL, three samples have been assembled: one sample of 434 texts from British media in the period 1990–2014, which total over 195,000 words, one from the German press, with 186 texts (137,917 words) from the 1950s to today and one from the French press, that is, 85 texts (67,503 words) for 2000–14.[10] Between them, they include over ninety body-related concepts that are currently applied to politics in the respective national discourse communities (see Appendix I). Due to the differing sizes and periods of coverage of the samples, no reliable statistical comparisons can be drawn; however, several broad patterns of usage that seem to be typical for the three national discourse communities can be identified and, at least tentatively, related to specific scenario versions.

5.3 *Body politic, corps politique, politischer Körper*: Traces of national discourse traditions in metaphor usage

(3) Britain has still not joined Europe. The *transplant of a European organ into the British body politic still requires constant reinforcement by immunosuppressant drugs.* (*Financial Times*, 17 January 2013)

(4) The Prime Minister knows that the free-market system is hard-wired into *our national DNA.* (*The Daily Telegraph*, 19 January 2012)

(5) The German question never dies. Instead, *like a flu virus, it mutates.* On the eve of unification some European leaders worried that it would resume *killer form.* (*The Economist*, 21 October 2010)

Examples (3) to (5) illustrate the wide range of applications of body-based metaphors in present-day British political discourse. Apart from the BODY concept and the notion of the LIFE CYCLE, concepts include of parts of the anatomy and their functions (twenty distinct sub-concepts), ILLNESS/DISEASE/INJURY concepts (thirty-three sub-concepts), THERAPY (eleven sub-concepts) and BODY AESTHETIC (four sub-concepts).[11] In comparison to medieval and early modern conceptualizations of the *body politic* concepts, we find both continuities and discontinuities. As can be expected, the great majority of specific sub-concepts of parts of the body and of illnesses and therapies that are recorded in BODYPOL is absent from the medieval and Renaissance texts, due to the development in medical/physiological knowledge.[12] Neither John of Salisbury nor Shakespeare could have conceived of *immunosuppressants, DNA* or *viruses*, as these concepts were not available to medieval and early modern physiology, which both still largely relied on the ancient Galenic medical philosophy that centred on the notion of humoral balance (Oswei 1973; Harris 1998: 22). Only the most prominent physiological and medical concepts, that is, HEAD, HEART, HAND, LIMB, ARM, LEG, BELLY, BLOOD, CANCER, INFECTION, WOUND, POISON, OPERATION-AMPUTATION, are common to the *Policraticus,* early modern writings and BODYPOL data.

On the other hand, all sub-concepts in BODYPOL, apart from the BODY AESTHETIC category, can be related to the two main themes for scenario building in this domain which John and Shakespeare already covered, that is, RELATIONSHIP (INTERDEPENDENCE AND HIERARCHY) OF DIFFERENT BODY MEMBERS AND ORGANS and BAD STATE OF HEALTH/CURE/THERAPY. Although it is mentioned a few times, the *body politic in good health* seems to be at no time a popular scenario; instead, it seems far more interesting for both historical writers and present-day journalists to comment on its pathological conditions and the chances of recovery and therapy.

The one conceptual area that sticks out as mostly represented in today's usage is the field of expressions relating to BODY AESTHETIC and referring to individual politicians. Within BODYPOL, they form a sub-strand of the public debate that is also distinctive in terms of its pragmatic stance, that is, irony and sarcasm:

(6) I am inventing a new diet: it's called the *Greek austerity diet. And I am putting myself on it right away.* ... The first and most obvious difference [to the EU-led economic austerity policy in post 2008-Greece] is that *my Greek Austerity Diet is entirely a scheme of my own devising. I voted for it. My own body politic took the decision.* (*The Daily Telegraph,* 14 November 2011, author: Boris Johnson (portly British Tory politician)

(7) *Body politic:* ... In what is perhaps the ultimate betrayal of the Celebrity 'Cool Britannia' culture he embraced upon entering Downing Street, *Heat* [magazine] this week prints a long-lens snap of *Blair resplendent in his Caribbean holiday podge – a sort of 'ripples and nipples' look.* (*The Independent,* 14 August 2007)

(8) Sorry, Gordon [= Gordon Brown, British Labour Prime Minister], but *your body politic doesn't match Putin's* (*The Observer,* 1 November 2009)

(9) Just last week [the pro-Conservative magazine *The Spectator*] landed yet another bruising punch on [British Labour Prime Minister] *Blair's solar plexus, a part of the body politic that Iain Duncan Smith* [= then the Conservative opposition leader] *has notably failed to reach.* (*The Independent,* 7 July 2002)

In example (7), the EU-critical, Conservative Mayor of London B. Johnson mocks his own body appearance and the concomitant need for a diet in order to denounce the European Union's austerity policy as applied to Greece; in (8) and (9), two former Labour prime ministers are being ridiculed for their non-photogenic body features as symptoms of political weakness and in (10) Tony Blair is depicted as a boxer who allegedly cannot be 'touched' by his official parliamentary opponent but is vulnerable to attacks from the magazine the *Spectator*.

In all these cases, the physical body (or body appearance) of a political leader is the ostensive target referent of the phrase *body politic*, but the use of that very phrase points to an implicit target, namely the politician's standing, power and status. There are a number of further ironical uses which, while not containing explicit wordplay on the double entendre of the term *body*, highlight grotesque aspects of 'corporeality' that are ascribed to an individual politician's standing vis-à-vis the whole *body politic*, such as those of *pustule, pimple, wart*, or *(ingrowing) toenail*. Their frequency in the English sample of BODYPOL is about 10–15 per cent, whereas in the French and German samples its occurrence percentage is between 2 and 5 per cent. It thus seems to occur in British public debates on a regular basis, mostly in polemical discourse, designed to ridicule the target referent. Significantly, it is also reminiscent of the historical *body politic – body natural* distinction. Of course, apart from conceptual historians, present-day British users of *body politic* are unlikely to make a conscious connection between it and ancient distinctions of the monarch's personal and virtual body. Nonetheless, this allusion and the resulting tension between the diverse metaphorical meanings of political body terminology is a distinctive, regular pattern in British public discourse.[13]

German political discourse has three main lexicalized items to express political BODY status: the phrase *politischer Körper*, which resembles *body politic* most closely, is represented in the German BODYPOL sample only four times and is outnumbered by the compound *Staatskörper* and its variant *Körper des Staates* ('state body'/'body of the state') with thirty-one occurrences, and the compound *Volkskörper* ('people's body') with fifty-two occurrences.[14] The terms *Staatskörper* and *Volkskörper* not only have a different thematic focus – STATE v. PEOPLE – but, more importantly, they occur in present-day public discourse in starkly different usage environments. The general term 'state body' (*Staatskörper* or *Körper des Staates*) can be applied to any nation or a multinational entity such as the European Union (translations into English and italics in the following examples by AM, for German original texts see notes):

(10) [According to a priest] all Russians are supposed to *unite in one authoritarian state body*. (*Berliner Zeitung*, 15 April 2014)[15]

(11) [On account of the EU's concerted crisis management] we are witnessing the historically unique act of Europe's political re-constitution: in substance, *a new political state body* is emerging. (*Die Zeit,* 16 December 2011)[16]

(12) At the Humboldt University in Berlin, the government has just set up a special 'expert centre' of eight scientists who check that Gender Mainstreaming is correctly *implanted in the state body.* (*Der Spiegel,* 30 December 2006)[17]

The 'people's body' (*Volkskörper*), on the other hand, is used in almost all post-1960 cases with a strong historical–ideological connotation of relating to (neo-)Nazism and to Nazi jargon[18]:

(13) The individual citizen drunk on Germanness became identical with the rabid *collective body of the people* (*Die Zeit,* 16 August 2012, referring to the photo of a drunken Neo-Nazi attacking an asylum-seekers' home in Rostock in 1992).[19]

(14) This *sick people's body* harbours a wounded soul. Katharina Rutschky sees the debate about biopolitics [i.e. about demographic decline] as symptom of a mass hysteria which has its deepest roots in the German traumas of the 20th century (*Die Welt,* 26 March 2006).[20]

(15) The *body of the people* body as a work of art. [Headline of a review of a book about Hitler's speeches on 'racial art', *Berliner Zeitung,* 24 January 2005].[21]

Even when there is no explicit link to the (Neo-)Nazi-ideology, readers are expected to be aware of the connotation in order to understand the reference of *people's body,* as in this comment from a left-wing Austrian magazine:

(16) No nuclear pollution of [literally: no atomic power in] *the people's body!* The anti- nuclear movement in Austria is sharply divided, for some groups have a cosy relationship with right- wing extremist environmentalists. (*Jungle World,* 25 August 2011)[22]

The emphatic rejection of *nuclear pollution in the people's body* in the first sentence of example (16) is a pseudo quotation, for which no actual reference is provided. In fact, it is unlikely that such a rejection has ever been uttered verbatim – rather, the purpose of the imaginary quotation is to denounce specific environmental groupings as being (too) close to Nazi-typical attitudes and ideology. In order to make sense of *Volkskörper* as an allusion, readers must be at least vaguely aware of its connection to (Neo-)Nazi jargon.

Historically, the use of the term *Volkskörper* can be traced back to the 1840s, and of the specific concept of the 'people as a body' as distinct from that of the 'state as a body' to the 1770s (Musolff 2010a: 127–8). From the mid-nineteenth century onward, it became quickly popular with racist, especially anti-Semitic, writers in Germany and it acquired quasi-terminological status in National Socialist ideology, where it was used to depict the German/Aryan race's 'Self' as being under attack from the Jewish *parasite race*, as repeated in Nazi propaganda from before the publication of Hitler's *Mein Kampf* until 1945 (Bein 1965; Rash 2006; Musolff 2010a: 23–68).

Since the intensification in Germany's critical engagement and 'coming to terms' with the Nazi past in the 1960s (Eitz and Stötzel 2007; Niven 2006; Schmitz-Berning 2000), *Volkskörper* has become a loaded, almost stigmatized term, which is reflected in the usage patterns recorded in the German BODYPOL sample. Before 1960 one can find it in newspapers and magazines being used interchangeably with *Staatskörper* and applied to all types of nation states. Since the 1960s, however, this indiscriminate or naïve use incurs censure, for example, in 1998, when the conservative German politician J. Schönbohm was criticized for having invoked the ideal of a homogeneous German 'people's body' as opposed to the notion of a 'multi-cultural' society in the debate about immigration. According to a critic, such a notion was likely to 'kindle the fire' of interethnic conflict.[23] To translate the term *Volkskörper* here or in examples (13–16) as *body politic* would be misleading because uncritical use of *Volkskörper* is taken as indicating either an extreme right-wing stance or political ignorance on the part of its utterer. The term's relatively high frequency in the German sample vis-à-vis the other body-political terminological variants is not a sign of its 'popularity' as such but rather of the degree of critical attention currently paid in German society to Nazi-reminiscent vocabulary.

As for French, translation into English might appear at first sight to be much easier, because *body politic* has the seemingly direct equivalent phrase *corps politique*. However, in the French sample of BODYPOL, we encounter several variants of *body politic* cognates, that is, *corps politique, corps électoral* and *corps social*, abbreviated in the annotations to the following examples as '[c-p]', '[c-e]' and '[c-s]' (translations by AM):

(17) The President *pulls the body politic [c-p] into a regression* that gives reason for concern. (*Le Nouvel Observateur*, 1 May 2012)[24]

(18) From Mitterrand to Sarkozy – an unstoppable *decline* of the presidential office and the *political system* [c-p]. (*Le Monde*, 5 March 2011)[25]

(19) The atomization of individual citizens under the shock of the [economic] crisis and *the splits in the body of society* [c-s] translate directly into radicalization and the surge of populisms in public life. (*Le Figaro*, 4 May 2012)[26]

(20) For more than 25 years, the political classes, both the (neo-)liberal right and the socialist left, have mismanaged *the ageing body of French society* [c-s]. (*Le Figaro*, 9 November 2010)[27]

(21) To note: a figure that was not highlighted during the election night, i.e. the 2.14 million void votes, 5.8 per cent of the whole *electorate* [c-e], which represents an extremely elevated level that is doubtless owed in part to the Front National voters of the first round. (*Éco* 121, 7 May 2012)[28]

As these examples show, the meanings of the phrases *corps politique, corps social* and *corps électoral*, are not identical but very closely related: the social, electoral and political bodies are all aspects of the same referent, that is, the politically active part of the French populace. Examples (17) and (18) depict the political institutions and classes as the body that cares (or fails to care) for · French society. This latter 'social body' is not to be confused with the 'political classes' themselves; rather, it is the whole nation (see examples 19, 20). The nation's manifest incarnation, however, are the voters in the national election (even if they spoil their votes, as is suspected for far right-wing sympathizers in 21). This 'electoral body' is the concrete manifestation of the 'political body' of the nation, which in turn is the politically active manifestation of the 'body of society'.

Such mutually defining uses of *corps politique, corps électoral* and *corps social* are found frequently in the French BODYPOL sample but have few counterparts in the English and German samples. Which discourse tradition can they be linked to? A commentary in the leftist newspaper *Libération* may help us, which highlights the *sick body politic* scenario in its title: 'The body politic: a sick patient in search of a therapy' (Boisnard 2005).[29] The article's author, the writer Philippe Boisnard, argues that the political classes must rethink their fundamental political assumptions, in particular the notion that French society and state are based on the notion of absolute obedience to the sovereign general will, which dates back to Rousseau's *Social Contract* (1762):

(22) In order to think of the political sphere in terms of the image of a body should require no more than to reread Rousseau's *Social Contract*. This metaphor is by no means neutral; it supposes that this body is directed by a singular unity of intention and that all members of society are only to be considered as its organs. (Boisnard 2005)[30]

It is impossible to provide here a detailed discussion of Boisnard's interpretation of Rousseau's political philosophy of state, but one quotation from *Du Contrat Social* (Book II, Chapter 4) that appears to support Boisnard's main point may be quoted:

(23) Just as nature gives each man absolute power over all his limbs, the social pact gives the political body absolute power over all its members; and ... it is the same power, directed by the general will, that bears the name of sovereignty. (Rousseau 1994: 120)[31]

If we follow Boisnard's reading, the relationship between the 'political' and 'social bodies' of the nation, which seems to underlie examples (17)–(21), can be traced back to the great French enlightenment thinker and his impact on revolutionary and republican thought.[32] Such an explication does not imply that every politician or journalist who uses the terms *corps politique* or *corps social* today must be aware of their conceptual link with Rousseau's philosophy. However, it seems plausible to assume that, thanks to Rousseau's prominent role in French education and public discourse, these definitions have become commonplace to this day. Unlike the English and German samples, the French one contains several interventions by public intellectuals, for example, the philosophers A. Renaud, G. Agamben and B. H. Lévy and the politician/writer R. Debray.[33] If intellectuals' and philosophers' voices play such an eminent role in public discourse, it is not surprising that key arguments and metaphors from philosophical texts and traditions play a greater role in French debates than in other national discourses. This philosophically oriented 'habitus' (Bourdieu 1990) of the French public seems to shape the conceptual and argumentative focus of the metaphor and distinguishes it from the historical, to some extent still guilt-obsessed focus on *Volkskörper* in the German public sphere, which harks back to the catastrophe of National Socialist rule, and the distinctive English wordplay on double-entendres of *body politic/natural* with respect to politicians' public status.

5.4 Historical explanations for the development of metaphor scenarios

Reviewing our findings about the historical development of the NATION (STATE) AS BODY METAPHOR so far, we note that it was borrowed and translated from medieval Latin into the European vernacular languages during the Renaissance as a cross-lingual/-cultural concept; since then it has branched out into divergent, though still interconnected, discourse traditions. These traditions are anchored in 'national' political cultures insofar as they include experiences, myths and famous/infamous precedents, which are easily understood by members of the respective discourse communities, whereas they have to be given extra explanation/paraphrasing when translated. The theoretical modelling of such long-term development of metaphors presents a challenge to CMT. Even if historical precedents of present-day conceptual metaphors such as that of the NATION AS FAMILY, NATION AS BODY, WORLD AS (GREAT) CHAIN OF BEING ETC. have occasionally been acknowledged by CMT proponents (e.g. in Lakoff 1996: 153; Lakoff and Turner 1989: 167–8), the main emphasis has always been on the synchronic study of metaphors as mappings that are grounded in everyday and, preferably, physical experiences. When CMT began to include cognitive 'embodiment' theory, the role of the body as a universal basis of human experience and conceptualization was further emphasized, with reference to neurophysiological data and to ontogenetically 'primary' experiences that were regarded as the basis of metonymies and 'primary metaphors'; these were in turn considered to be the building blocks of all complex metaphors (Grady and Johnson 2003; Gibbs 2005; Johnson 1987; Lakoff 2008; Lakoff and Johnson 1999). The explanatory model has remained essentially the same, with the modification that now a degree of inter- and cross-language semantic variation was allowed for, but only as a secondary phenomenon that was derived from differing combinations of underlying primary metaphors and metonymies (Kövecses 2005: 63–4; Yu 2008: 259).

Within the CMT framework the NATION (STATE) AS BODY metaphor can be accounted for only at a highly abstract level as a special case of a more general mapping ABSTRACT COMPLEX SYSTEMS ARE PHYSICAL OBJECTS (Kövecses 2002: 133–4 and 2005: 208–15). All culture-specific uses of the metaphor appear in this perspective as mere surface instances of one universal metaphor. Such an analysis is consistent with the general assumptions of CMT and can account for some broad cross-cultural differences of the conceptual architecture in emotion metaphors (Kövecses 2002, 2005; Yu 1998, 2003, 2008); it is, however, not suitable for the more fine-grained distribution patterns in our corpus data. Furthermore, the question of a discourse-historical motivation for such variation is not even raised in this perspective because the universal experiential basis is considered sufficient to motivate all BODY-based metaphors, including those in public political discourse.

However, CMT's 'escape from history' is only possible at the cost of making several implausible and counter-intuitive assumptions (Trim 2011a: 67–8, 2011b; Winters 2011: 5–8). If conceptual metaphors are seen as BODY-based in a strong sense of relating always to physically/physiologically measurable or phenomenologically given experiences, why do speakers not always use the metaphors in the same way? If the classic CMT approach was correct, recipients should always retrieve their meanings in the same way, which flies in the face of the notorious vagueness of metaphor in everyday and public discourses as well as of literary imagery. Metaphor acquisition would only apply to complex, secondary metaphors from this perspective, given that primary metaphors are assumed to be understood automatically by everybody – but how are users supposed to know the difference?

In view of these contradictions, a number of approaches have tried to 'reconcile' the cognitive approach with models of historical, diachronic language change, building on 'evolutionary' approaches in conceptual theory in general, for example, R. Dawkins' 'meme' theory and other naturalizing models of concept development (Aunger 2000; Dawkins 1989, 1999, 2004; Hull 1988, 2000; Sperber 1996, 2000). Extending this approach into historical linguistics, Croft (2000) proposes a two-step model of language change that consists of (i) innovation or 'altered replication', roughly analogous to 'mutation' in genetics, and (ii) selection or 'differential replication' (Croft 2000: 23–9). It is the latter aspect that is relevant to the entrenchment of semantic structures including metaphors in the discourse community; accordingly Croft and Cruse (2004) sketch an idealized 'life history' of metaphor from its starting point when 'a metaphor takes hold in a speech community and gets repeated sufficiently often …. First, its meaning becomes circumscribed relative to the freshly coined metaphor, becoming more determinate; second, it begins to be laid down as an item in the mental lexicon; third, it begins a process of semantic drift, which can weaken or obscure its metaphorical origins' (Croft and Cruse 2004: 204–5).

In contrast to the model of metaphor development in terms of the (limited) variation in combinations of universal, experientially grounded primary metaphors, this model of innovation and selection/propagation highlights the fundamental difference between the creation of metaphors, that is, first-time usage and understanding, and their diffusion and entrenchment in terms of discourse traditions. This distinction helps to see more clearly what different metaphor-analytical approaches can, and cannot, achieve. The CMT search for a perceptual and experiential grounding of metaphor mappings is of course perfectly legitimate, but is restricted largely to accounting for the initial formation of a metaphor. On the other hand, it is unsuitable for explaining its dissemination and variation aspects. It is only in socioculturally embedded contexts that metaphor variants are taken up or rejected by the users and that they change by way of recipients' reinterpretations of their use.

Sociohistorically situated and usage-based models of metaphor development have the 'disadvantage' of providing essentially interpretative post-hoc explanations of clusters of distribution, collocation and intertextual referencing relative to specific research corpora, such as EUROMETA and BODYPOL or those constructed by other metaphor researchers interested in real-life data (Cameron 2011; Cameron and Deignan 2003; Charteris-Black 2004, 2005; Hanne, Crano and Mio 2015; Koller 2004; Semino 2008; Low et al. 2010). In terms of their epistemological assumptions, they belong to theories of 'complex adaptive systems' that model conceptual and linguistic change as the non-teleological emergence and differentiation of 'metaphor paths' into culture-specific types of 'conceptual networking' (Frank 2008 and

2009; Frank and Gontier 2011). These models are largely compatible with Wodak's discourse-historical approach (DHA) referred to in Chapter 1, which views discourses as '"bundle[s] of simultaneous and sequential interrelated linguistic acts, which manifest themselves within and across the social fields of action as thematically interrelated semiotic, oral or written tokens"' (Wodak 2001b: 66).

The divergent discourse traditions in the use of the NATION AS BODY metaphor that we observed above can be understood as such 'bundles' of linguistic acts that are indicative of attitudes and ideological orientations in specific cultural communities of practice. The historical resonance of *Volkskörper* in German with its echoes of Nazi jargon, the interdependence of *corps politique, corps électoral* and *corps social* in French political culture, and the focus on the 'natural' overtones of the *body politic* in British public debates are examples of such discourse traditions. The empirical basis for their 'discursive reality' is the observable evidence in the distribution patterns of corpus data. To reach a full discourse-historical 'triangulation' in the DHA sense, we would need detailed evidence from social science and historical research, which has only been hinted at in the above sketches. However, even in the absence of a fully comprehensive interdisciplinary analysis, the corpus-based evidence presented in this chapter can go some way in reconstructing a plausible version of the discourse traditions in question.

5.5 Summary

The diachronic scenario analyses which we have discussed in this chapter illustrate the potential for more comprehensive contrastive studies of figurative discourse traditions. We have related the semantic variation of this metaphor across three languages to prominent historical formulations that go back decades or even centuries. It is not claimed that latter-day metaphor users are fully aware of the precise 'precedent' formulations; explicit referencing to specific texts is only typical in certain discourse registers, such as conceptual history research. However, it is claimed that the members of the respective communities have at least an approximate awareness of the discourse-historical status of phrases such as *body politic, corps politique* or *Volkskörper*, as being not only figurative but also connected to political memories, mythologies and famous (and infamous) formulations of ideologically charged concepts. In order to be accessible to the wider public, such awareness can only be non-expert, vague and simplistic. It may even be factually wrong in the same way as 'folk-etymologies' represent a form of 'knowledge' that is based on the erroneous reconstruction of historical information about lexical history, as in many 'forgotten' metaphors (Steen 2010: 176–8).

Similarly, discourse-historical awareness is incorporated in the source elements of a metaphor scenario in the form of allusive or associative meaning aspects rather than as evidence-based historical knowledge. This less-than-well-defined epistemic status makes it easy for public users, for example politicians or journalists, to deny the respective historical associations if they deem them to be embarrassing.[34] Their political and journalistic followers and opponents will, respectively, claim that their defence was credible or untrustworthy, on the basis of their political sympathies and allegiances. Is there any way in which the discourse-historical approach to metaphor scenario analysis can help to assess such claims and counterclaims on a non-partisan basis? In the following chapter we will study this question with regard to one of the historically most notorious metaphor scenarios of political discourse, that of the PARASITE ON THE BODY OF THE PEOPLE.

6

Parasites, scrounging and the question of deliberate metaphor

6.1 Parasites, metaphor and etymology

The derogatory categorization of individuals or groups as social 'parasites' seems to be a prototypical example of semantic mapping from the biological to the social domain, which functions to dehumanize and stigmatize the target referent as part of a BODY-based ILLNESS-/DEATH-scenario. In it, the PARASITE is conceived as a double threat: it draws its nutriment from the HOST BODY and at the same time infects it with a DEADLY DISEASE. If the BODY in question is to be saved, the PARASITE therefore needs to be completely destroyed.

This scenario acquired its most elaborate and infamous form in the discourse of extreme right-wing nationalists in post-First World War Germany who identified Jews as a parasite on the German and other national bodies, which needed to be exterminated on the widest possible scale. In the 'Third Reich' they used this scenario to first propagate and legitimize their plans and then, during the Second World War, to herald and boast about their implementation of the Holocaust. Since this genocide, those who use *parasite* metaphors to stigmatize others risk being accused of articulating a Nazi-like world view. On the other hand, *parasite* metaphors hold a fascination not just for racists and other extreme ideologues who subscribe to the extermination scenario, but also for popular science authors who use it to re-metaphorize biological entities (Combes 2005; Zimmer 2011), as well as for philosophers, writers and film makers (Serres 2007; Mitchell 2012). In this chapter, we look in detail at the implications of this enormous historical, political and ideological resonance. When we reconstructed the history of *heart, body and belly* metaphors in the preceding chapters, we found that their diachronic development was far from linear. In comparison with *parasite* metaphors, however, such complexity appears limited, for the latter's development involved several 're-metaphorization' phases, whose impact can still be observed in current-day usage.

In present-day parlance, parasites come in two main variants, that is, as bio-parasites (organisms that live on other organisms and can spread potentially fatal diseases), and as socio-parasites (individual persons or groups of people that allegedly live at the expense of a wider community). It is the latter sense that is usually considered as figurative, as well as derogatory and emotionally loaded, as the following examples show:

(1) South Wales man called Jews 'parasites'. ... Trevor Hannington, 58, pleaded guilty at Liverpool Crown Court ... to one count of inciting racial hatred by writing posts on the internet that *Jews were 'parasites feeding on others'* and 'utterly evil sub-beings'. (*WalesOnline*: 2010)

(2) Mick Philpott, killer of his own six children, was pretty evidently a nasty piece of work: bone idle and a *parasite upon the social security system*. (*Daily Express,* 12 April 2013)

(3) Iain Duncan Smith, the work and pensions secretary ... was about to deliver a speech on pensions reform when campaigner Willie Black began haranguing the MP, *calling him a 'parasite' and a 'ratbag' for pursuing social security cuts*. ... (*The Guardian,* 27 March 2013)

(4) *Bankers are giving Parasites a bad name.* (*ThinkLeftOrg,* 5 May 2012)

(5) I'm not a great phone hacker myself, but I feel kinship with the journalists who did it. *They are parasites who use other people's lives as material, and so am I. Journalism is parasitism.* It has to be. (*The Financial Times,* 17 February 2012)

As example (1) shows, use of the term *parasite* to stigmatize a group of people can be judged a racist criminal offence. Employing it against individuals, as in examples 2 and 3, on the other hand, is seen as an insult rather than as an offence; even when it is directed against the monarch, it is politically but not judicially penalized.[1] In ironic-hyperbolic use, as in (4) and (5), the context mitigates their insulting force, that is, the so-called 'parasites' appear to be 'not so bad after all', either because there are 'worse' cases ('bankers') or parasitism is deemed to be 'normal'.

Some dictionaries and encyclopedic websites suggest that the SOCIOPARASITE is derived from the BIOPARASITE (*Brewer's Dictionary of Phrase and Fable* 1999: 880; Wilkinson 2008: 238; https://en.wikipedia.org/wiki/Parasitism_(social_ offense), accessed 19 April 2013), and cognitive linguistic analyses have also assumed a uni-directional metaphorization of the concept.[2] This view is in line with CMT's basic assumption that metaphor 'allows us to understand a relatively abstract or inherently unstructured subject in terms of a more concrete, or at least more highly structured subject matter' (Lakoff 1993: 245). Etymology and historical lexicography, however, inform us that English *parasite* and its cognates in other European languages (e.g. French *parasite*, German *Parasit*, Italian *parassito*) are derived, via Latin, from the ancient Greek term *parasitos* (παρά-σιτος), which appears to have first denoted a religious official 'who ate the grain together' with others, that is, partook in communal religious meals in ancient Greece.[3]

Even in the ancient period, however, this meaning was widened to denote anyone – that is, not just priests – who lived at the expense of others, and in this extended sense the *parasite* as scrounger became a character in classical Greek comedy and was borrowed into ancient Roman comedy.[4] The main meaning of Latin *parasitus* was thus SOMEONE WHO EATS/LIVES AT THE EXPENSE OF OTHERS, and it is in this sense that the term was taken over by the early modern European vernacular languages from the late fifteenth/early sixteenth century onwards, mainly in humoristic references to a type of person that lives at the expense of others and repays the host with flattery and sycophancy.[5] By the early seventeenth century, the *parasite* character was already well established in English theatre, for instance, in Ben Jonson's 1606 comedy, *Volpone, or the Fox,* where the wily manservant Mosca ('The Fly') is termed 'a parasite', and in Shakespeare's *Coriolanus* (1608), where Caius Martius (Coriolanus) employs 'parasite' to designate a toadying courtier.[6]

6.2 Metaphorizations 'back and forth'

The biological meaning of *parasite* as an organism that draws its nutriment from and possibly does damage to another organism is attested in English and French only since the mid-seventeenth century, at first with respect to plants, for example, the mistletoe (Browne 2009 [1642]: 135. Using the domain-difference criterion, we have to classify this use as clearly metaphorical: the concept of 'X-FEEDING-ON-Y' is transferred from the social to the biological/botanical domain. 'Parasitological' studies in the scientific sense had of course been conducted long before that time but under different names; they had received an enormous boost through the invention and construction of accurate microscopes, which had made it possible to view tiny organisms that lived in and from bigger organisms.[7] However, it took until the eighteenth century for the BIO-PARASITE concept – and for its lexicalization under the term *parasite* – to become established, partly on account of controversies over its compatibility with the Christian doctrine of creation, which assumed a positive ethical bias that was difficult to reconcile with the detrimental effect of some bio-parasites on their hosts (Farley 1972).

In the context of the Enlightenment, the biological category PARASITE became so well known that it was re-metaphorized again in the last decades of the eighteenth century, this time in the opposite semantic direction, that is, from the biological to the social/political domain. One strand of this re-metaphorization occurred in the context of the French Revolution. E. Sieyès, one of its early leaders, used the PARASITE concept, though not yet the term, in his rally cry for the 'Third Estate' (1789), when he attacked the aristocratic privileges in the absolute monarchy as being equivalent to a system of 'botanical tumours that cannot live except on the sap of plants that they exhaust and deplete' (Sieyès 1989: 30). During the radicalization phase of the Revolution in the early 1790s, the denunciation of the monarch and the aristocracy as *parasites* was combined with *bloodsucker* and *vampire* metaphors.[8]

During the nineteenth and twentieth centuries, the revolutionary condemnation of the 'parasitic' *Ancien Régime* would serve as an ideological model for communist attacks on the bourgeoisie as a 'parasite body'.[9] In the Soviet Union, the phrase *parasites of the people* (ПАРАЗИТЫ ОБЩЕСТВА) was used up to the 1960s as a legal term to denote 'persons avoiding socially useful work and leading an anti-social, parasitic way of life'.[10] Similarly, in Maoist China 'enemies of the people' were denounced as *parasites*[11]; similar uses can be traced to the end of the twentieth century in revolutionary-terroristic literature (Rote Armee Fraktion 1987: 24). While the precise referents in the targeted social groups (e.g. royal family, aristocracy, 'bourgeoisie', 'capitalists', 'dissidents', 'imperialists') change across these texts, the core meaning of (socio-)*parasites* denoting members of a social class that lives at the expense of and damages the whole people remains relatively constant. It differs from the pre-revolutionary SOCIO-PARASITE concept in that it targets whole groups, not just individuals, and that it is based on a biological source concept. This metaphor version 'dehumanizes' its human referents in the specific sense that they are recategorized as belonging to a different kind of organisms, which is in scientific understanding incapable of 'mental states' (emotion or cognition) and hence of personal agency while its behavioural potential 'inspire[s] disgust and fear' (Tipler and Ruscher 2014: 222).

We may summarize the semantic developments of the parasite concept that we have surveyed so far as follows:

a) Originating in ancient Greece, the meaning of the term *parasitos*, and its Latin derivation, *parasitus*, was extended from designating a religious institution and its agents to a stock character of comedy a scrounger who lives at the expense of another person or group of persons. We can call these early stages in its semantic development SOCIO-PARASITE 1 (for the non-metaphorical reference to priests) and 1* (for the extended humorous meaning of 'scrounger' in general).

b) In the fifteenth to sixteenth centuries, the late Latin version of the term 'migrated' into the vernacular European languages in the form of calques while keeping its core meaning of 'servile, flattering scrounger' with pejorative connotations that were based on ethical disapproval and derision, but also included humorous elements. This early modern concept was applied to new target referents but remained within the main meaning tradition inherited from ancient comedy. We can designate this meaning as SOCIO-PARASITE 1**.

c) From the seventeenth century onwards, the term *parasite* was applied by analogy with SOCIO-PARASITE 1*/** in the characterization of biological entities that depended on other organisms, which led to a new meaning unit: BIO-PARASITE 1. This meaning is metaphorical but *not* 'experientially grounded' in the CMT sense of concrete bodily experiences informing abstract metaphorical concepts. Instead, only SOCIOPARASITE 1*/** can be considered as its source. Any awareness or classification of the physical or phenomenological 'experiences' of bio-parasites under this category label must have occurred after it had been coined. Of course, we are able to experience first-hand the effects of bio-parasites and observe some, like the mistletoe, with our own eyes. But that does not mean they were understood as *parasites* in a scientific sense before the science was developed and handed down to later generations.

d) From the late eighteenth century onwards, this biological meaning provided the basis of a new analogical application, that is, in the discourse of revolutionary radicalism, which led to a further metaphorical construction: SOCIO-PARASITE 2. It differed from the SOCIO-PARASITE 1-1** concepts in that it was derived from BIO-PARASITE 1 (i.e. through comparison with parasitic botanical and zoological species). Rather than denoting annoying but harmless individual characters in comedy or social satire, it became a class name for groups that were deemed to damage the whole of society and needed to be controlled or destroyed.

In a further re-metaphorization twist, the biological meaning of BIO-PARASITE 1 seems to have taken on some anthropomorphic implications from its SOCIO-PARASITE source, despite its scientific pedigree. In *On the Origin of Species*, Darwin found it necessary to warn against 're-humanizing' interpretations of bio-parasites when he integrated the BIO-PARASITE 1 concept into evolution theory: 'It is ... preposterous to account for ... this parasite [i.e., the mistletoe] by the effects of ... of the volition of the plant itself' (Darwin 1901: 5). Despite his warning, many popular representations of bio-parasites are riddled with anthropomorphisms to this day. Medical advice websites, for instance, characterize micro-organismic bio-parasites *as* if they were intentionally and deliberately 'insidious', 'harmful' or 'destructive', thus creating a re-humanized concept BIO-PARASITE 2. They also portray the respective bio-parasites, from a Euro- or US-centric viewpoint, as typical *immigrants*: thus, bio-parasites from Mediterranean regions that spread to Northern Europe are depicted as 'unwanted' or 'secret immigrants' who surreptitiously sneak into an unsuspecting and defenceless host population.[12] US anti-immigration blogs focus on immigrants across the Mexican border who carry (bio-)parasite-induced diseases. The blog, *MichNews.com*, for instance warned of a tapeworm parasite 'Taenia solium', which was 'moving along with [Mexicans immigrating into America] and passed among people'.[13] Here, the bio-parasite appears as an agent (= BIO-PARASITE 2) that uses the human socio-parasite (SOCIO-PARASITE 1** and/or 2) to spread from one country to another: a double PARASITE whammy, as it were, which blends popular beliefs about immigrants (e.g. that they come uninvited and deliberately secretly) with fears of illness-inducing bio-parasites.

6.3 Metaphor and racism

The application of the biologically grounded PARASITE concept to social groups in the last decades of the eighteenth century (SOCIO-PARASITE 2) was not confined to the ruling classes but was also employed to characterize one specific cultural-ethnic community, that is, the Jews. In his *Philosophy of the History of Mankind* (1784–91), the Baltic-German philosopher and cleric J. G. Herder (1744–1803) described Jews as a *parasitical plant* on account of their alleged dependency on other nations:

(6) God's own people who were once given their fatherland as a divine present have been almost since their inception a parasitic plant on the stems of other nations (Herder, *Ideen zur Philosophie der Geschichte der Menschheit*, quoted in Schmitz-Berning 1998: 460; translation: AM).

Herder's metaphor was obviously sourced from botanical organisms but could just as plausibly be applied to the general notion of a NATIONAL BODY, for which Herder, again, had already coined the term *Nationalkörper*.[14] Soon, the main term for the concept of a nation-specific political body became *Volkskörper* (see previous chapter), and in the course of the nineteenth century the metaphor of NATIONS AS BODIES and JEWS AS PARASITES were reinterpreted in Social Darwinist theories about human nations and races' 'struggle for survival' to fit the purposes of anti-Semitic polemicists (Evans 1997: 119–44).

In this perspective, the RACIAL SOCIO-PARASITE was no longer envisaged as a plant that was just taking advantage of its host by drawing nutrients from it but as an animal parasite on a human body, which endangered its life by infecting it with deadly diseases. In the social and economic crises following the First World War in Germany, the National Socialists developed this tradition further to the point where the parasitical threat to the German nation was deemed to require radical 'therapeutic measures'. Hitler spelt out this vision in *Mein Kampf,* first published 1925–6:

(7) The Jew was ... always a parasite in the body of other peoples. ...
He is and remains the typical parasite, a sponger who like an
infectious bacillus keeps spreading as soon as a favourable medium
invites him. And the effect of his existence is also similar to that
of spongers: wherever he appears, the host nation dies out after a
shorter or longer period. (Hitler 1992: 277; for the German original
compare Hitler 1933: 334)

Hitler's definition, which is reiterated throughout *Mein Kampf* and collocates with a wide range of vocabulary denoting disease-carrying organisms and their effects, such as *bacteria, bacilli, bloodsuckers, elements of decomposition, leeches, lice, maggots, rats, viruses, vipers* (Rash 2006: 155–6, 174), was the blueprint for the Nazi version of the JEWS AS PARASITES metaphor. Alfred Rosenberg, the Nazis' chief 'theorist' and later minister for the Occupied Eastern territories, depicted the slow destruction of a crab by the parasite 'sacculina' as the exact parallel to the influence of Jews on society in his pseudo-philosophical book *The Myth of the 20th century* first published in 1930 (Rosenberg 1936: 461). Joseph Goebbels, the Nazi Propaganda leader, defined Jews as an 'absolutely alien race' characterized by its 'parasitic features' (Goebbels 1934: 130); as minister from 1933 onwards, he saw to it that this message was reiterated on a daily basis until the end of the Third Reich. As the Nazis had almost complete control over the public media,[15] the JEWS AS PARASITES metaphor was continually reproduced, while 'deviant' explications or uses were forbidden and could only be uttered in private and clandestine contexts. In practical terms, being called a *parasite on the people's body* in Nazi Germany did not just amount to receiving an insult or a degrading characterization but was a death threat. Insofar as the genocide of European Jews was presented and even partially carried out by the Nazis as if it were a therapeutic/hygienic action, this metaphor can be said to have turned into a genocidal reality.

Historically, the JEWS AS PARASITES metaphor can be regarded as a variant of SOCIO-PARASITE 2 insofar as it has the same biological grounding and mapping direction, that is, application from a biological to a socio-political target referent. However, it is politically more radical for two reasons. Firstly, as defined in Nazi ideology, its target was a biologically defined group in a literal sense, that is, the alleged 'Jewish race'. Secondly, the Nazi version focused exclusively on fatally damaging bio-parasites for the source domain, and thus concluded that the perceived JEWISH RACE PARASITE had to be eliminated under all circumstances. Furthermore, the Nazi version of SOCIO-PARASITE 2 was blended with logically incompatible pseudo-religious ideas of devilish/demonic forces operating in world history (Bärsch 2002). This meant that the source notion of bio-parasites as unintentional agents (see above) was cancelled. Instead, the JEW AS PARASITE figure was held morally responsible for its supposed detrimental effects on the host nation. Focusing on this racist version of the SOCIO-PARASITE 2 meaning, we can thus distinguish an additional stage in the history of the X AS PARASITE metaphor:

e) Within a racist ideology such as Nazism, the SOCIO-PARASITE 2 concept can be further developed into the notion of a biological threat to the host society that must be eliminated at all cost. The concepts of BIO- and SOCIO-PARASITES are blended into the construct of a SUPER-PARASITE 2*, WHICH combines deadly dangerousness with devilish cunning. Cognitively, this blend is a new concept that serves the purposes of political propaganda. As such it belongs to a marginal register of public discourse but became mainstream in Nazi Germany.

6.4 Immigrants as 'parasites'

Unlike the Nazi regime, the racist SOCIO-PARASITE 2* concept survived the end of the Second World War. It is still popular with extremist political groups that want to express strong disapproval of other parts of society, which they perceive as being non-productive and destructive. It seems to be a special favourite with xenophobic anti-immigrant movements (Inda 2000). In present-day Germany, extreme right-wing websites allege that a Jewish-Russian 'invasion of scroungers' have settled as 'parasites' and that supporters of migration and multiculturalism are 'the worst parasites in our society'.[16] Another blog site gives a special twist to this denunciation by asserting that the very idea that immigrants could enrich one's 'home culture' is a 'parasite that is being put into the brains of our toddlers' by sinister leftist forces.[17] The continuity between such IMMIGRANTS AS PARASITES metaphors and the Nazis' JEWS AS PARASITES metaphor is evident.

In view of the historical 'precedent' of Nazi discourse (Keller-Bauer 1983), it could be argued that present-day use of the SOCIO-PARASITE 2* concept to stigmatize minorities or immigrants or any other groups of people is a continuation of the dehumanizing fascist discourse and should therefore be condemned and even persecuted by law. Against this view, however, it can be argued that such 'stigmatization of the stigma' is pointless for several reasons: (a) the SOCIO-PARASITE 2* concept, when used outside a totalitarian system is in 'free competition' with other derogatory metaphors and tends to be marginalized due to its inherent extremism, (b) such usage is not 'manipulative' or misleading because its users are aware of its figurative character and have freely chosen to express/understand their views of the topic in such a way, and (c) linguistic analysis should be ideologically neutral.

Lakoff's solution of this conundrum was to have his metaphor-analytical cake and eat it by drawing a neat line between a 'scientific', supposedly neutral, analysis of the FAMILY metaphors in US politics and an 'engaged' critique of their morality- and education-related 'entailments' (see Chapter 1). However, this solution seems to beg more questions than it answers, especially the question of how representative the occurrences of particular metaphors in public discourse truly are. With regard to present-day uses of the X AS PARASITE metaphor that resemble Nazi rhetoric, for instance, it would be good to know whether their dissemination and acceptance reaches beyond small, marginal groups of fanatical xenophobes and racists. In order to arrive at reliable conclusions, we need to go beyond the oft-repeated 'exemplary' analysis of small discourse samples that do not convey a comprehensive picture of its role in public discourse. In the remainder of this section we therefore present a pilot study that compares uses of the IMMIGRANTS AS PARASITES metaphor across different genres of immigration debates in Britain. It consists of a press corpus including broadsheet and tabloid newspapers as well as magazines, online discussion fora from the popular BBC 'Have your say' website and a sample of forty internet weblogs with readers' comments. Table 6.1 below gives an overview over the range and size of the whole corpus (word counts for blogs have been established through conversion into Word documents, which include some extra website material; their word count is therefore not as exact as that for the other media).

The first sample consists of press articles that have appeared in UK media, sampled from the online sites of the respective newspapers or magazines but without readers' comments, even if the media concerned operate comment sites. The *Have Your Say* sample, on the other hand, consists only of comments by members of the public who participated in the forum debates.

Table 6.1,

Media	Newspaper and magazine articles (2003–2014)	*Have your say* Online fora (April–June 2010)	Blogs (accessed December 2013)
Titles/key words	*Daily Express, Daily Mail, Financial Times, The Guardian, The Independent, The Observer, The Scotsman, The Spectator, The Sun, The Daily Telegraph, The Times.*	(1) Should politicians be talking about immigration? (2) How should immigration be tackled? (3) Are immigration rules fair?	40 websites, searched on WWW by key words: *immigration, parasites, UK*
No. of items	138 articles	2473 postings (566, 881, and 1026 for the respective fora; with 81 postings removed by BBC online forum management	40 websites
No. of words	130.756	333.518	89.950

It was compiled in spring 2010, when this topic was hotly debated in public as part of the general election campaign. The third sample, that is, blogs, was collected by a 'Google' keywords search designed to find websites containing *parasite* metaphors in relation to the immigration topic. The three samples evidently differ in their respective elicitation procedures, time frames and word counts and therefore cannot be regarded as statistically balanced. They are only intended as a heuristic basis for the comparative analysis of different media, and in particular for relating press discourse as produced by journalists (and, when quoted by the press, also by politicians) to readers' reactions.

The press and online forum samples show a high degree of consistency in the use of a relatively small set of standard scenarios, which account for more than 90 per cent of the data and confirm international research findings on (im) migration discourses.[18] They can be summarized as follows (italicized items are lexemes or phrases that reoccur with high frequency):

a) The SPACE-CONTAINER scenario: the nation(state) is conceptualized as a *container* with distinct *boundaries*, which separate those *on the outside* from those *inside*; immigrants are thus *outsiders* who want to *come/move into the container*. The *container* is often conceptualized as a *building* that has *doors* and other openings that can be *closed, open* or *half-open;* it is also seen as a vessel that has a *limited capacity* to include contents; if too many immigrants come in, this increases the *pressure* inside to *bursting point* and necessitates the erection of new *barriers.*

b) The MOVEMENT scenario (specific to immigrants as PARTICIPANTS): its most prominent version is that of a *flood, wave* or even *tsunami,* that *pours/ rushes* into the container. Two other recurrent scenario versions are those of an *invasion* and of *(benefit) tourism.* They all fit into the wider conceptual complex of a *mass movement,* as indicated by verbs such as *flock, pass through, overwhelm.* There are also a few instances of single immigrants being pictured as *swimming over;* this metaphor version is evidently motivated by Britain's geographical status as an island.

c) The ACTION scenario (specific to CONTAINER-insiders as PARTICIPANTS): these fall into two distinct groups: on the one hand, politicians and social groups that are viewed as (and mostly condemned for) *inviting, letting, allowing, bringing* immigrants into the country, and on the other hand those who try to *send them home, round them up, chuck* or *kick them out* or at least *limit, target* and *control* immigration. Even the lexical pair of *importing* and *exporting* is used. 'Ordinary' insider-citizens are depicted as noticing and reacting to an unwanted change in their living circumstances: one popular formula is the construction *when I/you walk down the street and see ….* A sub-scenario is that of VIOLENT ACTION, as indicated by terms such as *backlash, combustible issue, dangerous game, invasion, rivers of blood,*[19] *revolution, storm troopers, time bomb and weapon.*

d) The EFFECT scenario has three sub-scenarios: MIX, GAIN and SCROUNGE. The first one is mostly represented in the online commentaries and tabloid articles, referring as it does to an alleged mixing of cultures that *submerges, dominates* or *subjugates* traditional British culture. Its effect is that the insiders no longer recognize their surroundings 'when they walk down the street' (see above). This sub-scenario includes colourful formulations such as a vision of *Coronation Street* (a TV soap opera set in a terraced street, supposedly in the Manchester area) as having been *moved to Pakistan.* The GAIN sub-scenario is confined to the broadsheet press and small sections of the fora discussing immigrants that are among *best and brightest* of their respective home countries and provide an *economic benefit* to Britain: it is mostly used in arguments made in defence of continued immigration of certain elite groups (e.g., foreign students, skilled workers, business people). The last sub-scenario, which is of special interest here, is that of the IMMIGRANT-AS-SCROUNGER who *sucks, drains or bleeds the country dry* and *sponges off Britain*. It includes depictions of immigrants as *leeches, bloodsuckers* and *parasites*.

As part of the SCROUNGE sub-scenario, *parasite* imagery does occur across all three genres of press articles, blogs and online fora but its frequency, collocation patterns and argumentative contexts are markedly different. The press sample, even though it includes a number of strongly anti-immigration oriented texts, has only a few articles, in which immigrants are referred to by the authors as *parasites*; most of these uses are hedged and/or mixed with the GAIN scenario, for example, accusing the government of 'letting in parasites, [but] turning away entrepreneurs' (*The Daily Telegraph,* 25 March 2013). The great majority (c. 75 per cent) of articles in the press sample that include the term *parasite* quote it as being used by racist xenophobes.[20] *Parasite* imagery is evidently too strongly ideologically loaded to be used uncritically in the mainstream press. There are hardly any press texts from which readers could 'learn' an assertive use of *parasite* imagery, even though the SCROUNGE scenario is represented in about 25 per cent of all articles.

By comparison, the percentage of texts invoking the SCROUNGE scenario is smaller in the online forum sample, where it is present in just 251, that is, about 10 per cent of all 2,473 postings. In 90 per cent of all these postings, however, the scenario is used to assert that immigrants are indeed scroungers, and it collocates in many cases with the INSIDER-ACTION scenario that advocates radical measures against the *sponging* immigrants, for example, using the army to deport them. Explicit use of *parasite* vocabulary, however, is rare: it amounts to altogether fifteen instances in the sample; of these 50 per cent are directly targeted at immigrants, for example, in postings such as the following:

> **(8)** ... the willy nilly entry into this country of immigrants who come to do harm or to simply suck a living out of hard working middle income eaners [*sic*] (BBC, HYS-1, 30 April 2010).[21]

> **(9)** If they haven't been detected for ten years then they are either living via the proceeds of crime or tax dodging. And that makes them parasites and criminals (BBC, HYS-2, 30 April 2010).

> **(10)** ... the sort of immigrants who Labour has been busy encouraging ... naturally become potential Labour 'clients' of lazy spongers and parasites, almost guaranteed to vote for the party who will keep feeding them benefits (BBC, HYS-3, 9 June 2010).

In these and similar contributions, IMMIGRANTS AS PARASITES figure as a collective that have come deliberately to Britain (or have been invited to Britain by the

Labour Party, according to example 10) in order to exploit the country and engage in criminal activities. This characterization conforms to the more modern SOCIO-PARASITE 2 concept based on the biological source of PARASITE SPECIES. Arguably, example (10) comes close to the older SOCIO-PARASITE 1 concept of an annoying but relatively harmless 'hanger-on', insofar as the alleged client-role of immigrants for the Labour Party resembles that of the COURTIER PARASITE who served his 'master's' purposes. However, any humorous aspect that the comedy character may have had has been cancelled. The remaining co-text of the posting, which denounces the alleged 'Labour agenda … to flood the country with the world's dregs' as 'morally bankrupt and otherwise totally clueless', leaves no doubt that their existence is seen as obnoxious by the forum contributor.

The remaining 50 per cent of *parasite* instances in the *Have Your Say* debates, however, include critical thematizations of such uses as part of arguments defending the right of immigrants and also ironical counter-usage, similar to many of the press articles:

(11) This is a true story. A young man came to England from Zimbabwe to study business and finance. Whilst here his family were murdered, their farm and all their money seized. Our man had no other means of support, could not afford to pay his course fees and dropped out of his university course. Not convinced our immigration system would grant him asylum … our man bought a false passport from a man in a pub. By doing so he became an illegal immigrant. He never claimed a penny in benefits. … [comment 56] called this young man a parasite and a criminal. (BBC, HYS-2, 30 April 2010; *the reaction to 'comment 56' refers to the posting quoted as example (9) above*).

(12) Lets tackle the real problems of a lazy bunch of parasites feeding of the life blood of our hard working people, who consider benefits to be a God given right and work to be beneath them and stop bashing the hard working immigrants, just because they are fulfilling a vital place in our farms and factories (BBC, HYS-1, 29 April 2010).

Like the press, these comments ascribe the discriminating use of *parasite* imagery against immigrants to xenophobic parts of the British public; in some cases, such as example (11), they refer directly to a preceding anti-immigrant posting in the forum in order to disprove it by highlighting cases of 'non-parasitic' immigrants. Others, like the one in (12), use the *parasite* metaphor against other 'indigenous' groups ('lazy bunch of parasites feeding of the life blood of our hard working people, who consider benefits to be a God given right') whom they wish to criticize. Generally, neither the lexical collocations nor the argumentative contexts of these metaphor occurrences evoke the PARASITE-ELIMINATION scenario with its strongly racist, (pseudo-)biologically grounded presuppositions.

This picture completely changes when we study the blog sample (which is of course statistically incomparable to the other samples due to its predetermined 100 per cent rate of *parasite* text occurrences). Most of these blogs begin by emphatically asserting the *parasite* status of immigrants, often in headlines such as 'Foreign Immigrants are Parasites', 'Muselmanic Welfare Parasites Cost Britain £13+ BILLION A YEAR!', 'Britain: Muslim immigrants are the chief parasites'.[22] These statements are followed up in more than 80 per cent of cases by emphatic endorsements and assertions in the main text body of the blog and its further comments, which detail the parasites' alleged effect in graphic detail and combine this with racist hate speech that focuses on a stereotyped Muslim (in 15: Jewish) 'Other':

(13) Muslim immigrants in Europe are very often parasites. As a whole they do more bad than good for their host countries.[23]

(14) Parasitic Immigrants arrive here with their begging bowls out, to milk our hard won welfare & housing system. IDI Amin was not a nice guy but he had his country at heart, when he slung out its milking immigrants.[24]

(15) So Whitey, do you really feel like being the butt of the joke in the country your ancestors built? ... National humiliation from a bunch of mud parasites sent here by the JEW to destroy your genetic right to exist? *Am I making a mountain out of a molehill?*[25]

(16) The irony of the situation is inescapable: their [= the immigrants'] parasitical behaviour obliges governments, through taxpayers, to subsidize their adopted country's own destruction.[26]

Eight Blogs contain comments that are critical of the main anti-immigration thrust, but these are apologetic, arguing in detail about exaggerated statistics, the economic benefit that 'good' immigrants bring to Britain and issues of Human Rights legislation. The anti-immigration comments, on the other hand, not only describe their targets as criminal scroungers but elaborate on the bio-imagery by using collocations of *parasite* such as *leeches, locusts, rats, vermin, plague, germs,* and speculating on 'parallels' between bio- and socio-parasites. Several blog comments, for instance, focus on the 'curious' notion that 'parasites are suicidal' because they destroy themselves by destroying the host.[27] The blogs also include the 'double-parasite' *topos* found in US blogs mentioned earlier, that is, the concept of SOCIO-PARASITES CARRYING BIO-PARASITES, which in one case is used as a rebuttal of arguments that foreign doctors and nurses provide essential services: 'If we didnt have so many parasitic immigrants bringing nasty diseases and hordes of kids with them, we wouldnt need them at all!' (7 July 2013). Furthermore, they recommend radical counter measures to *root out, eliminate, cure this plague,* and they allege that if these measures are not soon implemented, the INSIDER group will be *exterminated.*

Overall, the vast majority of contributions to blogs that include the IMMIGRANTS AS PARASITES metaphor closely fits the racist SOCIO-PARASITE 2* concept in terms of biology-based scenarios, projected catastrophic outcomes and suggested 'practical solutions'. They are predominantly directed at Muslims and, so far, confined to the margins of public discourse, but otherwise there is little conceptual difference to Nazi propaganda.

6.5 Metaphors as deliberately chosen scenario elements

Our comparison of *parasite* metaphors in the debate on immigration across three media genres in Britain has shown that they form part of a narrative-argumentative scenario of social groups scrounging from the nation. They do *not*, however, show any uniform pattern of usage; rather, the findings differ strongly across the genres. Only the Blogosphere exhibits a consistent racist bias insofar as the IMMIGRANTS AS PARASITES metaphor collocates strongly with 'disgusting and dangerous organism' terminology and is employed in arguments that denounce immigrants as being detrimental to the INSIDER community. By contrast, such usage is explicitly criticized in the majority of contributions to the online fora and to an even greater extent in the press, even though these media genres themselves regularly employ the SCROUNGE scenario.

These findings highlight an important aspect in the relationship between scenario and metaphor. Some prominent metaphorical source themes seem to 'fit' scenarios and sub-scenarios particularly well, for example, the DOOR metaphor in the CONTAINER scenario, the WAVE-FLOOD metaphor in the MOVEMENT scenario, the PARASITE metaphor in the EFFECT scenario, but in principle another lexical 'filling' could also have been chosen for the scenario. Scenarios in themselves are not metaphor-specific or grounded in a particular source domain, but should rather be seen as conceptual patterns that emerge in discourse and are made narratively and argumentatively coherent by specific metaphors, which in turn makes them prime candidates for 'self-fulfilling prophecies' (see Chapters 1–2).

It would therefore seem plausible to assume that when scenarios are structured by a specific metaphorical filling, the speakers/authors have deliberately chosen to do so and that their listeners and readers are conscious of their semantic and pragmatic implications and the registers and ideologies they belong to. The *Have your Say* data leave no doubt that participants are fully aware of such implications with regard to the use of PARASITE metaphors as part of the SCROUNGE scenario: they all ascribe such use to anti-immigration and xenophobic/racist strands of the public debate. The meta-communicative disclaimers of some politicians who after having been 'caught' using racist metaphors pretend that they were 'not aware' of racist implications or of closeness to the discourse traditions of Nazi jargon only show that they are in fact acutely conscious of such traditions. Typically, they then try to convey their racist messages by slightly altered formulations, for example, in the form of hedged similes, which evoke the same scenario.[28] Given that speakers have a choice of which scenarios to use, how to fill them figuratively and which evaluations and 'solutions' to insinuate, such disclaimers must be judged disingenuous and deceitful. Whoever employs the PARASITE concept as part of the SCROUNGE scenario is doing so in full knowledge of its implications and of its polemical, insulting and defamatory bias.

The 'deliberateness' of figurative language use and reception in political and media discourse has been the issue of a more general theoretical debate among G. Steen, R. W. Gibbs, A. Deignan and C. Müller in the first issue of the journal *Metaphor and the Social World*,[29] which was triggered by Steen's earlier article on 'The paradox of metaphor' (Steen 2008). In that article, he had proposed the category of 'deliberate metaphor' in order to highlight metaphor use that is 'expressly meant to change the addressee's perspective on the referent or topic' and as a 'relatively conscious discourse strategy that aims to elicit particular rhetorical effects' (2008: 222–3). Steen offers the distinction between deliberate and non-deliberate metaphors as the solution of the 'paradox' that metaphor *analysis* always involves a differentiation between and comparison of source and target inputs but that the experimentally observed processing of metaphor, especially conventional figurative language, often short-circuits this comparison and relies instead on a quasi-automatic categorization procedure (2008: 232–8).

In response to Steen, Gibbs defends the classic CMT stance that all metaphor is being used non-deliberately in the sense that even though authors/speakers may compose their texts consciously, they *inadvertently* access and use any metaphors as conceptual structures unconsciously and automatically, without consciously comparing source and target. Hence, deliberate metaphor is deemed 'not essentially different from other forms of metaphoric language', which makes the deliberate v. non-deliberate distinction analytically superfluous (Gibbs 2011a: 21, 49). In their responses,

Steen, Deignan and Müller defend the category of 'deliberate' metaphor by distancing it from CMT's standard fare of clichéd figurative idioms and placing its analysis instead 'at the heart of metaphor theory: what is it that makes a metaphor vital, active, deliberate?' (Müller 2011: 64).

The analyses of x AS PARASITE metaphors, and of political metaphor in general that we have presented here support the 'pro-deliberateness' side of the argument, while putting the emphasis more on its social rather than psychological aspects. In common parlance, an action is judged to have been carried out 'deliberately' if its agent had a choice and can be held responsible for the action and its consequences. This does not imply that all aspects of metaphor construction have to be fully consciously reflected by all participants in a public debate. Even the most deliberate actions involve a lot of unconsciously performed partial sub-actions. Gibbs' main counterargument rests on an overgeneralized psycholinguistic perspective on 'deliberateness', that is, the truism that 'people's intuitions about their own conscious thought processes are often terribly misguided' (Gibbs 2011a: 40). Highlighting this aspect suggests that the interpretation of a speech action *as deliberate* rests only on introspection, that is, speakers' own 'intuitions' about the thought processes underlying their speech. However, such a reliance on introspection is not evidenced in research that focuses on deliberate metaphor use.

As regards political discourse, the denial of 'deliberateness' for both the production or understanding side is easily falsified. Metaphors in politicians' statements, press articles or internet debates such as the *Have Your Say* forum include extensive comments on and metarepresentational uses (quotations, allusions) of metaphors. The comments not only identify metaphors as figurative but also as belonging to specific discourse traditions, and assess them as being appropriate or inappropriate, correct or misleading, racist, polemical, hate-fostering or conciliatory etc. To arrive at such assessments, the commentators must presuppose that the metaphors in question were used deliberately; or else their comments would be pointless. In addition, commentators often also assume the speakers' awareness of the discourse tradition in which they are placing themselves, for example, Nazi-typical metaphors. Thus, even though the present-day memory of Nazi jargon in Britain may not be as detailed as in Germany or Austria, the majority of comments by *Have Your Say* contributors and press articles in the immigration debate corpus show that the British public is thoroughly familiar with the closeness of the IMMIGRANTS AS PARASITES concept to racist hate speech.

Gibbs insists that metaphor 'is not like murder in the sense that we may try to stay back and decide … whether that act was done deliberately or by accident' (Gibbs 2011a: 48). Apart from the fact that some political metaphors have, empirically, led to all too real mass murders in the course of human history,[30] the formulation 'not like murder' obfuscates the underlying issue of metaphorical discourse as a deliberate social action. *Like* murder and all other socially meaningful action, communicative uses of language are based on choices whose effects incur social and sometimes, legal, responsibilities. The fact that these choices can be more or less conscious (and that they are often denied by speakers if they get into difficulties) is neither here nor there. Socioculturally 'entrenched' conceptual frames and scenarios, even specific formulations, such as idioms, proverbs and conventional figurative lexis, may indeed make it all too easy for people to speak, act and think in clichés. But they are not thereby absolved from their social responsibility for having chosen such metaphors over others. Speakers also have the more specific choice between sticking to the conventional, unmarked version of a scenario and filling it with a particularly striking, persuasive, seemingly apt metaphorical formulation. The rhetorical and cognitive effects on their recipients, as documented in the latter's explicit interpretations and comments, range from mass acceptance, as in the historically catastrophic case of the Nazi metaphor of JEWS AS PARASITES, to sarcastic reinterpretation, resistant modification in counter-scenarios and explicit meta-communicative rejection in open debate.

6.6 Summary

In this chapter we have looked both at the long- and medium-term development of the metaphorical meanings of PARASITE and at synchronic, genre-related variations of one of their manifestations in British political discourse. Together, these analyses demonstrate the dynamic aspect of metaphor in political discourse. Historically, the concept of PARASITE was revealed to have been the object of several metaphorization impulses, starting with the extension of the terminology of archaic religious rituals in ancient Greece into the concept of the SOCIO-PARASITE individual that sponges off others. Subsequently, *parasite* terminology and meanings were transmitted via Latin into modern European languages, where they were first adapted to new referents (e.g. the Renaissance courtier) and later metaphorized by Enlightenment researchers into the scientific BIO-PARASITE metaphor in the seventeenth to eighteenth centuries. To achieve this, the scientists did not have to be aware of its classical pedigree; the starting point for their analogical coinage would have been the contemporary social understanding of *parasite* as designating a type of person who lived at the expense of others. This familiar notion served as the source for devising a category name for organisms that lived on and at the expense of other plants and animals.

Towards the end of the eighteenth century, this concept was re-metaphorized in a new semantic direction to denounce specific social groups as sponging off and damaging the whole nation conceived of as an animal and/or human body. Its nineteenth- and twentieth-century 'successor' versions can be roughly grouped into two main scenario versions, one highlighting the SPONGING-SCROUNGING aspect (directed either against privileged groups or against marginalized groups such as minorities a immigrants that allegedly did not work for their living), the other version highlighting a direct threat to the nation through blood poisoning and illness contamination (directed against a racially and/or religiously defined 'Other' that must be destroyed if the national 'Self' wants to continue living). The two scenario versions are not identical but share the analogy from biological species to social groups, which itself is to this day open and 'active' in all semantic directions, as the 're-re-metaphorization' of bio-parasites as 'selfish' minorities or immigrants has shown.

Both the long-term perspective over two millennia of PARASITE metaphorization and the medium-term perspective of the impact and aftershocks of the racist redefinitions and their genocidal applications in Nazism show very clearly that a unidirectional notion of the semantics of metaphor is untenable. Instead, the evidence of repeated re-metaphorization underlines the necessity of replacing the oversimplifying notion of metaphor as the mapping of 'concrete' source image schemas to 'abstract' target-domain concepts by a less rigid definition of metaphor: as a discursive, dynamic tool of assimilating any target topic to a more familiar set of concepts, in order to redirect and reshape its understanding by the respective communication partners. What is 'familiar' and what is 'topical' depends on the sociocultural context, not on intrinsic conceptual properties of the metaphor. In addition, the synchronic analysis of genre-specific variation of metaphor in British immigration debates demonstrated that both speakers/writers and hearers/readers operate a sophisticated, multilevel framework of conceptualization, in which they not only distinguish BIO- from SOCIO-PARASITES, but also gauge the fit of these concepts with varying scenarios and judge their political appropriateness against the historical pedigree of these scenario versions.

The finding of strong variation in the frequency, distribution and argumentative use of IMMIGRANTS AS PARASITES metaphors showed that its dehumanizing import crucially depends on the users' exploitation of the source scenario's outcome versions. The default outcome of the BIO-PARASITE scenario is the destruction of its host, whereas that of the SOCIO-PARASITE scenario is damage to, but not annihilation of the host. The IMMIGRANTS AS BIO PARASITES version thus suggests the existence of a deadly threat which must be countered by the most radical measures, that is, elimination of the parasite. It is only in this version that present-day uses of parasite imagery can be plausibly linked to historical precedents (Nazi and Stalinist usage) that advocated mass murder as a form of racial or social 'therapy'. Those who use the metaphor in this version today may, for obvious reasons of self-exculpation, disclaim the tradition they stand in, but their conclusions from the metaphor scenarios they use speak for themselves.

The picture of the average metaphor user that emerges from these analyses is not at all that of an 'unconscious' follower of discourse customs who automatically adopts entrenched concepts or frames, but that of someone who makes communicative choices and is aware of their contextual implications and their wider and sociopolitical and practical effects. Such awareness does not imply that all user are always 100 per cent conscious of the etymological and diachronic conceptual background, nor that they have a comprehensive synchronic overview of contemporary uses; they can of course be inconsistent in their use and erroneous in the interpretative hypotheses. But our evidence supports the assumption that metaphor uses are 'deliberate' in the sense of being chosen to fit specific socio-communicative purposes and incurring corresponding social and political responsibilities. The fact that these responsibilities are often disclaimed by politicians who adopt historically and/or ethically problematic metaphors only serves to underline their communicative significance. While the disclaimers may get a politician off the hook in terms of legal responsibility, the reaction to and criticism of such uses within the discourse community and even their own meta-communicative defence against such criticism are proof that political metaphors are neither coined nor interpreted automatically. On the contrary, they are consciously understood and debated as belonging to or initiating discourse traditions that can be and are evaluated politically and ideologically. No amount of disclaiming can absolve the discourse participants from their communicative responsibility of having made deliberate choices of the scenarios with which they operate in discourse and of the metaphors with which they fill those scenarios.

7

Nations as persons:
Collective identity construction

7.1 Introduction: Speaking for a nation

(1) Ladies and gentlemen, *Israel has extended its hand in peace* from
the moment it was established 63 years ago. On behalf of Israel and
the Jewish people, *I extend that hand again today. I extend it* to the
people of Egypt and Jordan, with renewed friendship for neighbours
with whom we have made peace. *I extend it* to the people of Turkey,
with respect and good will. *I extend it* to the people of Libya and
Tunisia, with admiration for those trying to build a democratic future.
I extend it to the other peoples of North Africa and the Arabian
Peninsula, with whom we want to forge a new beginning. *I extend
it* to the people of Syria, Lebanon and Iran, with awe at the courage
of those fighting brutal repression. *But most especially, I extend my
hand* to the Palestinian people, with whom we seek a just and lasting
peace. (Netanyahu 2011a)

This passage marks the start of Israeli prime minister Benjamin Netanyahu's
address to the 66th session of the United Nations General Assembly in
New York on 23 September 2011. It is structured by the rhetorical formula of
'hand-extension', which is based on a conventional but complex metaphoric-
metonymic-symbolic mapping: NATION AS PERSON, POLITICIAN (Netanyahu) FOR
NATION and HAND EXTENSION TO SHOW PEACEFUL INTENTIONS. Its use as a formula in
Israel's foreign policy towards its Arab neighbour states has been traced back
to the origins of the modern state of Israel and shown to have undergone
significant modifications in relation to Israel's own identity construction:
it evolved from a 'European model', based on pre-Second World War discourse

traditions over the 'Sabra' and 'Peacemaker' models to a 'postmodern model' as a 'device belonging to the world of public relations: The concept "peace" has been emptied of content; it has become illusory, something that neither the user nor the listener believes is possible to achieve' (Gavriely-Nuri 2010: 460).

Netanyahu's rhetorical hand extension has characteristics of the ritual invocation of a magic formula: after referring first to Israel as the 'agent' of the peace-symbolizing hand gesture, he takes over himself and rhetorically offers a sevenfold handshake to Israel's Arab neighbours, with some of whom his state is still technically at war. Most emphatically he extends his hand to the Palestinians, with whom his nation has been in armed conflict almost continuously since its inception in 1948 during Israel's 'war of independence' (Israel Ministry of Foreign Affairs 2015), which was experienced by Palestinians as a national catastrophe (*Nakba*), in which they lost most of their home territory (State of Palestine – Ministry of Information 2009).[1] Viewed from their side, the claim that the conquering state of Israel had 'extended its hand in peace' , as Netanyahu asserts, must sound cynical.

The hollowness of Netanyahu's peace-gesturing formula is revealed when he almost immediately afterwards accuses the Palestinians of consistently having 'refused to negotiate' with Israel for more than half a century, both under their former president Yassir Arafat and the current one, Mahmoud Abbas, who had addressed the United Nations earlier during the same morning session. A scenario is thus depicted in which one agent, that is, Israel has been extending its 'peace hand' for more than sixty years and the other agent has refused it and thus holds responsibility for the continuing hostilities. One might expect that agent 1 would lose patience with agent 2's intransigence after such a long time; however, at the end of his speech, Netanyahu 'magnanimously' allows Abbas a last chance to make peace with him, using the same *extended hand* formula one last time:

(2) Let's listen to one another. ... I'll tell you my needs and concerns. You'll tell me yours. And with God's help, we'll find the common ground of peace. There's an old Arab saying that you cannot applaud with one hand. Well, the same is true of peace. I cannot make peace alone. I cannot make peace without you. President Abbas, *I extend my hand – the hand of Israel – in peace. I hope that you will grasp that hand.* (Netanyahu 2011a)[2]

Netanyahu, as the formally authorized representative of a national UN member state, enacts here the collective identity of the nation state of Israel and uses the formula of *extending one's hand in peace* to (apparently) signal the will of his government, and thus his state (in terms of its international legal commitments), to 'make peace'. This makes good political and communicative sense, particularly in view of the audience he is addressing, that is, the United Nations, which have repeatedly demanded such a peace agreement and criticized Israel for not complying with these demands in recent decades.[3] For the purposes of his speech, Israel is assumed to be a single sovereign agent that can make certain commitments 'of its own free will', notwithstanding the political background knowledge on the parts of the speaker, his immediate audience and the wider international public, that Netanyahu and his government are only part of the political spectrum of Israel.

The representational relationship between a national collective and its virtual legal identity as a sovereign political agent, and the 'representation' of that identity by a concrete living person that acts as 'head of state' or 'head of government', is not only of interest for International Relations (IR) jurisdiction but also for metaphor theory. Lakoff and other cognitive linguists have interpreted such representations as being grounded in an underlying metaphor, THE (NATION) STATE IS A PERSON:

> As persons, states enter into social relationships with other states, which are seen typically as either friends, enemies, neighbours, neutral parties, clients, or even pariahs. States are also seen as personalities. ... Our policies are designed to be consistent with such metaphorical estimations of 'national personalities'. (Chilton and Lakoff 1995: 38–9)[4]

As evidence, Lakoff and Chilton refer to the famous tradition of conceptualizing the sovereign state as a human body, which is lexicalized as the *body politic* in English and has informed political philosophy and the theory of IR in the West since the Middle Ages, with further preceding traditions reaching back to Greek and Roman Thought in Antiquity (see Chapter 5). It has to be stressed, however, that BODY- and PERSON-based metaphors, though closely related, are not identical. While medieval thinkers such as John of Salisbury (see 5.2) used both metaphors as if they were congruent, modern political philosophy includes detailed theories of non-human 'state-bodies' and body- (or at least, head-)less 'state-persons'.[5] And while detailed body-state analogies have lost some of their popularity since the advent of scientific biology and medicine, the STATE AS PERSON metaphor plays to this day a central role in theories of the sovereign right of states to go to war and make peace with each other and the international legal commitments they enter into.[6]

This latter aspect is of particular significance for the Israel–Palestine relationship as part of the Middle East conflict system (Starr and Dubinsky 2015). Within it, leading politicians of both nations personify their states as agents: Netanyahu's performance of Israel's collective identity in the United Nations provides a good 'enactment' example of such a personification. The symbolic hand extension, which he offers rhetorically, can be interpreted as the special scenario version of the STATE AS PERSON metaphor that carries a conventionalized indication of peaceful intentions.

In the following sections we shall explore this issue further by analysing Netanyahu's and Abbas's UN speeches 2011–14 with specific regard to their 'nation-enactment' in front of a world audience[7] and by scrutinizing its underlying conceptual structure, that is, the STATE AS PERSON metaphor, as posited by Lakoff and Chilton.

7.2 From 'extended hands' to a 'new Nakba' in eight speeches

How easily recyclable the scenario of a nation state *extending the hand of peace* had already become by 2011 is evident when we consider its parallel use in the speech that Netanyahu's counterpart, the Palestinian president Mahmoud Abbas, gave on the same day an hour or so before Netanyahu spoke to the same audience:

(3) I am here to say on behalf of the Palestinian people and the Palestine Liberation Organization: *We extend our hands to the Israeli government and the Israeli people for peace-making.* I say to them: Let us urgently *build together a future* for our children where they can enjoy freedom, security and prosperity. Let us *build the bridges of dialogue instead of checkpoints and walls of separation* .... (Abbas 2011)

Abbas may have been a bit more specific than Netanyahu in explaining who he stood for by using 'we' to refer to his nation and the Palestine Liberation Organization (PLO) that formed its government and was his power base, but his rhetorical *hand-extending* gesture rested just as much on nation-personification as the Israeli prime minister's speech. In addition, Abbas exploited the metaphor of BUILDING by applying it to the alternative of peace-oriented policymaking ('build together a future', '[build] bridges of dialogue') vs. Israeli-authored, peace-obstructing concrete constructions such as 'checkpoints and walls of separation'. There is a lot one can do rhetorically with metaphorical 'hands'!

But Abbas did not restrict himself to the *hands* of his nation. In a passage which at least matched Netanyahu's rhetorical flourish, he depicted his own side as a (virtual) person with utmost 'openness of mind' for any peace offerings:

(4) We entered ... negotiations with *open hearts and attentive ears* and sincere intentions. ... Over the past year we *did not leave a door to be knocked or channel to be tested or path to be taken.* (Abbas 2011)

After thus emphasizing his own nation's continuous striving for peace, Abbas went on, like Netanyahu, to depict the opposite side as being hostile and unresponsive to this openness, always putting 'obstacles', 'blockages' and 'rocks' in the 'path' leading towards peace. However, in contrast to Netanyahu, he ended his speech not with a (pseudo-)personal appeal to his opponent to shake hands, but with an appeal to the Assembly and the UN Security Council, to formally recognize his nation as a state by granting legal UN recognition, for which he had recently applied.

Earlier in the speech, he had reminded the Assembly of the historic 1974 address to the same forum by his predecessor as Palestinian leader, Yassir Arafat, which also had contained a *hand-*based rhetorical formula that gained notoriety in its day. In this address, Arafat had issued a stark warning: 'Today I have come bearing an olive branch and a freedom-fighter's gun. Do not let the olive branch fall from my hand. I repeat: do not let the olive branch fall from my hand,' which was accompanied by a prominent 'wagging' gesture with his raised right hand index finger (Arafat 1974a, b).[8]

Now, thirty-seven years later, Abbas only quoted the 'Do not let the olive branch fall from my hand!' imperative as evidence of the Palestinian's 'affirmative pursuit for peace' while omitting his predecessor's more threatening hint at the 'freedom-fighter's gun' in the other 'hand' (Abbas 2011). By partly echoing Arafat, Abbas not only assumed that leader's authority but also construed Palestinian leadership as always having tried to make peace with Israel, which is as problematic a position as Netanyahu's corresponding stance (see above). Historically, the PLO, was, as Arafat's original statement made clear ('the freedom Fighter's gun'), committed to armed resistance against Israel. Since then, the PLO-backed 'Palestinian Authority' that governs the self-administered Palestinian territories and that Abbas took over from Arafat has renounced war as a means to solve its conflict with Israel but cannot realistically claim to speak for all Palestinians on this issue because their peace negotiation policies vis-à-vis Israel have for several decades been defied by their rival power holders in Gaza and South Lebanon, that is, Hamas and Hezbollah, respectively.

Notwithstanding the details and differences of Netanyahu's and Abbas's power and legitimacy bases, we may still regard them as being communicative 'equals' in the UN Assembly context, for they treat each other and are institutionally being treated in the Assembly as such in personifying their respective nations and taking the stance of offering peace to a uncooperative opponent. In this respect, their 2011 speeches mirrored each other to the point of repeating the metaphorical scenarios of *extending hands, building peace together, being ready to talk to each other*. Rhetorically, Abbas and Netanyahu appeared to be on the brink of falling into each other arms, to agree on a peace as quickly as possible.

Significantly, this close match between their communicative postures disappeared to a large extent in Abbas's and Netanyahu's UN speeches during the following years. In 2012, Abbas warned of a new *Nakba* and announced a unilateral initiative to achieve official UN recognition of Palestine at least as an 'Observer State' (i.e. not yet '[Full] Member' State), against Netanyahu's proclaimed preference for a bilateral peace treaty to be concluded before such recognition. Abbas still used the *extended hands* scenario to signal his acknowledgement that 'ultimately the two peoples must live and coexist, each in their respective State, in the Holy Land' (Abbas 2012), while providing no details about how this ultimate goal could practically be achieved. Netanyahu, for his part, devoted most of his 2012 speech to an appeal for sanctions against Iran's alleged nuclear armament programme, as a 'red line' that could not be breached (Netanyahu 2012). He briefly denounced Abbas's speech, which again preceded his own, as 'libellous' and recycled the formula of *sitting down together* with Abbas, to reach a 'compromise' that mainly fulfilled his own demands:

(5) We [Abbas and Netanyahu] have to sit together, negotiate together, and reach a mutual compromise, in which a demilitarized Palestinian state recognizes the one and only Jewish State. (Netanyahu 2012)

Netanyahu's insistence on effectively dictating the basic terms of any peace deal as a bilateral Israel–Palestine agreement instead of a UN-mediated treaty again belied his proclaimed willingness to 'negotiate together'. While not denying the Palestinian claim to statehood outright, he only allowed for it under the specific condition of 'a demilitarized Palestinian state'. Throughout the speech he identified Israel with the totality of the Jewish people in the world and throughout history, harking back to the days of King David, Joshua and the Maccabees to prove that there had always been a Jewish national identity and presence in the Middle East and in its 'eternal capital', Jerusalem (Netanyahu 2012). In view of this trans-historical identity of his own nation, negotiations with the Palestinians appeared in his speech more as a contemporary technical arrangement than a relationship between equals.

In 2013, the mismatch between the speeches (which this time did not take place on the same day) was even more pronounced. Netanyahu again started by invoking 'the Jewish people's odyssey through time' that began 'nearly 4,000 years' ago with 'Abraham, Isaac and Jacob' (Netanyahu 2013). This long-term view provided a link to compare present-day Iran's nuclear threat against Israel, which again formed his main topic, unfavourably with an alleged 'historic friendship between the Jews and the Persians', (for which he cited as 'evidence' King Cyrus's decree ending the Babylonian exile of the Ancient Israelites) and a reminiscence of Netanyahu's own grandfather being attacked by an anti-Semitic mob in Europe at the end of the nineteenth century, which had led him to become a Zionist and enabled the grandson to 'stand here today as Israel's prime minister' and defend his state against a new deadly threat, that is, Iran's nuclear armament. Netanyahu thus again posed as the leader-incarnation of Jewish national identity across the millennia, acting on behalf of all Jewry through the ages. He only briefly mentioned Palestinians as 'neighbours' and repeated the 2012 formula of 'mutual recognition, in which a demilitarized Palestinian state recognizes the Jewish state of Israel', but left out the detailed 'sitting down and speaking together' scenario (Netanyahu 2013).

Abbas started his 2013 speech by thanking the United Nations and celebrating its decision to accord Observer State status to Palestine, which he took to be a diplomatic victory for his government and an opportunity to emphasize equality with Israel in a new round of US-brokered negotiations that had started a few months earlier[9]:

(6) Our message stems from the idea that the two peoples, the Palestinian and the Israeli, are partners in the task of peace-making. This is why we *keep reaching out to the Israeli side* saying: let us work to make the culture of peace reign, *to tear down walls, to build bridges instead of walls, to open wide roads* for connection and communication. (Abbas 2013; italics: AM)

Abbas again used the literal/metaphorical ambiguity of REACHING OUT and BUILDING BRIGES/ROADS scenarios to appeal for Israeli–Palestinian cooperation as he had done two years before (see example 3); his change from an exclusive (Palestinian) 'we' to the inclusive (Palestinian and Israeli) 'us' expressed his strengthened confidence to negotiate for his nation on an equal footing with Israel. However, as Netanyahu's silence about the renewed negotiations in his speech indicated, the 'partnership' was more rhetorical than real. The negotiations were accompanied by hostile comments from both the Israeli and Palestinian public, only to be disbanded in spring 2014.[10] After their breakdown and a steady increase in missile attacks on Israeli targets from Hamas-controlled Gaza, the Israeli Defence Forces launched a military offensive against Hamas involving sustained bombardment and temporary invasion of Gaza with ground troops in July to August 2014.

Predictably, Abbas's and Netanyahu's ensuing speeches in the UN Assembly in September that year were largely devoted to blaming the other side for the casualties and destruction of this latest Gaza war. Less predictably, both speakers seemed to agree on the notion that Abbas, as 'president' of the 'State of Palestine', also spoke for the Palestinians of Gaza. Despite the fact that Gaza has been controlled *de facto* since 2006 by Hamas who explicitly opposed Abbas's negotiations with Israel and organized their military campaign in defiance of them, Abbas included Gaza in his 'Palestinian Authority' and on their behalf denounced the Israeli military campaign as a 'new war of genocide perpetrated against the Palestinian people' and as the 'new Nakba' that he had had warned against in 2012 (Abbas 2014). Regarding the now defunct negotiations, he claimed that his side had entered them 'with open minds, in good faith and with a positive spirit', whereas Israel, 'as usual ... did not miss the opportunity to undermine the chance for peace' by allowing 'at best' only for 'isolated ghettos for Palestinians on fragmented lands, without borders and without sovereignty over its airspace, water and natural resources' (Abbas 2014).

Unsurprisingly, Netanyahu defended Israel's campaign by highlighting its 'defensive' character in general, and specifically its attempt to carry out 'surgical strikes' against military targets, which were supposedly thwarted by Hamas' deliberate strategy to use civilians as human shields. For him, Hamas was part of a global coalition of terrorist Islamist organizations, which he listed in detail.[11] Abbas and his non-Hamas-controlled part of Palestine were mentioned in just one sentence:

(7) I say to President Abbas, these [incidents of Gaza civilians being used as human shields for rocket launch sites] are the war crimes committed by your Hamas partners in the national unity government which you head and you are responsible for. (Netanyahu 2014)

Netanyahu used the supposed 'national unity' of Palestine's two main regions (the West Bank and Gaza), and Abbas's nominal presidency over both to link his erstwhile negotiation partner to 'terrorists' with whom he could and would not negotiate. In terms of his immediate argumentative aims, the Israeli prime minister expressed a coherent stance against a supposedly unitary enemy, that is, the (supposedly united) Palestinians under Abbas's regime, but by doing so he delegitimized Abbas's authority and effectively deprived himself of his partner in negotiations. Later in his speech, Netanyahu even reverted to a historic Israeli government position vis-à-vis Palestine, that is, one that allocated political responsibility for Palestinians to the Arab nation states (Pappé 2010: 239–40):

(8) There is a new Middle East. It presents new dangers, but also new opportunities. Israel is prepared to work with Arab partners and the international community to confront those dangers and to seize those

opportunities. Together we must recognize the global threat of militant Islam ... and the *indispensable role of Arab states* in advancing peace with the Palestinians. (Netanyahu 2014; italics: AM)

By allocating and accepting (!) political responsibility for Hamas' military confrontation with Israel as the Palestinian Authority's responsibility, Netanyahu and Abbas both signalled a decisive – and ominous – change in their willingness to recognize each other publicly as negotiation partners. On the basis of their UN speeches, one might come to the depressing conclusion that the two sides have given up on any chance of recognizing each other in reality as legitimate national identities and are biding their time until new military facts are achieved that will force the other side to give in. Within a scenario of *states acting as persons,* the Israeli–Palestinian conflict is then viewed as a duel in which the opponents have reached a temporary pause in their fighting.[12]

7.3 Nations as persons with social identities

The above-cited exchanges between Netanyahu and Abbas in the UN Assemblies 2011–14 demonstrate how the NATION AS PERSON metaphor can be enacted and rhetorically exploited by political performers to achieve specific diplomatic and propagandistic effects in a public forum. The speakers do not just argue their case as individual politicians or even as power holders of specific parties or governments in their states, but as national leaders who 'speak for' and on behalf their peoples, despite any reservations that they or any observer may have about the validity of their assumed authority to do so. The UN General Assembly is of course a special environment, in which such symbolic role play is presupposed to apply to (and be accepted by) all speakers. It enables even the representatives of nations that are at war or in warlike conflicts to present and advertise their positions and to signal their intentions about how to continue or end the conflicts. It would be unrealistic to assume that Abbas and Netanyahu (or any other national leader speaking) would really sit down and negotiate together as a result of the public expression of their willingness to do so. Even if such a face-to-face conversation did take place, it would most probably happen in secret. The scenario depictions of *extending hands towards each other, sitting down, discussing with open hearts and open ears,* etc. primarily serve the purpose of rhetorical and theatrical performance of collective identities in front of a global public.

This performance aspect is not merely decorative; it provides crucial indications of how the respective collectives (as represented by their political elites) wish to be seen. Taking up the Chilton-Lakoff terminology quoted at the beginning of this chapter, such statements include projections of particular state 'personalities' that are meant to appeal to a worldwide audience as legitimate, coherent and likeable. However, the CMT account of the NATION AS PERSON metaphor has recently been subjected to critical scrutiny in a book entitled *The Language of Interstate Relations: In Search of Personification* (Twardzisz 2013). Its author, P. Twardzisz pursues two aims. Firstly, he argues against what he sees as a 'politicization of linguistic research' by CMT and CDA theorists who declare all political discourse to be non-objective, which in Twardzisz's view serves a leftist agenda (2013: 37). Secondly, he seeks to prove that interstate relations are not in fact thought of or linguistically manifested as metaphors at all but are instead mere 'semantic extensions' of simple referential devices (2013: 184–98). To prove these two points, he analyses the press coverage of IR in the magazines the *Economist* and *Newsweek* for state names in environments in which they appear as 'agents'.[13]

The set-up of his research corpus is *prima facie* very impressive: all opinion articles in the magazines for the period 1997–2010 were searched for 206 different tokens of the names of 192 states in five main grammatical environments: as subject of an active clause, as subject of a passive clause, in object position, in passive constructions with a state name in the 'by + name' phrase and in Saxon genitive constructions (Twardzisz 2013: 128–30). The mass of data is subdivided into five groups of state names according to their relative frequencies, and all observed *state as agent* constructions are scrutinized for examples that lend themselves to an interpretation of state names 'in a human sense' (2013: 131–2). The author concedes that this interpretation is 'burdened with some subjectivity' (2013: 131) and tries to illustrate his distinction between '+human' and '-human' cases by examples. Thus, state name + intransitive verb constructions such as *Syria repented, Hungary winked, France wept,* and also state name + transitive ones (*The US promised fresh beef, France devoted a lot of attention to ..., Spain spent little time over ...*) are classed as '+human' ('potential personifications'), but constructions such as *Turkmenistan developed its gas field, Vietnam ordered six submarines, Haiti spent $ 500m a year,* are excluded because the direct objects in such statements 'do not designate ... entities normally associated with humans' (2013: 132). As a justification for excluding 94 per cent (!) of all cases of the original data collection in this way,[14] however, Twardzisz's interpretative criterion seems highly questionable. It amounts to judging that, for instance, 'ordering a submarine' is not normally associated with humans. As it is only humans that can order submarines, such a proposition is inherently implausible. Of course most 'normal' people are never in a position to order submarines, but that is, after all, a sociopolitical circumstance concerning arms procurement, and not a function of what humans can 'normally' do.

Ordering, spending something, developing a project are in fact expressions referring to typical normal human activities, and their collocation with state names could therefore just as well be argued to be strongly indicative of personalization.[15]

Even if one allowed for Twardzisz's interpretation as a possible reading, it is still highly subjective. The overall result of his procedure, that is, excluding more than 90 per cent of all potential '+human' cases, suggests that the search criteria do not match the corpus construction. Twardzisz's data selection is solely defined by lexical and syntactic criteria, while metaphor is a semantic–pragmatic phenomenon, which is notorious for being manifested at textual rather than word or sentence level. Twardzisz takes it for granted that simple references to states by their names and specific syntactic constructions (the great majority of his examples being main clauses) are sufficient as evidence for his interpretations. The co-textual, stylistic and pragmatic information, which we have identified over the course of the preceding chapters as indispensable for the study of figurative language in political discourse, is largely missing. In contrast to other corpus-based studies where corpora and search criteria are carefully tailored to meet the needs of metaphor research, the impressive size of Twardzisz's corpus does not enhance the validity of his findings but only serves to immunize them from critical scrutiny.

In a separate chapter, Twardzisz tries to disprove the interpretation of state names and national leaders' names as metonymies of the 'part for whole' or 'whole-for-part' type, such as references to a national governments in terms of a person name (*Netanyahu, Abbas* …) or a state name (*Israel, Palestine* ….). He discusses at length theoretical disputes over the metaphor/metonymy distinction and alleges 'that the field is peppered with subjective claims, challenged with other subjective counter claims, both lacking substantial evidence' (Twardzisz 2013: 166). He argues, to some extent plausibly, against overinterpreting metonymies as *always* being loaded ideologically either through highlighting or through hiding specific referents. One of metonymy's main functions is, as he correctly emphasizes, that of a providing a 'shorthand name' (2013: 178–9). However, this function of shorthand referencing is by no means denied in metonymy theory.[16] There can be little doubt that semantic extension, metonymy and metaphor are closely related: semantic extension and metonymy can be the starting point for metaphor development in a diachronic perspective and many figurative texts and utterances contain various forms of combinations of them. But this empirical finding can surely best be used to 'unpack' the different figurative elements and analyse their relationships in detail rather than collapsing them into a minimalist category.

Twardzisz's sensible rebuttal of exaggerated assumptions about a supposedly pervasive, strongly figurative, and hence ideologically charged character of all news reporting and commenting only confirms previous empirical findings that the register of news reports is indeed not replete with metaphor in the sense of a high statistical frequency.[17] Like these analyses, his argument rightly corrects the claims of an omnipresence of the NATION(STATE) AS PERSON metaphor in press data (2013: 111–23), but its empirical basis should have been more clearly signalled as being limited to a narrow data selection in terms of register and syntactic constructions. However, as we saw in the preceding chapter, argumentative exploitation of metaphor varies greatly across media types, so that it is dubious to draw sweeping conclusions from one discourse genre and to another. In Chapter 8 we shall develop this critical argument further by looking at the reception and interpretation of political metaphors, including NATION AS PERSON metaphors.

The caveat against deriving sweeping conclusions about the pragmatic-discursive functions of metaphor and metonymy from too narrow a dataset also applies, of course, to the data from UN speeches presented above. They, too, form a sub-genre that provides a special context for qualitative interpretation. Furthermore, the small sample size effectively makes a quantitative analysis impossible. What, then, can a qualitative analysis show more than that of the NATION AS PERSON metaphor is used in UN Assembly speeches by national leaders to portray themselves as personifications of their respective states?

From the scenario-oriented perspective, we can ask what argumentative conclusions and evaluations hearers/readers are invited to draw concerning the public image of the respective nation states. In the first place it is probably uncontroversial to assume that nation personifications help to create an image of a unified social collective that is able to 'speak with one voice' and 'act' as a singular, independent agent. Such an image is more advantageous than a 'polyphonic' self-presentation as the basis for efficient diplomatic action. As to the more detailed, and more strongly figurative, depiction of specific 'character traits' of the *state-person*, it is also obvious that they should (be made to) appear in the best possible light for the purposes of addressing a widely recognized and internationally respected global political institution like the UN General Assembly. UN recognition is sought by all state leaders to gain support for their diplomatic endeavours, and the annual Assembly session provides the most prominent forum to do so. Hence, the most positive and plausible national 'self'-presentations and, in case of conflict, the starkest vilifications of the enemy side are only to be expected on such occasions – and they can easily be found in Abbas's and Netanyahu's speeches in the characterizations of one's own nation's 'Self' as continuously ready to *extend hands in peace, negotiate with open hearts*, and in the Other-portrayal as a *state-person* that is stubbornly *undermining* or *rejecting* any chance for peace.

Such 'Self'-vs.-'Other' identity construction has been the object of intensive study in sociopsychological Face Theory, as pioneered in the United States by E. Goffman and later adapted in linguistic and cross-/intercultural (im-)politeness theories.[18] Face Theory assumes that individuals have an interest in protecting their own self-esteem vis-à-vis others (as well as each other's mutual face within an in-group) from 'face-threats' or 'face-attacks'. Personal and social Face is thus established and negotiated in every communicative encounter and serves to create expectations and obligations about future behaviour that are assumed to be shared by the group.

In the context of interstate communication, as performed publicly by national leaders, the social identity that requires 'face-work' (Goffman) can be that of a leader claiming to represent a nation state or one of that nation itself. In the latter case, the figurative concept of SOCIAL FACE is productively applied via a further metonymy (INDIVIDUAL-FOR-WHOLE) to that national collective.[19] Speech acts that help to *establish, lose* or *save face* are then understood as expressing not just the public identities of their utterers but also those of the respective nations. The register of UN speeches, for instance, presupposes that speakers appeal to the Assembly as a neutral forum. Given the Member States' assumed commitment to abide by the UN Charter and international laws, they thus must be seen to do everything to achieve the peaceful resolution of their conflicts, however strongly adversarial their relationship with the 'conflict partner' may be. These institution-specific conditions of UN speeches go some way to explain the logically contradictory attempts to portray an opponent as stubbornly refusing any compromise but nonetheless to *extend one's own hand in peace,* which we observed in Abbas's and Netanyahu's 2011 and 2012 speeches.

Media comments on the conflict are also often couched in partly lexicalized versions of the SOCIAL FACE metaphor. The *New York Times* (15 July 2014), for instance, reported that Egypt helped Israel 'achieve a face-saving unilateral cease-fire' during the 2014 Gaza war, and the *Washington Post* (7 April 2014) stated that the Israeli government viewed the 2013 UN recognition of Palestine as a UN-Observer State as 'a clear slap in the face'. Such SOCIAL FACE interpretation of conflict diplomacy is *a fortiori* applied to national representatives who are either depicted directly as Faces or Face-holders for their nations. The *Daily Telegraph* (24 November 2012) judged that 'the price paid by ... Abbas for being the "acceptable face" of Palestinian nationalism' had been 'humiliation', and the BBC (22 September 2011) warned that if he came 'back from New York empty-handed' (as regards UN membership for Palestine), Abbas would 'lose face in front of Hamas'. Such Face-interpreting comments, which refer both to nations and to their leaders as Face-holders/-savers/-losers, can easily be found in the reporting of almost any international conflict.[20]

SOCIAL FACE-based idioms are especially attractive to journalists because they allow the assessment of complex diplomatic moves as if they were contributions to a face-to-face communication in which person agents as participants enhance, maintain or threaten each other's social identities. The precise referential identity of the conflict participants, in particular the question of whether they are the nations or the leaders acting on their behalf, is often left un(der)-specified, which answers the journalists' communicative twofold need for shorthand referencing (Twardzisz) and suggestive interpretation and evaluations. As we have seen in the Palestine–Israel debate, the latter aspects can be further elaborated discursively by assessing the respective speaker's performance in terms of its metonymic and metaphorical potential, for example, in scenarios of *extending hands* etc. Regardless of whether the referent is a nation or its leader, this Face-interpretation can work only on the basis of a presupposed scenario, in which the nations and/or their leader-speakers appear as the interactants that can 'save' or 'lose face' vis-à-vis each other within the projected social context in which they are operating (e.g. the UN Assembly). Without the assumption of such a scenario, the evaluation of diplomatic moves as Face-acts would be meaningless.

7.4 Two case studies

In this section, we will discuss two historical cases of political identity-construction through national Face-work. The first case is an attempt at enhancing a national 'Self' vis-à-vis other nations, which proved to be counterproductive; the second is a case of national Face attack and Face destruction that helped to legitimize genocide. The two historical sketches serve not only to illustrate the importance of national identity construction and the crucial role that national Face-work plays in it but also to clarify how its political success depends on its 'fit' with already established scenarios of social perception.

7.4.1 *National face-work gone wrong*

On 27 July 1900, Wilhelm II, Emperor of Germany, gave a farewell speech to troops that sailed to join the international Western expedition against the so-called 'Boxer rebellion' in China. Deviating from the prepared text, he exhorted the soldiers to behave 'like the Huns' against the Chinese in order to win historic glory. To the dismay of his chancellor and foreign secretary, who tried to impose a ban on this version,[21] Wilhelm's simile was published by a local newspaper, the *Weser-Zeitung,* on 29 July and, translated into English, by *The Times* on the next day. The (largely faithful) translation read:

> **(9)** No quarter will be given, no prisoners will be taken; Let all who fall into your hands be at your mercy. Just as the Huns a thousand years ago under the leadership of Etzel [= ancient German name of the

'Attila the Hun'] gained a reputation in virtue of which they still live in historical tradition, so may the name of Germany become known in such a manner in China that no Chinaman will ever dare to look askance at a German.[22]

This openly racist passage aroused immediate criticism, even in Imperial Germany itself. The opposition parties in parliament, that is, the Social Democrats and Liberals, attacked the government by citing letters from German soldiers serving in China, which were dubbed 'Hun letters' (*Hunnenbriefe*) in an obvious ironical allusion to Wilhelm's 'Hun speech' and contained explosive reports of atrocities ordered by the German officers.[23]

However, there can be little doubt that Wilhelm II intended the *Hun* comparison to be a commendation and praise of his soldiers, not an order to commit atrocities. For him, it was based on a simplistic analogy: the 'Huns' of late Antiquity were a warlike Asiatic people who had challenged the East and West Roman Empires and were remembered in history for their bravery and ferocity,[24] and the German expedition corps should show themselves equally warlike and brave. This would likewise guarantee them an honourable mention in the history books and scare off potential enemies in future (Wengeler 2005: 226). Wilhelm II's use of *Etzel*, which was not the historic name of the Hun leader (Attila) but the Middle High German version of the name of a character in the medieval *Nibelungenlied,* shows that he was not engaging in a reasoned historical comparison but using the name only as a vague reference to a 'great warrior' figure. For him and those parts of the German public who favoured imperial world politics (*Weltpolitik*), the *Etzel* reference fulfilled the Self-stereotype of their nation as being morally entitled to forcibly subdue and colonize nations on other continents (Rash 2012: 167–8). It was meant and understood as Face-enhancing 'Self'-praise: the Kaiser exhorting 'his' soldiers to establish a praiseworthy reputation of Germany as a proud warrior nation, afraid of nobody and to be feared by potential enemy-Others. Even those members of the Imperial elite who were embarrassed by the 1900 GERMANS-AS-HUNS comparison, such as B. von Bülow, foreign secretary at the time of the Kaiser's speech and later chancellor, were demanding that Imperial Germany should take its place 'in the sunshine' and join other world powers in the race for colonies (Bülow [1897] 1977: 166). The Kaiser's *Hun* comparison expressed the expansionist ambitions of the imperial German elite, albeit in embarrassingly crude imagery.

Fourteen years later, this belligerent self-aggrandizement of the Kaiser's *Hun* speech came to haunt the Germans at the outbreak of the First World War. Barely one month into the war, the same newspaper that had reported the *Hun* speech published a poem by the British Empire's most famous colonialist writer, R. Kipling, which exhorted its readers to 'Stand up and meet the war. The Hun is at the door' (*The Times*, 2 September 1914).[25] Kipling was by no means alone in recycling the *Hun* comparison as a powerful metaphor of Imperial Germany as an enemy-'Other'. British and, from 1917 onwards, US war propaganda produced a wealth of texts, posters and films that depicted Germany's war conduct as barbaric and depraved.[26] In these posters, Germany as *the Hun* featured as the absolute foe of Western/Christian Civilization, as a destroyer of homes and families, a rapist and murderer with blood-stained hands, with further accessories such as the spiked helmet, blood-dripping sword or bayonet, a plump, burly figure and a grimacing face surrounded by ruins and raped or murdered women and children.[27] Its personified nation-victim was Belgium, target of the German attack in the West, which needed to be defended, lest *the Hun's* expansionist drive should continue unabated.

To say that this version of the *German-Hun* link was the opposite of that intended by the Kaiser in 1900 would be an understatement. Wilhelm II's boast about his troops' military prowess equalling that of the ancient Huns was a hyperbolic comparison (see the 'Just as ...' construction in quotation (9), which matches the German original). By contrast, the First World War *Germany as Hun* metaphor, which continued to be in use during the Second World War,[28] applied a different, strongly pejorative stereotype of the *Hun* as an 'uncultured devastator', which had been in British usage since the early nineteenth century,[29] to the contemporary German Empire that had gone to war. It was integrated into the *WAR-AS-RAPE* scenario, which to this day is routinely employed for justifying war, for example, the 'Rape of Kuwait' by Iraq in the US-led 1991 Gulf War (Lakoff 1992). As part of this scenario, the *Hun* stereotype achieved the opposite effect of its intended purpose in Wilhelm II's morale-boosting speech. Germany's public Face was turned into that of an aggressor and perpetrator of crimes, that is, its internationally recognized collective identity as a nation-Self was largely reshaped into an abhorrent Other-stereotype.

7.4.2 *National face-destruction*

It is well known that the Nazis saw Jews as a racial, not a religious community: in his book *Mein Kampf*, Adolf Hitler reiterated this core element of his 'eliminatory' anti-Semitism on numerous occasions, and so did Nazi propaganda up until the end of the Second World War (Bein 1965; Chilton 2005; Hawkins 2001; Musolff 2010a). In line with this pseudoscientific framework, the Nazis' favourite metaphor to denigrate Jews was that of *parasites* that threatened the existence of the German *people's body* and therefore had to be annihilated. This racist viewpoint did not, however, contradict in any way the characterization of Jews as a nation/people. Hitler emphatically insisted on the 'peoplehood' (*Volkstum*) of Jews in *Mein Kampf* (Hitler 1933: 330–2, 1990:

272–3). This was perfectly consistent with the overarching National Socialist perspective of all peoples being characterized by their racial status. In the Nazis' ideological universe, a range of races existed, at the opposite ends of which stood the 'culture-creating' Aryans (best represented by the Germans) on the one hand, and their absolute enemies, the 'culture-destroying' Jewish people, on the other.

It goes almost without saying that this absolute Other of the Nazi German Self was accorded no 'human' social Face at all. The infamous Jew caricatures that populated Nazi media pictured them as contorted figures with stereotyped ugly features, facial expression and bodily posture. But such depictions had been (and still are) 'standard fare' for anti-Semitic propaganda material. They are not unique to Nazism and could not be relied upon to achieve the desired hate-inducing effect that was needed in the preparation of the German public to participate in the genocide of Jews in Europe after the outbreak of the Second World War. So, how did the 'sub-human' SOCIAL FACE of the Jewish people, as imagined in Nazi discourse, and its concomitant metaphors be 'validated' and made to look convincing? This study focuses on the Face-destroying strategies pursued in the film *The eternal Jew (Der ewige Jude)*, which the Nazi propaganda minister J. Goebbels released in 1940 as part of a miniseries of three films, together with *Jud Süss* and *Die Rothschilds*,[30] to bolster and legitimize anti-Semitism in the crucial period between the 'onslaught' (Friedländer 1998) on Jews in the November pogroms of 1938 and the start of systematic genocide in 1941.

By autumn 1940, when *The Eternal Jew* appeared in the cinemas, Nazi Germany had already witnessed mass deportations of Jews into the occupied territories won though the invasion of Poland, and also a never-ending series of anti-Jewish laws and administrative regulations that furthered their systematic isolation from the non-Jewish population (Friedländer 2007: 53–127). While the Jewish people were forced to disappear from public life in Germany, their supposed collective identity was reinvented according to the Nazi vision of the absolute enemy-Other. The three anti-Semitic films played a central role in this public reinvention of Jews. They had been ordered by Goebbels after the start of the war in September 1939 and were accorded massive resources as well as careful planning, with detailed input from Goebbels and Hitler (Welch 2007: 222–9, 239–57; Tegel 2007: 151–3). The films represented a concerted attempt to convince as many Germans as possible of the necessity to effect the 'annihilation of the Jewish race in Europe' as Hitler had put it in January 1939 (Domarus 1965: 1163, 1829). While the other films focused on historical Jewish figures, *The Eternal Jew* was presented as a political 'film contribution to the problem of world Jewry'. It set out to reveal the true identity of 'the Jew', which had become possible, thanks to the German conquest of Poland (*Film-Kurier*, 20 January 1941).[31]

Right from the start, the film introduced Jews as the 'origin of plague in humanity' and as 'a people of parasites' that had spread over the whole world to live off other nations. The film treated the theme of Jewish migration over the centuries at three levels: (a) as the original *modus vivendi* of the Jewish 'race' for the past 4,000 years, starting from Mesopotamia (!) across the world; (b) as allegedly exemplified by the Rothschild family's banks 'success' in spreading all over the world and causing the international banking crisis of the late 1920s; (c) by analogy with the migration patterns of rats that spread diseases such as plague, leprosy, typhoid, cholera, dysentery. This triple analogy (Jews as race/nation – Jews as a banking clan – Jews as illness-spreading rats), formed an intense filmic visualization of the *illness-therapy* scenario that was at the centre of Hitler's interpretation of recent German history. Its inferred 'problem solution' could only be that the annihilation methods for combating parasitic vermin had to be applied to their supposed human counterparts. It neatly equated the features of an 'eternal parasitic existence' with those of the 'Eternal Jew'. The film ended by presenting a clip of Hitler's 1939 speech, which spelt out the 'inevitable' conclusion, that is, 'annihilation'.

The Nazis showed the film in various versions and translations across all of Germany to school children and adult audiences and also in the occupied territories. Prior to and during the attack on the Soviet Union in 1941 the film was shown to army and police units that were directly involved in the Jewish genocide; it even found its way into the killers' political training manuals: 'The word of the Führer that a new war, instigated by Jewry, will not bring about the destruction of anti-Semitic Germany but rather the end of Jewry is now being carried out. ... This means not only removing the race of parasites from power, but its elimination from the family of European peoples'.[32]

For the Holocaust perpetrators, the combination of the *parasite-annihilation* scenario and the *Führer's* prophecy was evidently a sufficient affirmation of what they were already engaged in, that is, the murder of all Jewish persons they could get hold of. The impact on the general audience is harder to gauge, despite some evidence from the reports on popular opinion compiled by the secret police. In January 1941, they drew up an overall résumé from the reports that had come in from across the *Reich*, singling out for praise the film's convincingness in 'proving' that Eastern and Western Jews were of the same 'race' and that the migration patterns and effects of vermin and Jewish people were congruent. Such praise came, as the reports conceded, mainly from the 'politically active part' of the population, whereas squeamish cinemagoers had been scared off by 'disgusting scenes' (Kulka and Jäckel 2004: 440–1).

Arguably, the film had more the effect of updating the general public about the Nazis' latest strategies in the 'fight' against the Jewish enemy than eliciting new support. As such, the use of VERMIN, PARASITES and DISEASE metaphors in *The eternal Jew* only reiterated the well-known dehumanization *topos* of Nazi rhetoric. However, by being embedded in the double context of the Führer's prophetic speech of January 1939 and an ongoing new world war in 1940 (which Hitler's prophecy speech had defined as the condition for Jewish annihilation), the PARASITE-ANNIHILATION metaphor took on an additional practical meaning in Nazi propaganda. As the supposed arch-enemy of Germany, the Jewish people had had a minimal and distorted but still extant SOCIAL FACE; however, as a 'confirmed' PARASITE collective, they did not count even as a normal enemy, but only as a non- or sub-human existential threat to the German nation, which had to be exterminated at all costs. This extreme case of denial of any Self- or Face-status to Jews in Nazi discourse (which also found expression in the grotesque depictions of Jewish individuals in propaganda and in the physical mutilation of Holocaust victims' faces and bodies prior to and after their murders) demonstrates *ex negativo* the power of the NATION AS PERSON metaphor. The denial of social 'Self'-status through discursive destruction of collective Face stigmatizes the targeted social collective as being in imminent danger of physical extinction.

7.5 Summary

In this chapter we have investigated the personalization of nations, which has played a significant role in previous CMT- and CDA-oriented research and its critique (Twardzisz 2013). This contentiousness can easily be explained by the fact that the target topic could hardly be less ideologically explosive. The right of nation states to exist, their independence, sovereignty and integrity, all hang on its conceptualization as agents that can be held socially responsible for their behaviour towards each other and are in this aspect comparable to human persons. The metaphorization of the state/nation as a (quasi-)person thus goes beyond mere grammatical 'agency' and entails far-reaching politico-ethical evaluations. However, as argued throughout this book, it is less the global metaphorical concept A NATION STATE IS A PERSON than the discursively established scenarios in which it is embedded that is crucial for its argumentative and evaluative conclusiveness and its communicative force. As the historical examples of Kaiser Wilhelm's 'Hunnish' Self-Face construction and Hitler's JEW AS PARASITE Face-destruction showed, metaphors change their meaning when embedded in new scenarios that fit changing sociocultural circumstances. In the exchanges between Abbas and Netanyahu in the UN Assembly, we saw NATION AS PERSON construction at the micro-level, in the form of ostentatious identity-adjusting rhetorical formulas that negotiated egocentric and mutual Face in relation to changing situational and global political contexts. In such *Interaction Rituals* (Goffman 1967) the 'Self'- and 'Other'-identities of nations are graphically played out, to the point of real-life persons enacting them on behalf of their nations. Their performances are often interpreted meta-discursively by other politicians and the media as Face-loss or -gain.

By contrast, routine references to state names in agentive constructions, for example, in press reports, have only weak if any Face-implications and weak personalizing force. This 'negative' finding should, however, not be used to dismiss the NATION AS PERSON metaphor as an analytical concept. Instead, we should search for it where it can be found, that is, in emphatic identity-building discourses. As our two historical case studies showed, its political consequences could hardly be more momentous. Wilhelm II exposed German imperialist national pride to the extent that his personification, the *Hun*, could be turned into a grotesque symbol of brutality and barbarity. The Nazis' deliberate denial and destruction of any human-like 'personal' social Face for the Jewish people prefigured and served to advertise their murderous intentions.

Both the historical and the present-day case studies show that conceptual metaphors become politically effective if and when they are integrated into seemingly plausible scenarios with a minimal narrative structure and an argumentative and evaluative default bias. The scenarios of the NATION AS PERSON *extending hands in friendship* or *building bridges, rescuing a rape victim* or *defending its very existence against a fiendish parasitic enemy* are all 'good' scenarios in that respect. They are suggestive of an unambiguous conclusion/ solution for an urgent problem. The intermediary actions that the speaker presents as necessary for hearers/readers to perform, in order to attain that desirable goal, appear plausible and ethically legitimate: grasp the extended hand or 'muck in' as part of a team working together, come to the rescue of a fellow human in need of help or engage in self-defence. By contrast, Kaiser Wilhelm's scenario of *fighting bravely like the Huns* evidently was not a good scenario. First, it included a vague historical reference point, which was too far removed from the audience's experience to be of any 'clarifying' value. Secondly, its ethical value was at best neutral if not ambivalent, in any case not Face-enhancing. It was thus vulnerable to hostile reinterpretation. For the collective or someone acting on its behalf to be identified as a responsible quasi-person, it must be possible for the hearers/readers to evaluate their social Facework within a framework of commonly accepted ethical values. Helping, rescuing and self-defence are acceptable forms of action that enhance and maintain a person's Face in the respective discourse community, whereas *fighting like the Hun* is not.

The central issue is therefore not so much whether a conceptual metaphor A NATION IS A PERSON exists or whether it is pervasive, but rather in which specific scenarios it appears and which conclusions/solutions it is supposed to make seem plausible. Its argumentative and evaluative effectiveness depends on the kind of 'cognitive profit' that it yields, that is, in (over)simplifying a complex problem of political understanding and action into a seemingly simple issue that can easily be solved. The data examined in this chapter and earlier in this book show that the NATION AS PERSON metaphor, when it is situated in discourses, is made up of a combination of metaphoric and metonymic mappings. Its source-concept PERSON is usually, but not necessarily, associated with OWNERSHIP OF A BODY (that has various organs, limbs etc.). However, it *also* presupposes a social identity, a 'Self' that is socially accountable. This social identity is, in a second-order mapping, conceived of as the NATION AS PERSON'S Face, which it can establish, defend or lose vis-à-vis the other scenario participants.

For purposes of communicative efficiency and (pretended) 'clarity', this metaphor has often superimposed on it a PERSON FOR NATION metonymy that focuses on a national leader-figure who acts on its behalf. The inherent vagueness of this metaphor-metonymy combination (who exactly are the leaders representing? are they or their parties in charge or representative of their respective nations?) is not a conceptual deficiency but a rhetorical asset. It allows an emphatic version of the social Face metaphor, which can be associated with a 'real' personal face, to be applied to all of its scenarios and can on occasions even be physically enacted, as in Netanyahu's and Arafat's hand gestures in front of the UN Assembly. In conflict coverage in the media, journalists regularly employ social Face evaluation to interpret and reduce international conflicts to the (apparent) question of whether leader X (of nation X') has gained or lost face against leader Y (of nation Y'). While this secondary metonymy seems transparent enough to be implicitly understood by all users (so that they distinguish between political entities and the real persons in question), the transparency of the NATION AS PERSON metaphor is harder to estimate. This is not just a theoretical question, but an empirical issue, insofar it concerns actual metaphor understanding. So far, we have only presented indirect data, that is, follow-up interpretations of metaphor scenarios that are themselves an integral part of political discourse. In order to arrive at firmer conclusions, we need to access less 'mediated' data about the recipients' content understanding. In the following chapter we will discuss experimental findings on how the NATION AS BODY and NATION AS PERSON metaphors are in fact understood across different cultural contexts.

8

Understanding political metaphor

8.1 The unpredictability of metaphor understanding

NATION AS BODY and NATION AS PERSON metaphors seem to be grounded in the most immediate source domains imaginable: What could be more familiar to speakers than their own bodies and personalities? As we saw in previous chapters, however, the familiarity of the BODY as a source domain is not a sufficient reason to assume an experiential universality of these metaphors beyond a very general and abstract level: different cultural traditions vary in highlighting specific body aspects, for example, BELLY V. HEAD as source concepts and in interpreting their political significance (Chapter 5 above). Even within narrowly circumscribed national political cultures, the selection of sources for the NATION AS BODY metaphors and their interpretations have changed over time, so that we cannot assume a constant understanding of the state as a body.

As for the NATION AS PERSON metaphor, our discussion in the preceding chapter has shown that it, too, is based on an only seemingly universal FACE FOR PERSON metonymy, which is secondarily applied to the nation state (i.e. NATION AS PERSON WITH A SOCIAL FACE/IDENTITY). While SOCIAL FACE has been treated in some strands of linguistic 'politeness' theory as a universal notion of 'the public self image that every member of a society wants to claim for himself' (Brown and Levinson 1987: 61), many cross-cultural analyses have shown that this concept is in fact specific to the traditions of English-speaking countries and cannot account for the lexically and pragmatically more varied versions, for instance, in Asian cultures (Jia 1997; Pan 2000; Pan and Kádár 2012; Scollon, Scollon and Jones 2012; Watts, Ide and Ehlich 2005a, b; Yu 2008).

One important difference seems to be, for instance, a stronger emphasis on mutuality and conflict-avoidance of face-saving in a Chinese context, compared with a more 'egocentric' model of face-work in English, which is focused on enhancing and defending primarily the 'Self' against Face-threatening acts by other participants in a communicative event (Brown and Levinson 1987: 62–4). If the underlying FACE FOR PERSON metonymy is culture-specific, it stands to reason that its metaphorical application to nations, which leads to a combination of metaphor and metonymy or 'metaphtonymy' (Goossens 2003) of the type FACE FOR NATION AS PERSON, is also culture-sensitive. It would be an interesting research project for political metaphor analysis to investigate systematically the application of SOCIAL FACE metaphors on political and diplomatic issues in contexts that are significantly different from Anglo-American traditions.[1]

Most arguments about the cultural specificity of metaphors, however, concern only their 'production/usage-side', not their understanding by hearers or readers. It could be assumed that what is uttered metaphorically in public discourse is also always understood metaphorically, either fully or in parts or approximations, at least with regard to conventional metaphors. The terms *body politic, head of state, head of government,* etc., for instance, are deemed to have become lexicalized in English so that now they are learnt as part of English political vocabulary and, if unclear or not known, can be looked up in a dictionary.[2] The fact that some language learners may misunderstand them (e.g. through interference of 'false-friend' cognates in other languages) is no counter-argument to this assumption.[3] Participants in international public political discourse (e.g. politicians, journalists) are likely be at an advanced L2 acquisition stage and to have good access to competent L2 speakers. Even if initial misunderstandings occur, such speakers and hearers are likely to identify them and retrieve the intended meaning without much difficulty.

Nevertheless, there is still the possibility that recipients of a metaphorical utterance work out a meaning hypothesis that they think is the correct one and which remains unchecked or is even seemingly approved by the speakers who may not be aware of potential ambiguities, that is, an *undiscovered* misunderstanding. This assumption is not as far-fetched as it may sound. When teaching on a metaphor course for international MA students with very good English L2 competence at the University of East Anglia, I ran a class test to make sure that the term *body politic* (see above Chapters 4 and 5) had been correctly understood by the students. Approximately 50 per cent of them were Chinese, the other half was made up of British, US-American, European, Kurdish and Arab students. The instruction was informal and only asked students to explain the meaning of *body politic* with reference to their home nation. Here are eight exemplary responses from the first such class exercise (administered in 2011)[4]:

(1) Student A: 'The head of the body represents the Queen of England, as she is in charge of the whole country and she is royalty. The features of the head (eyes, nose, mouth and ears) represent the different official people, such as politicians, the Prime Minister, the Government'.

(2) Student B: 'If one organ or part of the national body suffers, the whole body would suffer from fever. In other words, having a healthy body requires healthy parts. As a nation, a problem in one area of a country should attract the attention of the whole people in that country'.

(3) Student C: '2 Heads: Head of state is the king? – Not sure anymore! Head of government are [Prime Minister] Rajoy and the big banks' presidents'.

(4) Student D: 'The face: president and government; the brain: oligarchs, members of parliament (make all decisions in essence); the hands: official and unofficial local authorities (including mafia groups); the mouth: the media – controlled by the oligarchs/MPs (dictate political ideology)'.

(5) Student E: 'Beijing: Heart and Brain, Shanghai: Face (economic center); Hong Kong and Taiwan: Feet; Tianjin: Hands (= army close to Beijing); Shenzhen: Eyes (= the first place open to the world)'.

(6) Student F: 'Beijing is the heart of China. ... The railway is the throat of China. Shanghai is the economic backbone of China. Tsingtao is the skeleton of Shandong province. Shenzhen is the liver of China; Tiananmen is the eye of Beijing. Nanjing is the face of Jiangsu; Szechuan is the hair of China; Xiangyang is the heel of China'.

(7) Student G: 'Beijing: brain (government); Shanghai: hug/arm (welcome to foreign people); Guangzhou: feet (keep China going); Hong Kong: face (familiar to everyone, representative); Taiwan: hair (we can live without hair but it is necessary for beauty)'.

(8) Student H: '... Taiwan: potential disease (maybe one time we have to fight against it and occupy it); Tibet: stomach (sometimes you feel uncomfortable); The head of the government: hair (if one goes down, always some other one will grow up)'.

Example (1) was produced by a British student, examples (2)–(4) by a Saudi Arabian, a Spanish and a Ukrainian student, respectively, and students E, F, G, and H are Chinese. While all answers are correct in the sense that they fulfilled the task, the responses fall into two distinct classes. The first four responses describe a political system in terms of a body's health and anatomy, even if, as in (4), substantial parts of the *body politic* seem to have been taken over by criminals or undemocratic forces. Responses (5) – (8), on the other hand, identify geographical places in China, including the politically separate state of Taiwan, and link them to parts of the human anatomy on the basis of functional correspondences between parts of the human body (*arm, brain, disease, eye, face, feet, hair, hands, head, heart, stomach*) and institutions or typical activities in the respective cities/provinces, and then associate these with further descriptive or evaluative explanations. These explanations serve to personalize the characterizations in the sense that they present the Chinese nation as presenting a *face* to the outside world, *hugging* those who are friendly towards it and actively *fighting* diseases.

The task of interpreting the phrase *body politic* as an instance of the NATION AS BODY metaphor had evidently been successfully fulfilled in *all* the above examples, but it is also evident that the responses represent significantly different perspectives. The first four responses differ in the national target referents but have in common the fact that they conceptualize the nation state and its institutions by functionally motivated analogies to the whole and parts of a human body. The analogies are not particularly precise but they are sufficient to indicate two main organizing principles, that is, that of a hierarchical ordering (*head/brain* = superior to rest of body) and that of the interdependence of all parts of the body. These two notions can be related to the *body politic* metaphor tradition in European/'Western' culture. The view of monarchs or other state leaders as *heads* of nations, of institutions as *organs*, and of the whole state as suffering if one part suffers illness or injury, which these answers articulate, is compatible with successive formulations of the NATION AS BODY concept by Western thinkers and poets since the Middle Ages, which have been reconstructed as a continuous tradition by historians of ideas. This tradition does not need to be consciously known by present-day users; its sedimented terminological traces such as *head of state, head of government, long arm (of the law), organ (of a party), heart (of the nation)* and prominent uses by contemporary politicians and media provide evidence of its continuity to this day. It thus seems not unreasonable to conclude that the British student's answer and the responses by the Arab, Spanish and Ukrainian students (all of whom had majored in English language and literature in their respective first degrees, and so may well have been familiar with *body politic* imagery in English political history and poetry) stand in a loose but still tangible connection to that tradition.

The Chinese students' responses, by comparison, clearly stand apart. In all of them, a basic mapping, GEOGRAPHICAL SHAPE OF NATION (CHINA) – ANATOMY OF A HUMAN BODY, seems to be presupposed, salient parts of which are selected according to PLACE FOR POLITICAL INSTITUTION/FUNCTION metonymies (e.g. *Beijing – seat of government, Shanghai, Shenzen, Hong Kong – internationally relevant economic centres, Taiwan – politically separate island state, Tibet – province with outlawed independence movement).* These metonymies are in turn analogically associated with functional interpretations of prominent body parts and organs, for example, *brain* or *heart* as controlling the rest of the body, *face, eyes, arms* as oriented to the outside world, *hair* as a variable physical property. Source domain consistency plays no major role, as example (5) shows, which treats *brain* and *heart* as functional equivalents that are simultaneously allocated to the nation's capital). These second-order analogies (based on primary metonymies) are loaded with specific evaluative interpretations, for example, in the depictions of Taiwan as one of China's *feet* (i.e. as an essential part of the nation's body), or as *hair* (beautiful but not necessary for survival) or as *disease* (to be combated) in examples (5), (7), and (8), respectively.

The contrast between the Chinese students' responses and the other examples lies not in a particularly imaginative interpretation or topical application of the NATION AS BODY metaphor – in examples (3) and (4), for instance, the Spanish and Ukrainian respondents also creatively apply the metaphor to topical issues in their countries – but in the metaphor-metonymy combinations that underlie its cognitive construction. It would be an overstatement to claim that these contrasting interpretations caused a 'misunderstanding' among the students; however, at the same time it was evident that for the Chinese respondents the basic geopolitical metonymy served as the foundation to construct the metaphor, whereas it played no significant role for the other students who focused on perceived functional similarities between body parts and political institutions. When the students discussed the results among themselves, they could easily understand each other but also agreed that their respective mental models of NATION AS BODY were different.

The Chinese students' versions could not be linked to 'Western' conceptual traditions in the same way as the non-Chinese responses, but that of course does not mean that they are without history. One possible link to historical traditions may be China's publicly imagined 'geobody' as part of its national identity. Callahan (2009) contends that contemporary Chinese visualizations of the nation's borders in historical and contemporary maps are characteristic of a 'Cartography of National Humiliation'. Based on the historical experience of having been for several centuries the victim of repeated colonialist and imperialist attacks by foreign powers up until the mid-twentieth century, Chinese cartography has served to articulate fears of future territorial dismemberment, for example, in a map from 1999 representing an 'international conspiracy to divide up the PRC [= People's Republic of China] into a clutch of independent states including Tibet, Manchuria, Inner Mongolia, East Turkestan, and Taiwan'

(Callahan 2009: 143). More recently, however, the author contends, the didactic goal of geopolitical maps in China is 'no longer primarily to recover lost territory' but to achieve 'symbolic recognition, acceptance and respect' (2009: 171). If geographical contours and locations are of such prominence in the public sphere of China, the grounding of conceptualizations of its *state organs* and *body parts* in geopolitical metonymies, which we observed in the Chinese students' answers, makes good sense. We can formulate the hypothesis that the conceptual architecture of the metaphor-metonymy combinations in the NATION AS BODY metaphor can vary in relation to culture-specific conceptual and discursive traditions, for example, by giving special prominence to the 'geobody' of the nation.

The 'evidence' consisting of four student responses differing from another four in an MA class in 2011 is of course not sufficient on its own to substantiate such a hypothesis; a much larger database is required. In the remainder of this chapter, I will present preliminary results of an attempt at such a widening of the database, which, though not yet fully conclusive, provide quantitative and qualitative data that help to interpret the initial findings and formulate more differentiated hypotheses. After the first encounter with different NATION AS BODY constructions that appeared to reflect divergent interpretations, I devised a simple questionnaire that asked students to paraphrase the NATION AS BODY/ PERSON metaphors in a few sentences and gave an unrelated example, so as not to prime informants' responses:

Questionnaire text:
The concept of 'nation' can be described by way of a metaphor or simile[*] that presents it in terms of a human body. Please apply this metaphor to your home nation in 5–6 sentences. Please state your native language(s), nationality, age, and gender at the bottom of the page.

Thank you very much for your cooperation!

guidance note: metaphor/simile = way of speaking/thinking of something in terms of something else (e.g. *Life is like riding a bicycle. To keep your balance, you must keep moving.* (Albert Einstein))

In an early version of the questionnaire, the first sentence included the ambiguous formulation '... a metaphor or simile [*] that presents [the nation] in terms of a human body/person', which conflated the two source domains of BODY and PERSON. (This ambiguity should be avoided in a follow-up study). Nevertheless, the great majority (80 per cent) of informants responded by interpreting the NATION AS BODY metaphor, the rest of them focused on the NATION AS PERSON reading. There were less than 1 per cent of 'mixed' answers, which underlines the distinctiveness of these two metaphors. Accordingly, the two sets of interpretations will be treated separately below. The survey protocol was to present the questionnaires as an exercise in lexical meaning retrieval, to administer and collect them in class within five to ten minutes in one of the first semester sessions and before any metaphor examples were introduced as part of a course syllabus. In this way, any priming effects of lecturers conveying specific model answers to the students were reduced to a minimum; however, such effects cannot be wholly excluded because the delivery in classes was not formally controlled.

This questionnaire was administered in seven more UEA seminar classes and, with the generous help of colleagues, in two other British universities and in Higher/Further Education institutions of nine more countries (China, Germany, Hungary, Israel, Italy, Norway, Poland, Romania and Spain), yielding altogether 648 completed questionnaires and involving participants from thirty-one different cultural and linguistic backgrounds (for an overview, see Appendix III), with more than 75 per cent being female students between the age of eighteen and twenty-five.[5] The pilot survey did not allow for a rigorous experimental set-up. Some answers were brief to the point of containing just one sentence and others included one-page mini essays of 250 words; some were invalid due to apparent misunderstanding or rejection of the task. Moreover, the linguistic cohorts vary widely, with the Chinese, German and Italian numbering more than 100 each, while some languages were represented by just one speaker. These conditions rule out any statistical analysis of the responses; however, such a quantitative study was not its purpose. The pilot survey aimed only at finding out (a) whether and how much semantic variation in the interpretation of the *body politic* metaphor, as applied to the nation, could be found and (b) whether any striking distribution patterns emerged that could tentatively be analysed as reflecting cultural traditions, with a view to preparing the ground for more rigorously controlled and quantitatively significant surveys. It is also important to bear in mind that the questionnaire did *not* elicit users' implicit understanding of the metaphors they were employing or their implicit understanding of other speakers' usage. Rather, they must be regarded as reflective interpretations of an explicitly presented metaphor that required some effort of semantic construal and its formulation in an answer. Thus, while the delivery was designed to exclude lengthy interpretation work, the answers represent in no way a record of users' automatic understanding but a conscious explanation of possible meaning(s) of *body politic*. It is impossible to give a comprehensive analysis of the data here; the following sections present some preliminary observations and discussions of examples that help to formulate further hypotheses concerning culture-specific traditions of metaphor scenarios.

8.2 Interpretations of the
NATION AS BODY metaphor

After the first encounter with contrasting interpretations of the BODY POLITIC concept as either an anatomy-/function-based or geography-based metaphor (as sketched above), it became soon clear that there is no 1:1 match of interpretations in relation to specific linguistic/cultural groups. For instance, British and US students' responses include geography-based readings that are fully compatible with Chinese students' answers:

(9) London, although located in the South East, can be considered as the 'head', directing operations as the brain does for the body. Birmingham, right in the centre of the country, could be said to act as the 'heart', controlling the flow of the 'blood' through the main arteries, including the M6 and M40 motorways and soon the high-speed rail link to London. Scotland and Wales are the 'limbs' to England's main body, on the periphery of the island but forming an integral part of our national identity.

(10) This is Britain, a vast, churning body of 48 million people, sucking in resources, processing them, and spewing out fumes and ideas. The mouth and nose are Dover and Portsmouth, sucking in the oxygen of European food and produce. It travels down the oesophagus of the motorways, arriving in the guts of the suburbs.

On the other hand, Chinese students in various countries[6] are just as likely as their European/US colleagues to construct the function-focused BODY PART-INSTITUTION mappings that seemed to be typical of the Western *body politic* tradition, and add humorous innovative applications of their own as in (14):

(11) The communist party of China is the head of the body. It leads the functions of the whole body system, which decides the entire national affairs. The government is the nervous system of the body, which is controlled by the head of the body.

(12) Laws are the eyes of our country. We are supervised by laws so that we dare not do something illegal.

(13) [If our country were a body,] every civilian is a cell. Any cell has its own function and it's indispensable. For instance, if all the cells on the foot left human body, this person would become a cripple. Just as a country without its masses will be an incomplete state.

(14) Corrupt officials are like fine hairs on China's arm. They grow there, thus humiliate the beauty of a lady by showing the world how they feed on people. … Corrupt officials are hard to be got rid of just like the hairs, being shaved off but later appearing to your eyes again.

However, interpretations such as (11)–(14) represent only a minority among the Chinese cohort's responses. The ratio of anatomy-/function-based vs. geography-based interpretations of the NATION AS BODY metaphor for the Chinese cohort is in fact exactly 1:3 (i.e. 16 vs. 48 responses). For the British/US cohort, this ratio is reversed, that is, 2.9:1 (26 function- vs. 9 geography-based interpretations). For other European/'Western' cohorts with sufficiently many responses, the preponderance of the anatomy-/function-based reading over the geography-based interpretation is equal or even more pronounced, as demonstrated in Table 8.1.[7]

Although the figures for the British/US and Chinese cohorts and those in Table 8.1 cannot be regarded as statistically validated, they do indicate a marked difference between Chinese and non-Chinese respondents for the *relative frequencies* of geography-based and anatomy/physiology-based metaphor interpretations. The great majority of responses by Chinese students is geography-based, whereas the European, US and Israeli students are far more likely to reproduce parts of the 'Western' tradition of conceptualizing the nation as a body of interdependent and hierarchically ordered members and organs.[8]

Table 8.1 Conceptual sources for *body politic* interpretations

	Anatomy/Physiology	Geography
German	61	4
Hungarian	16	5
Israel	14	2
Italy	84	27
Polish	11	0
Romanian	32	0
Spanish	16	5

In addition to thus providing further corroborating evidence in support of the hypothesis of at least two culture-specific tendencies in interpreting the *body politic* metaphor, the questionnaire corpus analysis also reveals two more interpretation perspectives, which focus (a) on viewing the nation as part/organ of a larger body and (b) on configuring it as part of one's own personal body. The former perspective can be observed in examples (15) – (17), the latter in examples (18) – (20):

(15) England is like an appendix, not very significant anymore but can still cause trouble and make you realise its [*sic*] there if it wants to [English L1 informant]

(16) Norway is a hand waving to the world. [Norwegian L1 informant]

(17) Italy is the leg of Europe. [Italian L1 informant][9]

(18) Israel is the heart of the Middle East. It is a main artery that transporting [*sic*] Merchandise for all the middle east. [Hebrew L1 informant]

Many of the examples of this type leave open the question of precisely which larger BODY-whole the nation belongs to. They also invoke folk-theoretical and symbolic encyclopedic knowledge as the conceptual grounding (*appendix* as a 'superfluous' organ, *hand*-waving as a symbol of friendliness). Some responses, however, specify the BODY target referent, as in (17) and (18). In further cases, it is the international community of nations that serves as the 'ground' against which the nation is profiled, for example, Germany as a FIST (on account of the two World Wars), Israel as a FINGERNAIL (on account of its size and being at the receiving end of design changes by outside powers) and China as the BACK of the world (on account of its 'basic' function for the global economy).

The alternative 'nation-as-part-of X' version, that is, NATION AS PART OF ONE'S OWN BODY, is not present in some of the smaller national cohorts but forms a recurring pattern across Chinese, British and German samples. Half of them are sourced, as in examples (19) – (21), from notions of HEART and BLOOD as the centre/medium of a person's identity, emotional existence and heritage:[10]

(19) Motherland likes [*sic,* presumably intended: *is like*] my blood. Blood is a part of my body so that I can't live without blood, and I also can't live if I lost my motherland. What's more, motherland likes my blood [*sic*], because I feel its warmth and at the same time it provides me the 'oxygen' and 'nutrition'. [Chinese L1 informant]

(20) The nation is the heart of each body, where feelings are. [Spanish L1 informant]

(21) The nation is our blood, lungs and hearts. Nation is like the blood in the veins. Nation is like the heartbeating. [Hungarian L1 informant]

These interpretation perspectives, which can perhaps be labelled 'NATION AS PART OF SELF' and 'NATION AS PART OF INTERNATIONAL/GLOBAL STRUCTURE', provide platforms for intricate and often polemical or humorous interpretations. They contrast with the two 'mainstream' readings discussed earlier, that is, the anatomy/function- and geography-based interpretations, which seem to be more standardized, repetitive and often have just minimal or no explanations (see examples (1) – (8)).

The latter, which make up the great majority of answers, may be seen as representing 'standard' interpretations of the *body politic* metaphor.

The less frequent NATION AS PART OF SELF and NATION PART OF INTERNATIONAL/GLOBAL STRUCTURE versions seem more likely to be triggered by the situational setting that motivated students to come up with imaginative answers. Nevertheless, these cases occur too often to be dismissed as exceptional and they, too, can be linked to usage traditions that we analysed in earlier chapters. Thus, the notion of one's nation as a CENTRALLY IMPORTANT ORGAN OF A LARGER BODY fits the CLOSENESS TO HEART scenario, and to link the *body politic* to one's own personal body is conceptually close to the ancient tradition of regarding the *body politic* as an attachment to the king's personal *body natural*. These concept- and discourse-historical links need to be explored in more detail before any conclusions can be drawn about their enduring significance in present-day metaphor understanding.

Overall, the systematic semantic variation in the responses to metaphor interpretation tasks throws in question the assumption of an automatic understanding of metaphors in the speaker's intended sense, which underlies much of the classic CMT literature. It opens up the possibility that seemingly unproblematic metaphorical communication may in fact *hide* differences in understanding. Doubtless, informants can interpret conventional metaphors very quickly and quasi-automatically when they are asked to produce just one meaning and also have been primed by source-related stimuli, as has been confirmed many times in psycholinguistic research (Gibbs 1994, 2005; Giora 2003; Glucksberg 2001, 2008; Glucksberg and Keysar 1993). However, our survey seems to show that with an open-ended question and less priming, responses to metaphor interpretation tasks can be much more varied and imaginative, and this variation can show systematic distribution patterns that are linked to culture-specific traditions. The degree to which respondents may be aware of these traditions still remains to be explored further.

8.3 Interpretations of the
NATION AS PERSON metaphor

Roughly one fifth of all responses (131 out of 648) focused on the PERSON concept as the source for the metaphor interpretation, with the Chinese cohort providing the bulk of this group but also with examples from the German, Israeli, Italian, Norwegian, Romanian, Spanish and Polish cohorts. As we saw in Chapter 6, the NATION AS PERSON metaphor lends itself to argumentative elaboration and exploitation. Many of the questionnaire responses show the informants' interpretative efforts to argue and present conclusions about their own nation's politics, ethics and (SOCIAL) FACE vis-à-vis other nations. Again, it must be stressed that these responses do not represent spontaneous, let alone 'automatic' understanding performances. On the other hand, as in the case of NATION AS BODY examples, they do show recurring patterns that provide insights into cultural tendencies of metaphor interpretation.

The majority of responses from the Chinese cohort list character traits or activities of PERSON TYPES, as in the following examples:

(22) Our nation is like a mother, who covers her children under her protection. China is like a giant person who moves forward step by step. China is a teenager still full of energy to do things. ... China is like an actor, who plays different roles on the world stage.

(23) China welcomes and gives warm hugs to foreigners who come to China. China is growing up day by day. China wears a beautiful dress to show her elegance to the whole world. China fights against violence bravely. China kissed the India and comforted them [*sic*] in a very kind way.

The characterizations of one's nation as a MOTHER or a BEAUTIFUL WOMAN dominate the Chinese sample: they account for thirty and sixteen occurrences respectively, out of total of seventy responses (sixty-six of which were given by female respondents). These are also represented in Israeli, Italian, Polish, Romanian, Serbian, Spanish responses, but, curiously, not in the German and British cohorts. The latter do contain FATHER characterizations (one quoting the term 'fatherland' as evidence), but the number of occurrences (seven across the overall corpus) is too small to be indicative of any sociocultural trend. It would, however, be interesting to compare this finding with US-American metaphor interpretation data in view of the alleged predominance of (STRICT) FATHER models of the NATION AS FAMILY metaphor (see Chapter 2).

The main MALE figure in the NATION AS PERSON characterizations, however, is the OLD WISE MAN/(GRAND)FATHER/TEACHER figure who looks after his family as competently and caringly as the MOTHER figure does. This type is represented across several 'national' cohorts, as the following examples show:

(24) China is a father who has survived many vicissitudes but still has infinite power. Hong Kong, who had been abandoned helplessly, is his favourite daughter among lots of children. Nowadays, after the excited and impressive coming, her father does all he can and does his best to compensate for this abandoned thing. (Chinese L1 informant)

(25) Our nation is just like an old man, full of cultural deposits, he is also a good teacher who told us so many things. ... (Chinese L1 informant)

(26) My nation looks like a 65 year old man, who is wise and clever but he hasn't be able to use his intelligence to become happy. ... (Greek L1 informant)

(27) Britain is an easily likeable friend. ... [He] is ancient but is experiencing revitalisation. ... (English L1 informant)

(28) As Abraham Avinu [Abraham our father] signed an alliance between god and his body, so does the land of Israel and all of it's [*sic*] citizens with god. ... (Hebrew L1 informant)

(29) When a group of people or a person is in pain he [Romania] is going to get help. (Romanian L1 informant)

This WISE TEACHER figure collocates strongly with other characterizations that focus on wisdom and competence (including the roles of LAWYER, DOCTOR, PACIFIST, PHILANTROPIST), which altogether account for fifty-three responses. By contrast there seem to be only two responses that come close to the STRICT FATHER model, both of which betray no great liking or positive bias on the part of the interpreter:

(30) My country is like a muscular, middle-aged man. He ... has scarfs [*sic*] all over him, but still stands tall. He is white an [*sic*] catholic, but shows respect to others. ... He has a strict facial expression, even if he tries to smile. (German L1 informant)

(31) My Government is like a selfish father. His 'kids' are affected by his decisions without being asked. ... (Spanish L1 informant)

Characterizations of one's own country as a BABY/CHILD only occur in responses by Chinese (9), Norwegian (2), Nigerian (1) and Belorussian students (1), relating as they do to these nations' (relatively) recently regained statehood or economic/political strength. What emerges overall from these recurring characterizations is the picture of an EXTENDED FAMILY, in which NURTURE, SOLIDARITY and COMPETENCE are of prime importance.[11] The two main results that can be gleaned from these data are (a) a marked preference for MOTHER-type nation concepts, especially among Chinese respondents and (b) the lack of STRICT FATHER-type characterizations even for MALE-indexed NATION characterizations across all 'national' cohorts.

There is a small sub-group of NATION AS PERSON interpretations in terms of national politics. These are sophisticated constructions that allude to topical and/or historical aspects, taking a specific political stance. Some of the NATION AS PART OF SELF responses cited above (NATION AS BLOOD/HEART, Germany as FIST, Norway as WAVING HAND) already hint at such perspectives, but their formulation can be more elaborate and illustrative, as the following examples show:

(32) Despite being a fairly young nation, Norway is already a full-grown petroholic. Like most addicts, Norway might appear well-functioning for longer periods of time. ... Still, Norway frequently turns into a state of denial. (Norwegian L1 informant)

(33) The Romanian nation ... knows too well the price of hardship and whose hard work has left deep marks on its soul. It ... puts a lot of soul in everything it does. ... It has not learnt yet that mind and reason should prevail over soul and heart. (Romanian L1 informant)

(34) The soul of my nation is the mentality the people have. Body and mind didn't work together properly the last 100 years that's why its has [*sic*] been seriously ill at least two times. (Polish L1 informant)

In these examples, nation-specific experiences of economic development, crisis and conflict are reinterpreted as personality traits, with the NATION AS PERSON metaphor providing a platform for political comments. True to stereotype, one English example highlights perceived national characteristics in a humoristic and self-ironical manner, far removed from any 'automatic' metaphor interpretation:

Example (35)

Questionnaire: NATION AS BODY metaphor

Andreas Musolff, University of East Anglia

Task: The concept of "nation" can be described by way of a metaphor or simile[*] that presents it in terms of a human body/person. Please apply this metaphor to your home nation in 5-6 sentences. Please state your native language, nationality, age, and gender at the bottom of the page.

Thank you very much for your cooperation!

Your native language (L1)	Nationality	Age	Gender
English	British	19	Female

[*] **guidance note: metaphor/simile** = way of speaking/thinking of something in terms of something else
(e.g. *Life is like riding a bicycle. To keep your balance, you must keep moving.* (Albert Einstein))

The above sketch would merit an analysis in terms of multimodal metaphor theory, specifically cartoon theory,[12] which cannot be provided here. It skilfully exploits the stick man depiction to represent the characteristics of a stereotypical English collective Self: obsessed with historical legacy, self-doubt, but also endowed with a lingering imperial courage (guts), ritually obeying habits such as tea-drinking and queuing. While stereotyping to the point of caricature, it also strongly personalizes that Nation-Self through depicting its facial expression and general posture – and clearly showing that it has a heart!

8.4 Summary

In this chapter we have investigated empirical data from a pilot questionnaire corpus about the reception/understanding aspect of political metaphor, which in many studies is assumed to simply mirror the meaning intended by the speaker. Our principal finding is that metaphor understanding and interpretation is at least as variable as metaphor use and production, if not more so. Even for a centuries-old mapping such as that between the human body/person on the one hand and the (nation) state and society on the other, understanding is neither automatic nor universal but, on the contrary, variable and culture-specific/-sensitive.

This variation is particularly visible in the striking contrast between the two main preferred/most frequent versions of corporeal conceptualizations of the nation in the questionnaire responses. Chinese responses clearly favoured interpretations based on a geography-institution metonymy, which was interpreted further metaphorically, for example, Beijing as the *heart* of China, on account of it being the seat of government. The majority of European/US/Western responses, however, reproduced the hierarchically organized, anatomy-and/or physiology-based analogies to political institutions that have been the staple of Western political theories since the Renaissance. In addition, two less frequent but still noticeable interpretation patterns emerged from the pilot survey: the conceptualization of the nation as an organ/part of a larger (international or global) body and its 'reverse' version, that is, the understanding of the nation as part of the individual Self's own body. Some of these latter response-types gave rise to highly elaborated interpretations that used the basic scenario of a nation state 'acting like a person' to achieve special argumentative, polemical and ironic effects. This ties in with our findings of similar pragmatic exploitation of metaphor scenarios in internet fora debates (Chapter 6) and in the SOCIAL FACE interpretations of collective identities in international relations and their media coverage (Chapter 7).

Even though our findings from the pilot study cannot be regarded as statistically conclusive, they open up a new field for empirical research into the relationship between metaphor production and reception. If the hypotheses about preferred and non-preferred interpretations are corroborated in quantitative studies that involve representative and balanced groups of informants, they would help to develop the theory of metaphor interpretation further and enhance our understanding of the social emergence and entrenchment of political stereotypes. In additional experiments, the relationship between interpretation under test-like conditions (as exemplified here) and implicit user-understanding could be explored and related to informants' awareness of culture-specific traditions.

This latter perspective is especially relevant for the second group of responses that we discussed, that is, interpretations of the NATION AS PERSON metaphor. On the one hand we found evidence for the conceptualization of the state as an AUTHORITY FIGURE IN A FAMILY, with the great majority of responses focusing on the role of a NURTURING AND WISE PARENT, stereotypically represented as MOTHER. This version embeds the nation personification in an EXTENDED FAMILY scenario, which seems to account for many roles that a nation state can fulfil. Apart from this main pattern stand the exceptional cases of interpretations that produce stance-taking, polemical or humorous comments on the historical, political or social stereotypes about one's own nation. The cited interpretative personifications of allegedly typical German STRICTNESS, Norwegian PETROHOLISM, Romanian SOUL-CENTREDNESS or EMPIRE-MEMORY AS A BURDEN on the English nation are based on pre-established typecasts that serve the respective writer as an object for endorsement, critique or humorous questioning and trigger further pragmatic and rhetorical effects. In the light of these findings, the assumption of a naïve hearer/reader who understands and accepts 'automatically' the ideological bias of political metaphors becomes less and less plausible. If readers vary to such an extent in their metaphor interpretations, as shown above, and also creatively de- and reconstruct metaphors to fit new scenario versions, it is hard to claim that their understanding is unconscious and automatic, let alone that they also 'buy into' the ideological bias and ballast that comes with it.

Without such an assumption of the hearer/reader's naivety and gullibility, the notion of 'manipulative' use of metaphor in the sense of the speakers/ writers' intended meaning being blindly and passively received and reproduced becomes questionable on several counts. First, it conflates the hearer's cognitive reconstruction of the (likely) intended target reference with an ideological acceptance or approval, based on a lack of critical consciousness. Secondly, the assumption that metaphors are understood only at face value by the average member of the public betrays an arrogant self-empowerment of metaphor critics/therapists as having special insights into metaphors' hidden meanings, which they impart to the supposedly naïve language users. Finally, it absolves these recipients of their responsibility for letting themselves be manipulated. They can then pretend that a 'misunderstanding' of, for instance, the depiction of other social groups as 'parasites' on their collective Self's body (see Chapters 6 and 7) prevented them from understanding its propagandistic function of announcing and legitimizing xenophobic or indeed genocidal violence. In this version, the notion of 'manipulative' metaphor becomes a convenient excuse for political and social disengagement.

On the other hand, the emergence in the survey of distinct preferences of metaphor interpretation among specific linguistic and national groups does provide evidence of culture-specific default conceptual patterns that can be related to particular discourse traditions. This finding shows that many respondents indeed rely on socially dominant scenarios that are entrenched in their respective discourse communities. However, it does not show or imply that they did not have any alternative(s). Obviously the entrenched dominant scenario version provides an easily accessible and socio culturally 'acceptable' model to follow, but it is neither the only one available nor is it exempt from reflexive or meta-linguistic comment and critique. Unlike the necessity to understand the mere target metaphor referent, the decision to accept, endorse and disseminate the whole metaphor scenario that it is embedded in, together with its ideological bias, is in the gift of the interpreter.

9

Conclusion:

How does scenario analysis fit into cognitive metaphor studies?

This book has focused on the analysis of political metaphor and argued in favour of a new methodological approach, that is, scenario analysis, as best suited to do justice to its multifunctionality and its discourse-historical situatedness (Frank 2008; Frank and Gontier 2011; Musolff 2011; Wodak 2001b; Zinken 2007). The notion of scenarios enabled us in the first place to go beyond mere categorization of metaphors based on domains by searching for recurring argumentative, narrative and stance-taking patterns in corpora of present-day metaphor use and analyse their frequency and collocation clusters. These clusters of metaphor occurrences were then related to political tendencies, media registers and discourse traditions, and evaluated in terms of popularity and prominence in the respective discourse communities. The scenario-oriented approach helped us to refine our understanding of the metaphors' degree of entrenchment in their sociocultural setting and the power to 'frame' its discourses.

This framing power depends not just on the repeated use of particular source concepts but also on their (apparent) argumentative plausibility and interactional appeal, which invites the hearers/readers to accept specific conclusions and solutions as unproblematic or inevitable. Some uses of political metaphor, such as those of POLITICS AS WAR/DUEL or HUMANS AS PARASITES, gained enough power and attractiveness to turn words into action. This momentous social force can most plausibly be explained by the seeming 'naturalness' of the underlying scenarios, which reduces a complex social reality into an ethically 'black-and-white' problem definition with an unambiguous solution.

This initially micro-historically oriented perspective was then widened to a long-term diachronic review of the conceptual history of some metaphor scenario uses, which can be traced back over centuries and millennia. Such dominant 'master scenarios' (e.g. NATION AS BODY, NATION AS PERSON, NATION/GROUP OF NATIONS AS FAMILY) show culture-specific variation at intra-national, national and supra-national level. The more widely they are used, however, the more likely they are to hide or obscure culture-specific assumptions, as could be observed in international political discourses conducted in English as lingua franca. Political leaders from different, and indeed opposing, communities can construct the discursive identities (SOCIAL FACE) of their collective Selves in ways that mirror or even repeat each other. The underlying conflicting scenario assumptions are thus 'glossed over' while still informing the speakers' actual argumentative and strategic purposes.

The importance of variation in metaphor scenarios was further underlined in findings from questionnaires that elicited students' metaphor interpretations. As the responses to the NATION AS BODY/PERSON survey (Chapter 8) made clear, the assumption of uniform and automatic understanding processes for political metaphors is unrealistic. Even within relatively homogeneous cultural groups, variation was found to be pervasive; furthermore, there are deep-seated differences in the combination of metaphorical and metonymical mappings that make up the scenario versions. In our data, the most basic conceptual BODY source unit could be the geographical shape of one's country, the institutional hierarchy of state and society, the speaker's/writer's own physical body or even combinations of these three. The fact that these different scenario versions could all be formulated in lingua-franca-English and restated in an *X is Y* formulation is no proof of universality. As discursive phenomena, metaphors can of course be translated and reformulated in all languages, including English. But this general translatability does not imply that they are uniformly understood. Rather, the interpretation responses showed systematic variation, which we linked to sociocultural factors. These findings need further empirical investigation and may involve methods of 'variationist' sociolinguistics in the Labov-Trudgill tradition, that is, specifying corpus-based scenario patterns that can be related to social variables in user and interpretergroups.[1]

The scenario-based approach revealed the necessity to distinguish between four levels of 'metaphor understanding': (a) *metaphor reception* in the sense of the hearer's identification of the target referent, (b) *semantic reconstruction* of the likely version of the speaker's intended 'informative' meaning, (c) *interpretation* in the sense of the hearer appreciating the respective piece of discourse as figurative and (d) its ideological *acceptance* as a 'convincing' argument that suggests specific political conclusions and perhaps further practical 'solutions'. Of these, only the first two can plausibly be said to constitute a (semi-) automatic process of accessing the maximally relevant informative intention that can be ascribed to the speaker (in the sense of 'relevance theory'-oriented approaches).[2] The third level involves the processing of metaphorical discourse as a 'deliberate' (Steen 2011) figurative formulation, which goes beyond automatic response, although it may still happen largely unconsciously. By ascribing deliberateness (rather than mere intentionality) to the speaker's use of metaphor, the hearer becomes at least vaguely aware of its non-literal status and can, if he or she so chooses, recycle, criticize or comment on that metaphor use as a communicative precedent. As we have seen, the discourse-historical career of many political metaphors is characterized by a significant degree of such referencing of usage precedents by way of allusion to or (selective) quotation and modification of previous scenario versions.

At the level of 'acceptance', metaphors are integrated as scenarios, complete with seemingly self-evident default conclusions, into the hearer's worldview. To ascribe automaticity to such ideological internalization is, we have argued, tantamount to depicting the average (or at least the 'uneducated') metaphor recipient as a naïve and gullible communicator who blindly subscribes to whatever happens to be the dominant scenario version in his or her discourse community. Such an assumption is devoid of empirical evidence and also contradictory, in that its extreme version would not even allow for 'remedial' enlightenment by a metaphor expert: How could anyone who has been imprisoned in a specific conceptual metaphor ever become amenable to criticism and deconstruction of that metaphor by others? Empirical evidence such as the findings from the interpretation tasks (Chapter 8) as well as the dialogic and creative scenario reinterpretations in online fora (Chapter 7) suggest that average, non-expert metaphor interpreters are fully capable of handling variable metaphor scenario versions and of choosing and refining them to fit the relevant argumentative and interactional contexts. They must therefore be deemed to be communicatively and ethically responsible for these choices.

What are the implications of this scenario-oriented approach for the general study of metaphor and figurative language? Of course, not all metaphor uses are political. There are many lexical items, idioms and grammatical constructions that have a non-literal semantics as their main meaning but no political import whatever. Poetic and other artistic metaphor uses may be related to political issues, but their intended effect on the recipient is predominantly an aesthetic one. However, all metaphors – from the most hackneyed and clichéd idioms to sophisticated and even hermetic artistic metaphors – convey a 'surplus' of meaning that cannot be paraphrased in literal formulations. Like a 'buy one, get one free' offer, they provide an added meaning aspect in terms of pragmatic (argumentative, interactional and meta-representational) effects, at little or no extra construction and processing cost. This added meaning makes them especially popular in all types of discourse, including political registers. But in the latter the added communicative value of metaphor takes on special significance because all political utterances and their interpretations are continually contested and renegotiated. This contrasts significantly with figurative idioms in general, which are as stable and uncontested as the literal definitions of 'natural kinds' that we find in a dictionary or an encyclopedia. After all, hardly anybody argues about the standard meaning of phrases such as *foot of the mountain* or *table leg*, just as nobody argues much about the standard meaning of the words *foot* or *leg*.

At the other end of the metaphoricity spectrum, that is, in poetic and maximally creative usage, disagreement about a metaphor's meaning is often treated as a matter of artistic and hence interpretative freedom. But this 'tolerant' view often implies a perspective on metaphor as not being representative of 'normal'/average language and instead constituting a special, extraordinary or even deficient type of language use. Such attempts to exclude metaphor from 'normal' language use have rightly been refuted by Conceptual Metaphor Analysis. The (relative) semantic indeterminacy of artistic metaphor is owed not to its metaphoricity but to it being part of a language register that is dominated by the poetic function (Jakobson 1960), that is, a focus of the speech event's expressive form. The meaning of poetic metaphors in whatever genre is no mere cross-domain mapping of concepts for the purposes of informing the readers/hearers about facts or influencing their beliefs and attitudes. Poetic metaphor aims first and foremost to achieve artistic effects, and this requires sustained and sophisticated interpretative work. If subtle and/or profound enough, interpretation may change the recipients' understanding of the world and of their human existence in it. But such a communicative effect is typically multifaceted and fosters contemplation rather than specific, short-term changes of opinions and attitudes.

Political discourse, on the other hand, is characterized by competitive debate and dispute because its participants aim to gain a power advantage over each other, through offering their audiences new nuances of meaning and interpretations, which promise to lead to new initiatives in the political process. Its dominant functional type is not poetic but polemical and interactional: influencing others' beliefs and attitudes and suggesting new courses of action. Political metaphor thus serves primarily as a means to change meanings, and hence, to change social and political attitudes. This susceptibility to continuous change would not be possible without its ability to provide cognitive and emotional access to default narrative and argumentative scenarios that provide conceptual platforms for the adoption of ideological and tactical stances, as well as for secondary, meta-representational commenting. It is precisely because they are 'packaged' in specific scenarios that metaphors can be meaningfully changed, by way of formulating divergent scenario versions. The scenario-oriented analysis of political metaphor usage thus provides a test case for demonstrating both metaphors' communicative multifunctionality and their twofold significance for cognition: they are both the product of and a means to shape thought, emotion and social perception.

At the core of the cognitive account of metaphor lies the link between linguistic data and conceptual structures. Some studies assume that the link can be short-circuited, in the sense that language mirrors mental (and even neural) structures and therefore provides direct access to what people are thinking when they communicate, whether literally or figuratively. However, as with all communication among human beings, it is possible that speakers are lying or are being deliberately vague in their metaphorical utterances, and there is no *a priori* guarantee that their intentions are understood, let alone accepted by their hearers. This is especially true for political communication, where all concepts, including figurative ones, are continuously contested, leading to a succession of debates about what a particular metaphor use is supposed to mean. These debates have as their focus 'real' issues of sociopolitical import, but that import depends on the convincingness and success of their discursive scenario constructions. To be successful in the speech community, political metaphors need not be grounded in universal experience, though this will undoubtedly help. But they must fit in with discourses already familiar to their recipients, so that they can be recognized as a basis for argumentative conclusions. It is this recognizability that has kept the notion of *Britain at the heart of Europe* alive for twenty-five years, as we have seen in Chapter 4. Launched in 1991 as an optimistic-sounding slogan, and having suffered all kinds of reinterpretation and satirical de-construction since then, it still provides a discourse frame for politicians and journalists to advertise their stance on a possible British exit from the European Union in 2015. The larger master scenarios, such as NATION AS BODY, NATION AS PERSON, and NATION AS FAMILY have been debated in Western cultures for centuries and even millennia. What makes them recognizable is not a precise reproduction by users and receivers, but rather an awareness of them as shorthand narratives with a default argumentative, emotional and interactional appeal that have become commonplace in the respective discourse community.

In a few cases, a specific formulation, such as the *Britain at the heart of Europe*, slogan can be traced back to a 'launch event' (the 1991 speech by John Major), but this initial context was soon forgotten. What helped the slogan to stay in usage was the application of a long-established, entrenched idiom (*X at the heart of Y*) to an enduring and disturbing topic of debate in the British polity. The HEART OF X scenario could thus develop into a familiar frame that gave its users a narrative context in which they could make sense of the varying issues in the Britain's relationship with the European Union, from potential participation in the 'euro' currency at the start of the 1990s to the possibility of a 'Brexit' in the mid-2010s. A successful metaphor scenario seems to be the most likely one that reassures its users of participating in the crucial public debates of their community while at the same time allowing for new, meaning-changing applications that make the metaphor seem convincing.

Analysis of metaphor scenarios is not a replacement of but a complement to other levels of cognitive metaphor study, such as Conceptual Metaphor Theory, Blending or Conceptual Integration theory, metaphor identification analysis and the study of the conceptual-pragmatic interface. Focusing, as it does, on narrative, as well as on argumentative, evaluative and interactional patterns of metaphor usage, it provides an interface to text-linguistic and discourse-analytical dimensions of the linguistic investigation of figurative language. Unlike some theory-driven approaches, it takes as its starting point corpus-based evidence of naturally occurring, documented use and experimentally elicited interpretation. Both these methods are still being further developed and therefore subject to criticism and refinement: many of the findings presented here can only be regarded as indicative and in need of further testing. Nevertheless, the recurrence of scenario clusters across synchronic and diachronic samples and their systematic semantic variation which can be related to culture-and group-specific tendencies of sociopolitical perception and argumentation show their central importance for discourse as the communicative construction of our world.

In the last chapter of *Metaphors we live by*, Lakoff and Johnson assert that 'in the area of politics and economics, metaphors matter more, because they constrain our lives' (1980: 236). The reason for metaphors' constraining force lies, according to the founders of CMT, in their ability to 'hide aspects of reality' (1980: 236–7). We agree with Lakoff and Johnson on the (phenomenological) insight that all metaphors, and for that matter, all cognitive constructs 'hide' aspects of reality, in the sense that such constructs can never represent the totality of (experienced) reality. We also agree with them in highlighting the social significance and potential dangerousness of political metaphors. But we do not agree with their contention that metaphors 'constrain' peoples' lives. In this, Lakoff and Johnson rely uncritically on an imprisonment imagery that assumes 'blind acceptance' (1980: 237) on the part of the receiver. This assumption may fit in with their view of metaphor understanding as automatic processing, but it is not supported by evidence of documented public political discourse. The figurative discourses that have been discussed in this book are characterized by pervasive (though systematic) semantic variation, pragmatic modification and meta-representational commenting. None of the speakers/writers, nor, as the preceding chapter demonstrated, any of the hearers/readers accepted the respective metaphors blindly. Even the endorsements of a metaphor scenario that is dominant in a culture-specific tradition are based on interpretative actions. The communicative, social and political responsibility for any action ensuing from political metaphors thus lies with their users and interpreters.

Appendix I: Source concepts of the metaphor NATION AS BODY in British, French and German media in BODYPOL

Concepts	Sub-concepts	Language-specific samples		
		English	French	German
BODY (GENERAL)				
	1. BODY	X	X	X
	2. ORGANISM	X		X
	3. IMMUNE SYSTEM	X	X	
	4. VITALITY			X
- LIFE-DEATH				
	5. BIRTH	X		
	6. LIFE	X		X
	7. DEATH	X	X	X
ANATOMY-PHYSIOLOGY				
	8. ANATOMY			X
	9. ARM		X	
	10. ARTERIES	X		
	11. BELLY	X		X
	12. BLOOD	X		X
	13. BRAIN/MIND		X	X
	14. CAPILLARIES			X
	15. DNA	X		
	16. FOOT			X
	17. GALL BLADDER	X		

(Continued)

Concepts	Sub-concepts	Language-specific samples		
		English	French	German
	18. HAND	X		
	19. HEAD	X	X	X
	20. HEART	X		
	21. LEG		X	
	22. LIMB/MEMBER		X	X
	23. LIVER	X		
	24. LUNG			X
	25. MUSCLES	X		
	26. ORGAN		X	X
	27. ROOT CANAL	X		
	28. SKELETON		X	
	29. NERVES			X
	30. SOLAR PLEXUS	X		
	31. TOENAIL	X		
STATE OF HEALTH				
- GOOD STATE OF HEALTH				
	32. HEALTHY	X	X	
	33. IMMUNITY	X		
	34. VIRILITY		X	
- BAD STATE OF HEALTH				
	35. ALLERGY	X		
	36. BOIL			X
	37. BUMP			X
	38. BLOOD CLOT	X		
	39. CANCER	X	X	X
	40. CANKER	X		
	41. CIRRHOSIS	X		
	42. COMA	X		
	43. CYST	X		
	44. DISEASE	X	X	
	45. EPIDEMIC, PANDEMIC	X		
	46. FEVER	X		X
	47. GANGRENE		X	

(Continued)

Concepts	Sub-concepts	Language-specific samples		
		English	French	German
	48. HEART ATTACK			X
	49. INFLUENZA	X		
	50. INFECTION	X		X
	51. NEURALGY	X		
	52. PAIN	X		
	53. PARALYSIS	X		
	54. PATHOLOGY	X		
	55. PLAGUE	X		
	56. ROT, DISINTEGRATION	X	X	
	57. SCLEROSIS	X		
	58. SICK MAN	X		
	59. SYMPTOM	X		X
	60. TEMPERATURE			X
	61. TUBERCULOSIS			X
	62. TUMOUR	X		X
- AGENT OF DISEASE				
	63. ALIEN BODY		X	X
	64. BLOODSUCKER-LEECH			X
	65. CONTAGION	X		
	66. MICROBES			X
	67. PARASITE	X	X	X
	68. POISON	X		X
	69. SPLINTER		X	
	70. TENTACLES	X		
	71. VERMIN		X	
	72. VIRUS	X		X
	73. ZIT	X		
- INJURY				
	74. BRUISE			X
	75. DISEMBOWEL	X		
	76. DISMEMBER	X		
	77. FRACTURE		X	
	78. GERM WARFARE	X		
	79. WOUND	X	X	X

(Continued)

Concepts	Sub-concepts	Language-specific samples		
		English	French	German
- THERAPY				
	80. AMPUTATION			X
	81. CLEANSING			X
	82. DIAGNOSIS			X
	83. DOCTOR			X
	84. DIET	X		
	85. INFUSION			X
	86. LIFE-SUPPORT MACHINE	X		
	87. MEDICINE	X	X	
	88. OPERATION	X		X
	89. PROBE			X
	90. RELIEF	X		
	91. ROOT CANAL TREATMENT			X
	92. SEX CHANGE			X
	93. THERAPY	X	X	X
	94. VACCINATE		X	
BODY AESTHETIC				
	95. PIMPLE	X		
	96. PUSTULE	X		
	97. WART	X		
	98. BODY APPEARANCE	X		

Appendix II: Source concepts and English lexis in the metaphor field centred on THE (NATION) STATE IS A (HUMAN) BODY in BODYPOL

Categories	Sub-Cs	Lexical items
BODY		
	1. BODY	body, body politic
	2. ORGANISM	organism
	3. IMMUNE SYSTEM	(auto) immune system, immunity
- LIFE-DEATH		
	4. BIRTH	birth, born, embryo
	5. LIFE	revive, survive
	6. VITALITY	vital
	7. DEATH	dead, death, deceased, bury, last rites, turning off the life-support machine, six feet under, body politic snatchers
ANATOMY		
	8. ARTERIES	arteries
	9. BELLY	belly
	10. BLOOD	bleeding
	11. BRAIN	brain
	12. DNA	DNA, genes
	13. FACE	face

(Continued)

Categories	Sub-Cs	Lexical items
	14. GALL BLADDER	gall bladders
	15. HAND	hand
	16. HEAD	head
	17. HEART	heart
	18. LIMB	limb, part
	19. LIVER	livers
	20. LUNG	lung
	21. MUSCLES	muscles
	22. NERVE	nerve
	23. ORGAN	organ
	24. SKIN	skin
	25. SOLAR PLEXUS	solar plexus
	26. TOENAIL	toenail
	27. TORSO	torso
STATE OF HEALTH		
- GOOD STATE OF HEALTH		
	28. HEALTHY	on the mend, off the sick list, recover, in rude health, in good health
- BAD STATE OF HEALTH		
	29. ALLERGY	Allergy, allergic
	30. CANCER	cancer, cancerous, metastasize
	31. CANKER	canker
	32. CIRRHOSIS	cirrhosis
	33. COLLAPSE	breakdown, collapse
	34. COMA	coma
	35. CYST	cyst
	36. DISEASE	ailments, disease, diseased, illness, malaise, sick, sick man
	37. FEVER	febrile
	38. INFLUENZA	flu
	39. INFECTION	infection, infected
	40. NEURALGY	neuralgic
	41. PAIN	ache, pain, painful
	42. PANDEMIC	pandemic
	43. PARALYSIS	paralysis, cripple(d)

(Continued)

Categories	Sub-Cs	Lexical items
	44. PATHOLOGY	pathologies
	45. PLAGUE	plague
	46. ROT, DISINTEGRATION	rotten heart of Europe
	47. SCLEROSIS	eurosclerosis, eurosis
	48. SYMPTOM	symptom
	49. SYNDROME	syndrome
	50. THROMBOSIS	blood clot
	51. TUMOUR	tumour
- INJURY		
	52. DISEMBOWEL	disembowel
	53. DISMEMBER	dismember
	54. WOUND	wound
- AGENT OF DISEASE		
	55. CONTAGION	contagion
	56. GERM	germ warfare
	57. LEECH	leech
	58. PARASITE	parasite
	59. POISON	poison, toxic, cyanide, toxin
	60. VIRUS	(flu) virus, superbug, MRSA
	61. ZIT	zit
- THERAPY		
	62. CURE	cure, course of treatment
	63. DIET	diet
	64. DISINFECT	disinfect
	65. DOCTOR	doctor
	66. LIFE-SUPPORT MACHINE	life-support machine
	67. MEDICATION	antidote, drugs, medication, medicine, remedy,
	68. OPERATION	ops, bypass, remove
	69. RELIEF	relief
	70. ROOT CANAL TREATMENT	lifted from the root canals
	71. SIDE EFFECT	side effect
	72. TRANSPLANT	transplant

(Continued)

Categories	Sub-Cs	Lexical items
BODY AESTHETIC		
	73. PIMPLE	pimple
	74. PUSTULE	pustule
	75. WART	wart
	76. BODY APPEARANCE	hard-bodied, 'moobs' (man boobs). podge, portly, 'ripples-and-nipples' look

Appendix III: Linguistic/ cultural background of questionnaire participants

Linguistic/Cultural background	Number of participants
Albanian	1
Arabic	7
Bemba	1
Chinese (Mandarin + Cantonese)	156
Dutch	1
English (UK)	36
English (US)	6
Estonian	1
French	3
German	114
Greek	1
Hebrew/Israeli	34
Hungarian	23
Indonesian	1
Iranian (Farsi)	2
Italian	119
Japanese	4

(Continued)

Linguistic/Cultural background	Number of participants
Korean	1
Kurdish	2
Latvian	1
Lithuanian	1
Norwegian	5
Polish	16
Portuguese	1
Romanian	64
Russian	2
Serbian	1
Spanish	40
Turkish	2
Ukrainian	1
Yoruba	1
Overall	**648**

Notes

Chapter 1

1 Libertad! online (2015): Kommune I (24 May 1967) (translation: AM).

2 For a detailed analysis of bin Laden's text and comparison with Bush's rhetoric in terms of distance and deictic polarization, see Chilton 2004: 165–72.

3 A Google search for 'metaphor' and 'politics' from September 2014 generated more than twenty-four million hits; for detailed bibliographies, see Dirven, Hawkins and Sandikcioglu 2001; Dirven, Frank and Ilie 2001; Carver and Pikalo 2008; Barcelona and Ruiz de Mendoza Ibáñez 2015.

4 For a detailed discussion of Twardzisz's critique of CMT, see below, Chapter 7.

5 See Chilton 2004; Fairclough 1995, 2005, 2014; Wodak 2007; Wodak and Chilton 2005.

6 For CDA's understanding of 'hidden ideologies' as collectively 'normalized' 'knowledge' structures, see in particular van Dijk 1998, 2008, 2014. Conceptual metaphors that are no longer perceived as being figurative and instead have become established as unquestioned 'knowledge' can thus be viewed as fulfilling these ideology conditions (see Charteris-Black 2004 and 2005; Goatly 2007).

7 See, for example, *The Times,* 31 October 1992: 'Worst Treaty in Town', which quoted the former British prime minister M. Thatcher denouncing 'misleading analogies' that compared EU integration to a train leaving the station. For analysis of examples from the German unification debate, see Schäffner 1991.

Chapter 2

1 In *Metaphors we live by*, Lakoff and Johnson introduced a basic distinction between 'structural', 'orientational' and 'ontological' metaphors but later conceded that this division was artificial, as the different categories overlap (Lakoff and Johnson 2003: 264).

2 See Kövecses 2002: 3–9; Lakoff 1987a: 68–90; Lakoff and Johnson 1980/2003: 252–4; Taylor 1995: 40–65.

3 Another common case of metonymy, which we will encounter in many text examples in this and further chapters, is that of the WHOLE FOR PART relationship, for example, 'Europe' (literally, a geographical label) standing for the European Union (multi-state confederation that does not, strictly speaking, cover the whole continent of Europe).

4 See Jackendoff and Aaron 1991; Pinker 2007: 235–76; Rakova 2002; Wierzbicka 1986.

5 See Gallese and Lakoff 2005; Feldman and Narayanan 2004; Gibbs 2005: 194–7; Lakoff 2008: 26–30; Lakoff and Johnson 1999: 569–83.

6 See Hickok 2014 for a critical in-depth discussion of the details of the neurophysiological evidence and its instrumentalization for 'embodiment theory'; on the alleged link to metaphors, see especially pp. 126–43.

7 See Kempson 1977: 141–4; Lyons 1977, vol. 1: 145, 165.

8 For the use of 'semantic field' theory in metaphor analysis, see Kittay (1987: 229–92). Critics (Stern 2000: 242–3; Croft 2003: 164; Musolff 2004a: 73–5) have highlighted the *ad hoc* character of the boundary definitions of these fields and a lack of clarification of their epistemological status.

9 See Hoffman 2004; Hodges 2011; Kellner 2003; Silberstein 2002.

10 See Musolff 2000: 172–200, Knowles and Moon 2006: 31–3, 98–100, 103–4; Goatly 2007: 80; Elkins 2010.

11 For war-based metaphors in medicine/health discourse, see Balko 2010; Docherty 2002; Druce 2013; Larson 2008; Reisfield and Wilson 2004; Semino 2008: 164–6, Sontag 1978; in sports news: Charteris-Black 2004: 117–34; Hamilton 2012; Pinar Sanz 2005: 116–19; in business-related discourse: Charteris-Black 2004: 142–6, Herrera and White 2000; Koller 2004: 64–112.

12 Goatly (2007: 72–83) chooses an even more general level of abstraction by positing a conceptual metaphor theme ACTIVITY IS FIGHTING.

13 Musolff et al. 2001; Musolff 2004a. The English-language EUROMETA sample, which we will largely rely on here, is based on British print and online media texts from the period 1990–2014; specifically, they are sourced from: *BBC Online-News, Channel 4-Online, Economist, Financial Times, New Statesman* (formerly: *New Statesman & Society*), *Scotsman, Spectator, Daily Express, Daily Mail, The Daily Telegraph, The European, The Guardian/Observer, The Independent, The Scotsman, The Sun, The Times/Sunday Times*. Special thanks go to students at Aston, Durham and East Anglia Universities in Britain who helped in the collection and domain classification of EUROMETA.

14 Musolff 2010a, 2010b, 2013.

15 For the application of corpus-driven and corpus-based approaches in metaphor studies, see Deignan 1999, 2005, 2008; Deignan and Semino 2010.

16 *Peter Crisp, Ray Gibbs, Alan Cienki, Graham Low, Gerard Steen, Lynne Cameron, Elena Semino, Joe Grady, Alice Deignan* and *Zoltán Kövecses*.

17 Pragglejaz Group 2007; Steen 2007; Steen et al. 2010.

18 These domains are MOVEMENT, BUILDING-CONSTRUCTION, TECHNOLOGY, NATURE, GROUP-DISCIPLINE, ECONOMY, LOVE-FAMILY, LIFE-BODY, GAME-SPORT, WAR-FIGHTING, PERFORMANCE (plus, possibly: MYTH), see Musolff 2004a, 2010b.

19 For the genre-specific function of metaphorical expressions in headlines, see De Knop 1985, 1987; Herrera-Soler 2006; Neagu and Colipcă-Ciobanu 2014; Vandenberghe, Goethals and Jacobs 2014.

20 This understanding of 'framing' contrasts with that of Lakoff who locates full 'frame'-access even at individual word- or proposition-level (2004a: 3).

21 See for example, Gowland and Turner 1999: 310–21; Karolewski and Suszycki 2011; Scully 2014: 123.

22 Lakoff and Johnson 1980/2003: 156. For the sociological and socio-psychological sources of 'self-fulfilling prophecy' theory, see Merton 1948; Watzlawick, Beavin and Jackson 1967: 78, 135.

23 This notion of frame emergence through metaphor use in discourse links to other discourse-based or 'discourse-dynamic' approaches in metaphor studies (Cameron 2011; Cameron and Deignan 2006; Zinken 2007; Zinken, Nerlich and Hellsten 2008) but focuses more specifically on the question of how sociocultural entrenchment can (*not*: must) result from metaphorical framing.

24 For the concept of the 'community of practice' and its relationship to social identity-construction and speech communities, see Holmes and Meyerhoff 1999.

Chapter 3

1 *New Oxford Bible* (2001): Old Testament: 111, 927, New Testament: 127.

2 See for example, *The Guardian*, 24 May 2015: 'Brexit: would it mean dancing to our own tune, or being out of step with the world?'; *The Daily Telegraph,* 6 May 2015: 'Brexit threat looms over Britain's election and Europe's fate', *The Economist,* 4 May 2015: 'The Brexit dilemma'.

3 For an enthusiastic endorsement, see the preface to *Don't Think of an Elephant. Know your values and frame the debate* by the democrat governor and 2004 presidential candidate, Howard Dean (Dean 2004) and Blogs such as http://effectmeasure.blogspot.de/; for criticism of the 'therapeutic' and politicizing approach in linguistics cf. Hutton 2001; Twardzisz 2013: 37–62.

4 A similarly flawed attempt of 'deducing' political developments from speculative cognitive hypotheses has been made by Lakoff, together with P. Chilton and M. Ilyin, to describe the international debate about the 'Common European House' slogan, which was coined in the late 1980s by the last Soviet leader M. Gorbachev, as evidence of a culture-determined misunderstanding generated by conflicting conceptual models based on the domain HOUSE (Chilton and Ilyin 1993; Chilton and Lakoff 1995). According to their analyses, the lexemes *dom* in Russian and *house* in English access different, culture-specific mental models of the general concept of HOUSE (i.e. BUILDING FOR HUMAN HABITATION), on account of the (alleged) fact that the Russian HOUSE stereotype is a communal apartment block, whereas the Western HOUSE stereotype is supposed to be a free-standing, owner-occupied family home. Therefore, they hypothesize that '[when] the metaphor was translated out of Russian into the language and cultural setting of other European states, the entailments were different (Chilton and Lakoff 1995: 54), which led to a misconstrual of Gorbachev's policies in the West and ultimately to their rejection. Corpus-based studies (Bachem and Battke 1991; Musolff 2000) have, however, shown that British and German media, which may be counted in the 'Western' camp – were perfectly capable of debating and in some parts, endorsing, the 'communal apartment block' version of the metaphor during the 1980s and early 1990s. The demise of Gorbachev's slogan in the 1990s had arguably more to do with the collapse of the Soviet Union than with contrasting metaphorical 'entailments'.

5 See Deignan 2010: 360–2; Musolff 2001, 2004a, 2006, 2009, 2010; Semino 2008: 219–22; Sinding 2015.

6 In environmental and ecological planning, formalized scenario construction and testing has become an important policy tool; see Pérez-Soba and Maas 2015, Schwartz and Ogilvy 1998, van der Heijden 2005, Zurek and Henrichs 2007.

7 For the saga of the *Franco-German couple* in the British press, see Musolff 2009a.

Chapter 4

1 *Shorter Oxford English Dictionary* (2002), vol. 1: 1213. *At the heart* is recorded in this sense since the sixteenth century. As the heart is, literally speaking, a body organ, which is attributed in this basic sense only to zoological organisms, its use with the modifier *of Europe* fulfils the MIP-VU criteria.

2 For overviews ad comparisons with other (mainly: geographically motivated) HEART metaphor uses in British and German debates about the European Union, see Musolff 2004b, 2013b.

3 In addition to example (1), see for example, *The Daily Telegraph*, 14 July 2015: '[PM Cameron] should ... study closely the unstoppable process of integration that has once again been shown to be at the heart of the EU, and reflect that the only viable British relationship with the EU is one that keeps this country at a healthy distance from [it]'; *New Statesman*, 5 March 2015: 'Forget leaving – Britain does best at the heart of Europe'; *Financial Times*, 1 January 2015: 'The growing uncertainty surrounding the future of the UK at the heart of Europe has been very damaging to the UK.'

4 For inter- and cross-cultural variation concerning the position, shape and ingredients of the heart as container of emotions, see Kövecses 1986, 1990, 1995, 2000.

5 These *X at the heart of Europe* ascriptions refer to various European politicians and countries; however, none of them includes the UK. In his

autobiography, Major claims to have 'used the phrase "heart of Europe" before [the speech in Germany], during the election for leadership of the Conservative party' (Major 2000: 269), but these recollections, if accurate, are not reflected in EUROMETA, most probably on account of the fact that those inner-party debates were not widely reported in the public media in all details.

6 For a detailed description from Major's own perspective, see Major 2000: 312–41.

7 *The Times*, 31 August 1994; *The Guardian*, 3 September 1994; for analysis, see Musolff 2000a: 70–8; Tassinari 2006.

8 The press themselves noted the dissociation of positive *heart of Europe* references from the 'Euro'-specific statements (see for example, *New Statesman*, 5 March 1999; *The Guardian*, 28 June 1999).

9 See for example, near-identical promises by the Labour prime ministers Blair and Brown to *put/keep Britain at the heart of Europe* (*London Evening Standard*, 23 November 2001; *Daily Express*, 23 November 2009).

10 From a Relevance-theoretical viewpoint, irony is explained an 'echoic' utterance in which speakers implicitly express their dissociative attitude to an attributed thought or utterance, thus denouncing it as 'ludicrously false (or blatantly inadequate in other ways)' (Wilson and Sperber 2012: 130). For the general status of irony and sarcasm within Relevance Theory, see Sperber and Wilson 1995: 237–43; Wilson and Sperber 1992.

11 The French government even did the magazine the honour of officially condemning its article, which, predictably, only encouraged British EU-sceptical commentators to recycle the catchy headline (*The Daily Telegraph, Daily Mail*, 16 December 2012).

12 See, for instance, reporting on statements by US officials (*Financial Times*, 10 January 2013: 'Stay at heart of Europe, US tells Britain', *The Independent,* 27 November 2013: 'Irish ambassador … urges Britain along path at heart of Europe', *Financial Times,* 23 February 2014: 'Merkel calls for Britain to remain at heart of Europe.'

13 For the long-standing debate over 'dead' vs. alive metaphors, see Goatly 1997: 31–40; Lakoff 1987b; Müller 2008.

14 The canonical formulations of blending theory are Fauconnier and Turner 1998, 2002, Turner and Fauconnier 2003. Lakoff and Johnson (2003: 261) claim an overlap between their approach and CIT (2003: 261–4); for a more critical comparison, see Grady, Oakley and Coulson 1999.

15 *Brewer's Dictionary of Phrase & Fable* 1999: 1279.

Chapter 5

1 For the origins and conceptual history of the fable, see Guldin 2000: 101–3; Hale 1968, 1971: 26–8; Koschorke et al. 2007: 15–26; Nestle 1927; Patterson 1991: 111–37; Peil 1985; Schoenfeldt 1997.

2 For literary analyses of the punning metaphor-expansion in *Coriolanus*, see Jagendorf 1990; Muir 1959; Patterson 1991: 118–26; Peltonen 2009; Spurgeon 1993: 347–9.

3 For overviews of these broad conceptual strands, see Archambault 1967; Charbonnel 2010; Coker 1967; de Baeque 1997; Dhorn van Rossum and Böckenförde 1978; Guldin 2000; Hale 1971; Harris 1998; Kantorowicz 1997; Koschorke et al. 2007; Maitland 2003; Mouton 2009; Musolff 2009, 2010a, b, 2011; Nederman 1992, 2004; Sawday 1995.

4 For the Latin original of *Policraticus*, see John of Salisbury (1909).

5 John's special concern for the *feet/peasants*, as a special object of Christian care and solidarity among all body members, has been related to the 'medieval humanism' tendencies in France; see Liebeschütz 1950; Bass 1997: 203–10 and Guldin 2000: 57–8.

6 Shogimen (2008: 103) has compared John's 'notion of medical treatment as the eradication of the causes of diseases', which 'highlighted coercive and punitive aspects of government as the final solution to political conflicts', with contemporary medieval, Japanese notions of 'medical treatment as controlling physical conditions', which put a greater emphasis on 'daily healthcare and preventative medicine', that is, preventative measures, thus indicating a historic cross-cultural contrast in scenarios of the metaphor POLITICAL REFORM AS MEDICAL TREATMENT.

7 See for example, Fortescue 1997 [1468–71]: 20–1; for analysis: Bertelli 2001; Kantorowicz 1997.

8 See Hale 1971; Harris 1998; Musolff 2010a; Patterson 1991; Skinner 1978.

9 For the links between Foucault's discourse concept and Critical Discourse and Discourse-Historical Analysis, see Chilton 2005: 19–20; Faiclough 1989: 28–30; Wodak 2005.

10 Samples also exist for Italian, Russian, Dutch and Spanish as well as for American English, but so far they are too small for meaningful comparisons.

11 For a detailed overview, see Appendix II.

12 The 'knowledge' relevant for use as metaphor source has to be understood as popular, non-expert information because scientific expertise about bodies is socially restricted and far too complex to be useful for familiarization of abstract concepts such as the 'nation state'. We also have to bear in mind that our human body knowledge itself is not immediately accessible but culturally mediated and itself 'grounded' in metaphor, as any history of popular medicine will attest. For a striking example of a reversal of social and biological grounding of metaphors, see the following chapter.

13 Examples such as (6)–(9) rely on the assumption that the politician as a part of the body politic needs to be strong (in order to survive a punch to

the solar plexus) or a valuable limb (in contrast to mere toenail – or pustule – status). In all these cases, an idealized body concept is presupposed, against which other bodyforms can be judged. While such judgements and their underlying assumptions about 'ideal bodies' would probably be considered sexist, ageist, racist and offensive, were they publicly applied to 'real-life' bodies, they seem to be acceptable when used metaphorically.

14 In addition, *Nationalkörper* ('national body') is attested but just with one occurrence (*Die Zeit*, 19 May 2005).

15 'Ich fragte einen mir bekannten Priester, was denn unsere Spiritualität ausmache. … die Antwort [lautete,] dass alle Russen sich in einem obrigkeitlichen Staatskörper zusammenschließen sollten'.

16 '… [es] findet … der geschichtlich einzigartige Akt einer politischen Neugründung Europas statt. … – in der Sache entsteht gerade ein neuer politischer Staatskörper'.

17 'An der Berliner Humboldt-Universität hat die Regierung eigens ein "Kompetenzzentrum" eingerichtet, in dem acht Wissenschaftler darüber wachen, dass Gender Mainstreaming korrekt in den Staatskörper eingepflanzt wird'.

18 The exceptions are some ironical uses, for example, one ridiculing opinion polls as being akin to probing the people's body with a thermometer (*Frankfurter Rundschau*, 13 January 2013: 'der Demoskop [führt allwöchentlich seine Stimmungssonde in den Volkskörper ein').

19 '… der deutschtrunkene Bürger [verschmolz] mit dem tobenden Volkskörper'.

20 'Im *kranken Volkskörper* steckt eine verletzte Seele. Katharina Rutschky sieht in der Debatte um die Biopolitik das Symptom einer Hysterie, die ihre tiefste Ursache in den deutschen Traumata des 20. Jahrhunderts hat'.

21 'Kunstwerk Volkskörper'.

22 'Kein Atom im Volkskörper! Die Anti-AKW-Bewegung in Österreich streitet derzeit heftig. Denn einige Gruppen … pflegen einen unkritischen Umgang mit rechtsextremen Umweltschützern'.

23 *Die Zeit*, 18 June 1998: Wer die Homogenität eines ‚deutschen Volkskörpers' ins Feld führt, der gießt Öl ins Feuer der Ghettos'.

24 '… le président [= Nicolas Sarkozy] … entraîne le corps politique français dans une consternante régression'.

25 'Mitterrand à Sarkozy: une irrésistible érosion de la fonction présidentielle et du corps politique'.

26 'L'atomisation des individus sous le choc de la crise et la divergence du corps social trouvent une traduction directe dans la vie publique avec la radicalisation et la poussée des populismes'.

27 'La classe politique, droite libérale et gauche socialiste confondues, a malmené depuis plus de vingt- cinq ans le vieux corps social français'.

28 'A noter un chiffre peu souligné lors de la soirée électorale, à savoir les 2,14 millions de votes nuls et blancs, soit 5,8% du corps électoral, un niveau extrêmement élevé, qui correspond sans doute à une part de l'électorat frontiste du premier tour'.

29 'Le corps politique, un malade à la recherche de sa thérapie'

30 '... de penser la dimension politique à l'image d'un corps, il n'y aurait qu'à relire Rousseau, ... *Du contrat social*, ...] Cette métaphore n'est pas anodine, elle suppose que ce corps soit dirigé par une seule unité intentionnelle ... et que tous les membres de la société ne soient plus considérés que comme organes de celui- ci'.

31 'Comme la nature donne à chaque homme un pouvoir absolu sur tous ses membres, le pacte social donne au corps politique un pouvoir absolu sur tous les siens, et c'est ce même pouvoir qui, dirigé par la volonté générale, porte ... le nom de souveraineté'. For further pertinent passages depicting the *corps politique* see Rousseau 1990: 82, as well as the *Discours sur l'économie politique* (Rousseau 2002); for interpretations of Rousseau's linkage between society and state, see Derathé 2000; Bertram 2003; Wraight 2008.

32 See de Baecque 1997; Guilhaumou 1989 and Sinding (2015) who applies *body politic* scenario analysis to the writings of Edmund Burke and Thomas Paine.

33 See Renaud 1995; Agamben 1995; Lévy 2012; interview with R. Debray, Denis Podalydès and Olivier Py, in *Le Monde*, 5 March 2011.

34 Such denials are, for instance, routine in the case of *Volkskörper* and other terminology that carries Nazi associations; see Musolff 2013a; Wodak 2013.

Chapter 6

1 *The Guardian*, 17 November 2009: 'Labour candidate who called Queen "parasite" faces sack.'

2 See Charteris-Black 2005: 182–4; Chilton 2005; Hawkins 2001.

3 See Hassl 2005: 2–5; Lewis and Short 1984: 1301; Liddell and Scott 1869: 1193; *Shorter Oxford English Dictionary*, vol. 2: 2096.

4 See Antonsen-Resch 2005; Arnott 1968; Damon 1998; Gullestad 2012.

5 For English, see *Shorter Oxford English Dictionary*, 2: 2096 and Nevalainen 1999: 444; for French, see Robert 1977: 1356; for German, where *Parasit* seems to have quickly become a synonym of the older term *Schmarotzer* ('beggar'), see Duden 2013: 615.

6 Jonson 1966: 38; Shakespeare 1976: 146 (Act I, Scene 9, line 45).

7 See Cox 2002: 603; Zimmer 2011: 2–4.

8 See de Baecque 1997: 85, 102–6; Desmet, Rooryck and Swiggers 1990; Hamerton-Kelly 1996: 79; Schama 1989: 72–3.

9 See Figes 1996: 603–27; Lenin 1989: 381–492; Marx 1960: 149–58.

10 See Beerman 1961; Fitzpatrick 2006. I am indebted to Veronica Bowker, David Lilley and Ekaterina Sintsova for drawing my attention to the Russian sources.

11 See Lu 1999; Lynteris 2013.

12 See for example, *healingdaily.com, dailyparasite.blogspot, allergyescape.com.* (accessed 18 December 2014). http://www.amren.com, 2004 (accessed 10 April 2013).

13 http://MichNews.com, 2004 (accessed 8 January 2012; withdrawn since 2013).

14 Herder [(1777], *Deutsches Museum. Von Ähnlichkeit der mittleren englischen und deutschen Dichtkunst, nebst Verschiednem, das daraus folget,* quoted in Schmitz-Berning 1998: 667.

15 Abel 1990; Evans 2005, 2008; Welch 2007.

16 See http://unglaublichkeiten.com, 2003 (accessed 10 April 2013), http://www.wahrheiten.org, 2010 (accessed 10 April 2013), for an overview, see Posch, Stopfner and Kienpointner 2013.

17 See http://aryanmusic.net/news.php, 2010 (accessed 10 April 2013).

18 See Böke 1997; Charteris-Black 2006; Cisneros 2008; Hönigsberger 1991; Jung, Niehr and Böke 2000; KhosraviNik 2010; KhosraviNik, Krzyżanowski and Wodak 2012; Musolff 2012; Richardson and Colombo 2013.

19 The *rivers of blood* phrase alludes to the Conservative politician Enoch Powell's speech of 20 April 1968, in which it appeared as a quotation from Virgil's *Aeneid*, prophesying civil war (Charteris-Black 2011: 27–8). In most articles in the sample, this speech is referred to only as an exemplary case of dangerous xenophobic rhetoric; the online commentaries and Blogs include both positive and negative evaluations.

20 See for example, *The Scotsman,* 4 January 2014: 'The attempt of the far right to present the citizens of these countries as parasites … is as absurd as it is repellent'; *The Guardian,* 5 February 2013: 'The government is telling us that the coming Romanians and Bulgarians are ill-educated, parasitic benefit tourists. These people deserve better'; *The Spectator,* 27 April 2013: 'People like me: non-EU immigrants … are all viewed as grasping parasites.'

21 Quotations from the online fora have been anonymized and are identified only by reference to the respective *Have Your Say*-sample (numbering 1–3) and the date of the posting. Omissions are indicated by '…' and all special notations, highlighting, typographic and other errors in the postings have been preserved.

22 See http://www.stormfront.org/forum/; http://sheikyermami.com/muselmanic-welfare-parasites-cost-britain-13-billion-a-year/; http://jonjayray.wordpress.com/2007/10/03/britain-muslim-immigrants-are-the-chief-parasites/ (all accessed 15 December 2013).

23 See https://answers.yahoo.com/question/index?qid=20141206204434AALHoSO (accessed 15 December 2013).

24 Comment posted to http://www.weeklygripe.co.uk/a294.asp on 14 November 2012 (accessed 15 December 2013).

25 Posted to http://expeltheparasite.com (n.d) (accessed 15 December 2013).

26 Posted to http://answers.yahoo.com/question/index?qid=20120624051236AAds2v0, (n.d) (accessed 15 December 2013).

27 This pseudo-scientific observation can already be found in Hitler's JEWS AS PARASITES metaphor in *Mein Kampf*; see Hitler 1933: 334.

28 For recent such cases in German-speaking countries, see research on the late Austrian politician J. Haider's *immigrants as parasites* denunciations (Pelinka 2001; Pelinka and Wodak 2002), xenophobic imagery used by the Swiss far-right politician D. Lüthard (Musolff 2013a) and on comparisons between benefit-receivers and parasites by German politicians (Blasig 2005; Bundesministerium für Wirtschaft und Arbeit 2005; Matussek 2010; Sarrazin 2010).

29 See Deignan 2011; Gibbs 2011a, b; Müller 2011; Steen 2011. Charteris-Black 2012 suggests the term 'purposeful' as a replacement for 'deliberate'.

30 See Bosmaijan 1983; Rash 2005, 2006; Fabiszak and Kaszubski 2005; Hawkins 2001; Musolff 2010a; Schwarz-Friesel and Kromminga 2014.

Chapter 7

1 For the historical debate about the Nakba and its long-term effects, see Masalha 2003; Morris 2004; Pappé 2010.

2 The video recording of this speech shows Netanyahu raising his hand above the lectern during the last part of this passage, possibly simulating the initiation of a handshake (see Netanyahu 2011b).

3 See Netanyahu 2011: 'It's here [i.e. the UN assembly] year after year that Israel is unjustly singled out for condemnation.'

4 For further cognitive work based on the STATE AS PERSON metaphor, see in particular Kövecses 2002: 60–2; Lakoff 1992, 2004a: 71–2; Charteris-Black 2004: 76 and 2005: 44, 173–4.

5 See for example, Hobbes [1651] 1996; Rousseau [1762] 1990, [1755] 2002; for analysis see Mouton 2010.

6 See for example, Clausewitz [1832] 1998; Grotius [1625] 2005; Schmitt [1927/1932] 2002; for analysis see Fabiszak 2007: 75–91.

7 The English text versions of the eight speeches (delivered by Netanyahu in English and by Abbas in Arabic) have been compiled from the internet and cross-checked with those on the official UN website (UN General Assembly 2015); they amount to 27,636 words altogether.

8 On other uses of the extended hand metaphor by Arafat, see Gavriely-Nuri 2010: 461, 464.

9 See *Haaretz*, 29 July 2013: 'Difficult choices ahead'. Kerry launches Israeli–Palestinian peace talks, seeking 'reasonable compromises'.

10 See *Times of Israel* 4 April 2014: 'As talks flounder, sides prepare for blame game'; *The Palestine Chronicle*, 3 April 2014: 'Palestinians Must Abandon the "Peace Process".'

11 Netanyahu 2014: 'So when it comes to their ultimate goals, Hamas is ISIS and ISIS is Hamas. And what they share in common, all militant

Islamists share in common: Boko Haram in Nigeria; Ash-Shabab in Somalia; Hezbollah in Lebanon; An-Nusrah in Syria; The Mahdi Army in Iraq; And the Al-Qaeda branches in Yemen, Libya, the Philippines, India and elsewhere. ... Militant Islam's ambition to dominate the world seems mad. But so too did the global ambitions of another fanatic ideology that swept to power eight decades ago. The Nazis believed in a master race. The militant Islamists believe in a master faith.'

12 For a famous description of war as an 'extended duel', see Clausewitz 1998: 27–8, 205–6.

13 Initially, the *Time* magazine was also considered: Twardzisz 2013: 127–8.

14 The '+human' hit rates for the five different sub-categories range from 2.11 per cent to 5.7 per cent; see Twardzisz 2013: 149.

15 Such an interpretation is, for instance, proffered by Farkas (2014) in her analysis of metaphor in the three post-Second World War Hungarian constitutions. She identifies the verbs *protect, fight, respect, preserve, own, manage, assist, provide, cooperate, serve, (not) being entitled to* as the chief collocates of *state* in agentive constructions and comes to the conclusion that 'metaphorical occurrences of the concept of the state overwhelmed non-metaphorical ones' and 'surfaced almost exclusively as personification' (Farkas 2014: 110–1).

16 See Barcelona 2003; Bierwiaczonek 2013; Littlemore 2015; Panther and Radden 1999.

17 See, for instance, Nerlich and Koteyko 2009; Steen et al. 2010, which are cited by Twardzisz himself: 2013: 126.

18 See Goffman 1959, 1967, 1972; for the development of Face theory in linguistic pragmatics, see Brown and Levinson 1987; Culpeper 2011; Scollon, Scollon and Jones 2012; Watts, Ide and Ehlich 2005.

19 See Epstein (2011) and Mikalayeva (2011) for productive applications in modelling negotiation behaviour in IR Theory.

20 EUROMETA and BODYPOL corpora include examples of *Face*-interpretation for conflicts between Ukraine and Russia, Greece v. EU and China v. USA (see *The Sunday Times*, 21 December 2014: 'Europe seeks face-saving retreat for Putin over Ukraine'; *The Economist* 31 January 2015: 'The task for European governments is to find a way for [Greek prime minister A. Tsipras] to retreat from his demands without losing face altogether'; *The Guardian*, 5 January 2001: 'If the US loses face, the hawks who argue for a tougher overall policy-line on China may definitively prevail.') SOCIAL FACE idioms are not considered by Twardzisz who only includes clauses that include the verb *face* (e.g. *France faces growing fears, Japan faces condemnation*, Twardzisz 2013: 132) in his search.

21 See Bülow 1930: 359–60; MacDonogh, 2000: 244–5; Röhl 1988: 21.

22 *The Times*, 30 July 1900; quoted after *Oxford English Dictionary on historical Principles*, 1989, vol. VII: 489. For the German versions of the speech and their editorial history, compare Matthes 1976: 85–8; Behnen 1977: 244–7 and Sösemann 1976.

23 Such reports were of course officially denied by the government, but the German war minister, H. von Goßler, conceded the possibility that 'His Majesty's speech might have been open to misunderstandings', not least through establishing the reference to the 'Huns' (see Hufer 2003; Ladendorf 1906).

24 See *Oxford English Dictionary on historical Principles*, 1989, vol. VII: 489; for the popular view of the Huns in nineteenth-century Germany, see Brockhaus (1838), vol 2: 427.

25 'For All We have and Are', for the full text, see Kipling 1994: 341–2; for its biographical context and reception, see Matin 1999.

26 Messinger 1992: 137–9; Schneider and Wagener 2007; Taylor 2003: 186; Thacker 2014: 48, 63, 162–3.

27 The contextual reference of such depictions were the reports of German war atrocities especially against civilians in Belgium; see Messinger 1992: 70–84; Cull, Culbert and Welch 2001: 25; Taylor 2003: 178–80; Wilson 1979; Zuckerman 2004.

28 *Oxford English Dictionary on historical Principles*, 1989, VII: 489; *Brewer's Dictionary of Phrase and Fable* 1999: 596; similarly, Hughes 2006: 243–4; Ayto 2006: 43. In current usage, the *Hun* epithet only occasionally resurfaces in tongue-in-cheek statements, often related to football, and in articles that discuss lingering anti-German resentments (e.g. *The Observer* 28 November 2004: 'Stop making fun of the Hun').

29 *Oxford English Dictionary on historical Principles*, 1989, vol. VII, 489.

30 See Wulf 1966; Mannes 1999; Tegel 2007; Welch 2007; Vande Winkel and Welch 2007. The film was preceded 1939–40 by a touring exhibition under the same title; see Friedländer 1998: 253–4; Kallis 2005: 194–5, 199.

31 For detailed film-historical analyses of the film, see Hornshøj-Møller 1995; Hornshøj-Møller and Culbert 1992.

32 *Mitteilungsblätter für die weltanschauliche Schulung der Ordnungspolizei*, Folge 27; 1 December 1941; quoted after Matthäus 2004: 300.

Chapter 8

1 Shida (2002) has argued that US–Chinese diplomatic relationships have in the past suffered from unacknowledged effects of 'distinctive ... face-saving cultures'.

2 See for example, *Brewer's Dictionary of Phrase and Fable* 1999: 149; Deignan 1995: 2; *Shorter Oxford English Dictionary* 2002, I: 258.

3 Research into L2 metaphor acquisition has become a burgeoning area of applied metaphor analysis in its own right; see for example, Littlemore and Low 2006, Littlemore, Chen, Koester and Barnden 2011; MacArthur and Littlemore 2011; Nacey 2013; Philip 2010; Piquer-Piriz 2010; Wang and Dowker 2010.

4 The responses have been edited and normalized for English spelling and grammar, but no content has been added or changed.

5 I am grateful to the colleagues and students of the universities of Aston, Birmingham and East Anglia in the UK; Heidelberg University (Germany); the Eötvös Lorand University in Budapest (Hungary); the universities of Estremadura and La Mancha in Spain; Hadassah College and Hebrew University in Israel; the University of Verona (Italy); Oslo University (Norway); Cracow College 'Stairways School of English' (Poland); the University of Bucharest (Romania); the University of Verona (Italy) and Hangzhou Normal University in the People's Republic of China.

6 The Chinese students' samples were collected across five different institutions in Britain, Germany and China, the largest cohort being that at Hangzhou Normal University (= 135).

7 The counting procedure underlying this table and all other quantified statements in this chapter is an enumeration of relevant answers per completed questionnaire. Some questionnaires had to be discounted because they contained irrelevant answers. On the other hand, some questionnaires included several relevant answers that fell into different categories (e.g. function vs. geography-based and further, see below). In these cases, each correct answer was counted separately, so that the respective questionnaire was taken twice (and in a few cases, three times) into consideration. The justification for this counting procedure was that the focus of the pilot study was on ratios of response categories, not on numbers of questionnaires.

8 Geography-based responses were also recorded in questionnaires filled in by Japanese, Kurdish and French students, but their cohort numbers are too low to allow for any meaningful comparison.

9 Interpretation of Italy as the 'leg of Europe' make up 22 per cent of all responses in the Italian cohort, often with explicit reference to the stereotypical characterization of Italy as 'Europe's boot', which provides a plausible source motivation (Watts 2009: 107).

10 Other examples conceptualize the nation as one's own FEET/LEGS (for 'standing up and going forward in the world'), HANDS ('creating the people') or EYES ('noticing the democracy and equality enjoyed by general citizens as well as the corruptions and irresponsibility of some government parasites').

11 Two recurring roles that do not fit this model are those of the FIGHTER/WARRIOR (seven occurrences) and of the GIANT (six occurrences). They seem to be motivated by the immediate topical and argumentative context of the respective answers: in the first place a focus on a nation's competition or conflict with another nation, and in the second place, a focus on China's territorial vastness. In addition, there are a few other characterizations (e.g. WRITER, SINGER, GODDESS, FIRE-FIGHTER), but they occur in such low numbers as to preclude their analysis as culture specific.

12 For an analysis of the pictorial metaphor, see especially Forceville 1996, 2009; Forceville and Urios-Aparisi 2009; Philips 2003; for the wider field of the multimodal metaphor, including gestures, see Cienki and Müller 2008; Müller et al. 2013, 2014; Norris 2011.

Chapter 9

1 Tagliamonte (2012: 87) includes metaphorization among sociolinguistic variation patterns but only cites examples of diachronic metaphorical and metonymic extension. A comprehensive sociolinguistic account of metaphor would have to include synchronic variation and link it to historical traditions and usage tendencies. For the methodological background, see Labov 1972; Trudgill 2011.

2 For the basic relevance-theoretical account of metaphor as a form of 'loose uses of language' that involves an interpretive relationship between propositional form and speaker's thought, see Sperber and Wilson 1995: 231–7. The relevance-theoretical account can be seen as partly compatible with the CMT approach in focusing on the inferential processing of figurative meaning (see Gibbs and Tendahl, 2006, 2011; Sperber and Wilson 2008; Tendahl 2009; Tendahl and Gibbs 2008; Wilson 2011; Wilson and Carston 2006).

Bibliography

Abbas, M. (2011), Statement before the United Nations Assembly, 66th session, 23 September 2011, http://gadebate.un.org/sites/default/files/gastatements/66/PS_en.pdf (accessed 19 January 2015).

Abbas, M. (2012), Statement before the United Nations Assembly, 67th session, 27 September 2012, http://www.haaretz.com/news/diplomacy-defense/full-transcript-of-abbas-speech-at-un-general-assembly-1.386385 (accessed 19 January 2015).

Abbas, M. (2013), Statement before the United Nations Assembly, 68th session, 26 September 2014, http://mondoweiss.net/2013/09/general-assembly-transcript.html (accessed 19 January 2015).

Abbas, M. (2014), Statement before the United Nations Assembly, 69th session, 26 September 2014, http://www.un.org/en/ga/69/meetings/gadebate/26sep/palestine.shtml (accessed 19 January 2015).

Abel, K. -D. (1990), *Presselenkung im NS-Staat: Eine Studie zur Geschichte der Publizistik in der nationalsozialistischen Zeit*, Berlin: Colloquium Berlin.

Aesop (2002), Aesop's *Fables*, translated by L. Gibbs, Oxford: Oxford University Press.

Agamben, G. (1995), La double identité du peuple, *Libération*, 11 February 1995.

Ahrens, K. (2011), 'Examining conceptual metaphor models through lexical frequency patterns: A case study of U.S. presidential speeches', in S. Handl and H. -J. Schmid (eds), *Windows to the Mind: Metaphor, Metonymy and Conceptual Blending*, 67–184, Berlin: Walter de Gruyter.

Ahrens, K. and S. M. Y. Lee (2009), 'Gender versus politics: When conceptual models collide in the US senate', in Kathleen Ahrens (ed.), *Politics, Gender and Conceptual Metaphors*, 62–81, Basingstoke: Palgrave Macmillan.

Antonsen-Resch, A. (2005), *Von Gnathon Zu Saturio: Die Parasitenfigur und das Verhältnis der römischen Komödie zur griechischen*, Berlin/New York: W. de Gruyter.

Arafat, Y. (1974a), Statement before the United Nations Assembly, 29th session, 13 November 1974, http://www.al-bab.com/arab/docs/pal/arafat_gun_and_olive_branch.htm (accessed 30 January 2015).

Arafat, Y. (1974b), Statement before the United Nations Assembly, 29th session, 13 November 1974, https://www.youtube.com/watch?v=LVXN6EiqKFY (accessed 30 January 2015).

Archambault, P. (1967), 'The analogy of the body in renaissance political literature', *Bibliothèque d'Humanisme et Renaissance*, 29: 21–63.

Arnott, W. G. (Summer 1968), 'Studies in comedy, I: Alexis and the parasite's name', *Greek, Roman and Byzantine Studies*, 9 (2): 161–68.

Aristotle (1991), *The Art of Rhetoric*, translated by H. C. Lawson-Tancred, London: Penguin.

Aunger, R. (ed.) (2000), *Darwinizing Culture. The Status of Memetics as a Science*. With a foreword by Daniel Dennett, Oxford: Oxford University Press.

Ayto, J. (2006), *Movers and Shakers: A Chronology of Words that Shaped Our Age*, Oxford: Oxford University Press.

Bachem, R., and K. Battke (1991), 'Strukturen und Funktionen der Metapher *Unser Gemeinsames Haus Europa* im aktuellen politischen Diskurs', in F. Liedtke, M. Wengeler and K. Böke (eds), *Begriffe besetzen. Strategien des Sprachgebrauchs in der Politik*, 295–307, Opladen: Westdeutscher Verlag.

Bakewell, S. (2013), 'How we're herded by language', *The Guardian*, 6 September 2013.

Balko, R. (2010), The Drug War Metaphor: Increasingly Literal. *reason.com* [Blog], 6 October 2010, http://reason.com/blog/2010/10/06/the-drug-war-metaphor-increasi/ (accessed 24 June 2015).

Barcelona, A. (2003), 'Clarifying and applying the notions of metaphor and metonymy within cognitive linguistics: An update', in R. Dirven and R. Pörings (eds), *Metaphor and Metonymy in Comparison and Contrast*, 207–77, Berlin and New York: Mouton de Gruyter.

Barcelona, A. and F. J. Ruiz de Mendoza Ibáñez (eds) (2015), *Bibliography of Metaphor and Metonymy*, https://benjamins.com/online/met/ (accessed 6 June 2015).

Bärsch, C. -E. (2002), *Die politische Religion des Nationalsozialismus*, Munich: Fink.

Bass, A. M. (1997), 'The metaphor of the human body in the political theory of John of Salisbury: Context and innovation', in B. Debatin, T. R. Jackson and D. Steuer (eds), *Metaphor and Rational Discourse*, 201–13, Tübingen: Niemeyer.

BBC (2010a), Have your Say: Should politicians be talking about immigration? http://www.bbc.co.uk/blogs/haveyoursay/2010/04/should_politicians_be_talking.html (last accessed 15 December 2013).

BBC (2010b), Have your Say: How should immigration be tackled? http://www.bbc.co.uk/blogs/haveyoursay/2010/04/how_should_immigration_be_tack.html.

BBC (2010c), Have your Say: Are immigration rules fair? http://www.bbc.co.uk/blogs/haveyoursay/2010/06/are_immigration_rules_fair.html (last accessed 15 December 2013).

Beermann, R. (1964), 'Soviet and Russian Anti-Parasite Laws', *Soviet Studies*, 15 (4): 420–9.

Behnen. M. (ed.) (1977), *Quellen zur deutschen Außenpolitik im Zeitalter des Imperialismus 1890-1911*, Darmstadt: Wissenschaftliche Buchgesellschaft.

Bein, A. (1965), 'Der jüdische Parasit', *Vierteljahreshefte für Zeitgeschichte* 13: 121–49.

Bertelli, S. (2001), *The King's Body. Sacred Rituals of Power in Medieval and Early Modern Europe*, University Park, PA: Pennsylvania State University Press.

Bertram, C. (2003), *Rousseau and The Social Contract*, London: Routledge.

Bierwiaczonek, B. (2013), *Metonymy in Language, Thought and Brain*, London: Equinox.

Bin Laden, O. (2001), Videotaped Address, 7 October 2001, http://www.press.uchicago.edu/Misc/Chicago/481921texts.html (accessed 3 May 2014).

Black, M. (1962), *Models and Metaphors*, Ithaca: Cornell University Press.

Blasig, R. (2005), 'Clements Parasiten', *Braunschweiger Zeitung*, 25 October 2005.

Böke, K. (1997), 'Die "Invasion" aus den "Armenhäusern Europas" Metaphern im Einwanderungsdiskurs', in M. Jung, M. Wengeler and K. Böke (eds), *Die Sprache der Migrationsdiskurse. Das Reden über die "Ausländer" in Medien, Politik und Alltag*, 164–93, Opladen: Westdeutscher Verlag.

Boisnard, P. (2005), 'Le corps politique, un malade à la recherche de sa thérapie', *Multitudes. Revue politique, artistique, philosophique*, 50, http://multitudes. samizdat.net/ (accessed 10 February 2013).

Bourdieu, P. (ed.) (1990), 'Structures, habitus, practices', in *The Logic of Practice*, 52–79. Stanford, CA: Stanford University Press.

Brewer's Dictionary of Phrase and Fable (1999), edited by A. Room, London: Cassell.

Brockhaus (1838), *Brockhaus Bilder-Conversations-Lexikon*, Leipzig: Verlag Brockhaus.

Brown, P. and S. C. Levinson (1987), *Politeness: Some Universals in Language Usage*, Cambridge: Cambridge University Press.

Browne, Sir T. (2009), *Pseudodoxia Epidemica: or, Enquiries into Commonly Presumed Truths*, Oxford: Benediction Classics (First published 1642).

Bülow, Prince B. von (1977), 'Erklärung im Reichstag zu Grundfragen der Außen-politik', in M. Behnen (Hg.) (1977), *Quellen zur deutschen Außenpolitik im Zeitalter des Imperialismus 1890-1911*, 165–66, Darmstadt: Wissenschaftliche Buchgesellschaft, (originally in *Stenographische Berichte über die Verhandlun-gen des deutschen Reichstages*, 4. Sitzg., 1897).

Bülow, Prince B. von (1930), *Denkwürdigkeiten*, edited by F. v. Stockhammer, vol. 1, Berlin: Ullstein.

Bundesministerium für Wirtschaft und Arbeit (2005), *Vorrang für die Anständigen – Gegen Missbrauch, 'Abzocke' und Selbstbedienung im Sozialstaat. Ein Report vom Arbeitsmarkt 2005*, Berlin: Bundesministerium für Wirtschaft und Arbeit.

Bush, G. W. (2001), Address to Congress, 20 September 2001, https://www. youtube.com/watch?v=_CSPbzitPL8 (accessed 23 June 2015).

Callahan, W. A. (2009), 'The cartography of national humiliation and the emer-gence of China's geobody', *Public Culture*, 21 (1): 141–73.

Cameron, L. (2011), *Metaphor and Reconciliation. The Discourse Dynamics of Empathy in Post-Conflict Conversations*, London/New York: Routledge.

Cameron, L. and A. Deignan (2003), 'Combining large and small corpora to investigate tuning devices around metaphor in spoken discourse', *Metaphor and Symbol*, 18 (3): 149–60.

Cameron, L. and A. Deignan (2006), 'The emergence of metaphor in discourse', *Journal of Applied Linguistics*, 27: 671–90.

Carr, R. H. (1906), 'Introduction', in R. H. Carr (ed.), *Plutarch's Lives of Coriolanus, Caesar, Brutus and Antonius in North's Translation*, v–xxxv, Oxford: Clarendon Press (Reprint 2009, Milton Keynes: Lightning Source).

Carver, T. and J. Pikalo (eds) (2008), *Political Language and Metaphor. Interpreting and Changing the World*, London: Routledge.

Charbonnel, N. (2010), *Comme un seul home. Corps politique et corps mystique*, 2 vols, Lons Le Saunier: Aréopage.

Charteris-Black, J. (2004), *Corpus Approaches to Critical Metaphor Analysis*, Basingstoke: Palgrave-Macmillan.

Charteris-Black, J. (2005), *Politicians and Rhetoric. The Persuasive Power of Metaphor*, Basingstoke: Palgrave-Macmillan.

Charteris-Black, J. (2006), 'Britain as a container: Immigration metaphors in the 2005 election campaign', *Discourse & Society*, 17 (5): 563–81.

Charteris-Black, J. (2011), *Politicians and Rhetoric. The Persuasive Power of Metaphor*, Basingstoke: Palgrave-Macmillan.

Charteris-Black, J. (2012), 'Forensic deliberations on "purposeful metaphor",' *Metaphor and the Social World*, 2 (1): 1–21.

Chilton, P. (2004), *Analysing Political Discourse: Theory and Practice*, London: Routledge.

Chilton, P. (2005a), 'Manipulation, memes and metaphors: The case of *Mein Kampf*', in L. de L. de Saussure and P. Schulz (eds), *Manipulation and Ideologies in the Twentieth Century*, 15–43, Amsterdam and Philadelphia: Benjamins.

Chilton, P. (2005b), 'Missing links in mainstream CDA: Modules, blends and the critical instinct', in R. Wodak and P. Chilton (eds), *A New Agenda in (Critical) Discourse Analysis: Theory, Methodology and Interdisciplinary*, 19–51, Amsterdam and Philadelphia: John Benjamins.

Chilton, P. and G. Lakoff (1995), 'Foreign policy by metaphor', in C. Schäffner and A. Wenden (eds), *Language and Peace*, 37–55. Aldershot: Ashgate.

Cienki, A. (2004), 'Bush's and Gore's language and gestures in the 2000 US presidential debates: A test case for two models of metaphors', *Journal of Language and Politics*, 3: 409–40.

Cienki, A. (2005), 'Metaphor in the "Strict Father" and "Nurturant Parent" cognitive models: Theoretical issues raised in an empirical study', *Cognitive Linguistics*, 16: 279–312.

Cienki, A. (2008), 'The application of conceptual metaphor theory to political discourse: Methodological questions and some possible solutions', in T. Carver and J. Pikalo (eds), *Political Language and Metaphor. Interpreting and Changing the World*, 241–56, London: Routledge.

Cienki, A. and C. Müller (2008), *Metaphor and Gesture*, Amsterdam and Philadelphia: Benjamins.

Cisneros, J. D. (2008), 'Contaminated communities: The metaphor of "Immigrant as Pollutant" in media representations of immigration', *Rhetoric & Public Affairs*, 11(4): 569–601.

Clausewitz, C. von (1998), *Vom Kriege*, Berlin: Ullstein.

Coker, F. W. (1910), *Organismic Theories of the State. Nineteenth-Century Interpretations of the State as Organism or Person*, New York: Columbia University.

Combes, C. (2005), *The Art of Being a Parasite*, translated by David Simberloff, Chicago: The University of Chicago Press.

Connolly, B. (1995), *The Rotten Heart of Europe*. London: Faber.

Cox, F. E. G. (2002), 'History of human parasitology', *Critical Microbiology Reviews*, 15 (4): 595–612.

Croft, W. (2003), 'The role of domains in the interpretation of metaphors and metonymies', in R. Dirven and R. Pörings (eds), *Metaphor and Metonymy in Comparison and Contrast*, 161–205, Berlin and New York: Mouton de Gruyter.

Croft, W. (2000), *Explaining Language Change: An Evolutionary Approach*, London: Longman.

Croft, W. and D. A. Cruse (2004), *Cognitive Linguistics*. Cambridge: Cambridge University Press.

Culf, A. (1996). 'Tabloids are condemned over Euro 96 own goals', *The Guardian*, 30 October 1996.

Cull, N. J., D. H. Culbert and D. Welch (2001), *Propaganda and Mass Persuasion. A Historical Encyclopedia 1500 to the Present*, Santa Barbara, CA: ABC-Clio.

Culpeper, J. (2011), *Impoliteness: Using Language to Cause Offence*, Cambridge: Cambridge University Press.

Damon, C. (1998), *The Mask of the Parasite. A Pathology of Roman Patronage*, Ann Arbor, MI: University of Michigan Press.

Dawkins, R. (1989), *The Selfish Gene* (New edition), Oxford and New York: Oxford University Press.

Dawkins, R. (1999), *The Extended Phenotype. The Long Reach of the Gene*, Oxford: Oxford University Press.

Dawkins, R. (2004), 'Viruses of the mind', in Latha Menon (ed.), *A Devil's Chaplain. Selected Essays*, 151–72, London: Phoenix.

Dean, H. (2004), 'Foreword', in G. Lakoff (ed.), *Don't Think of an Elephant! Know Your Values and Frame the Debate. The Essential Guide for Progressives*, ix, White River Junction, VT: Chelsea Green Publishing Company.

de Baecque, A. (1997), *The Body Politic. Corporeal Metaphor in Revolutionary France 1770-1800*, Stanford, CA: Stanford University Press.

Deignan, A. (1995), *Collins COBUILD English Guides 7, Metaphors*. London: HarperCollins.

Deignan, A. (1999), 'Corpus-based research into metaphor', in L. Cameron and G. Low (eds), *Researching and Applying Metaphor*, 177–99, Cambridge: Cambridge University Press.

Deignan, A. (2005), *Metaphor and Corpus Linguistics*, Amsterdam and Philadelphia: John Benjamins.

Deignan, A. (2008), 'Corpus linguistics and metaphor', in R. W. Gibbs (ed.), *The Cambridge Handbook of Metaphor and Thought*, 290–4, Cambridge: Cambridge University Press.

Deignan, A. (2010), 'The evaluative properties of metaphors', in G. Low, Z. Todd, A. Deignan and L. Cameron (eds), *Researching and Applying Metaphor in the Real World*, 357–73, Amsterdam and Philadelphia: Benjamins.

Deignan, A. (2011), 'Deliberateness is not unique to metaphor: A response to Gibbs', *Metaphor and the Social World*, 1 (1): 57–60.

Deignan, A. and E. Semino (2010), 'Corpus techniques for metaphor analysis', in L. Cameron and R. Maslen (eds), *Metaphor Analysis: Research Practice in Applied Linguistics, Social Sciences and the Humanities*, 161–79, London: Equinox.

Degani, M. (2015), *Framing the Discourse of a Leader: An Analysis of Obama's Election Campaign Speeches*, Basingstoke: Palgrave Macmillan.

De Knop, S. (1985), 'Linguistic and extralinguistic aids for reconstruction and interpretation of metaphors in headlines', in W. Paprotté and R. Dirven (eds), *The Ubiquity of Metaphor*, 243–62, Amsterdam and Philadelphia: Benjamins.

De Knop, S. (1987), *Metaphorische Komposita in Zeitungsüberschriften*, Tübingen: Niemeyer.

Derathé, R. (2000), *Jean-Jacques Rousseau et la science politique de son temps*, Paris: Vrin.

Desmet, P., J. E. Rooryck and P. Swiggers (1990), 'What are words worth? language and ideology in French dictionaries of the revolutionary period', in J. E. Joseph and T. J. Taylor (eds), *Ideologies of Language*, 162–88, London and New York: Routledge.

Dhorn-van-Rossum, G. and E. -W. Böckenförde (1978), 'Organ, Organismus, Organisation, politischer Körper', in O. Brunner, W. Conze and R. Koselleck (eds), *Geschichtliche Grundbegriffe. Historisches Wörterbuch zur politisch-sozialen Sprache in Deutschland*, vol. 4, 519–622, Stuttgart: Klett-Cotta.

Diede, M. K. (2008), *Shakespeare's Knowledgeable Body*, Berne: Peter Lang.

Dirven, R. (2003), 'Metonymy and metaphor: Different mental strategies of conceptualisation', in R. Dirven and R. Pörings (eds), *Metaphor and Metonymy in Comparison and Contrast*, 75–111, Berlin and New York: Mouton de Gruyter.

Dirven, R., B. Hawkins and E. Sandikcioglu (eds) (2001), *Language and Ideology. Volume I: Theoretical Cognitive Approaches*, Amsterdam and Philadelphia: Benjamins.

Dirven, R., R. M. Frank and C. Ilie (eds) (2001), *Language and Ideology. Volume II: Descriptive Cognitive Approaches*, Amsterdam and Philadelphia: Benjamins.

Dobski, B. J., and D. A. Gish (eds) (2013), *Shakespeare and the Body Politic*, Lanham, MD: Lexington Books.

Docherty, J. (2002), Four Reasons to Use the War Metaphor with Caution. *Mediate.com* http://www.mediate.com/articles/docherty.cfm#.

Domarus, M. (1965), *Hitler. Reden und Proklamationen 1932-1945. Kommentiert von einem deutschen Zeitgenossen*, 4 vols, Munich: Süddeutscher Verlag.

Druce, V. (2013), 'Military metaphors in medicine: Waging war', *Reflections on Science Communication from Imperial College London* [Blog], 8 February 2013. http://refractiveindex.wordpress.com/2013/02/08/military-metaphors-in-medicine-waging-war/ (accessed 31 January 2015).

Duden (⁵2013), *Das Herkunftswörterbuch. Etymologie der deutschen Sprache. Der Duden in 12 Bänden*, edited by J. Riecke, vol. 7, Berlin, Mannheim and Zürich: Duden/Bibliographisches Institut.

Eitz, T. and G. Stötzel (2007), *Wörterbuch der 'Vergangenheitsbewältigung': Die NS-Vergangenheit im öffentlichen Sprachgebrauch*, Hildesheim: Olms.

Elkins, J. (2010), 'The model of war', *Political Theory*, 38 (2): 214–42.

Epstein, C. (2011), 'Who speaks? Discourse, the subject and the study of identity in international politics', *European Journal of International Relations*, 17 (2): 327–50.

Evans, R. J. (1997), *Rereading German History, 1800-1996. From Unification to Reunification*, London and New York: Routledge.

Evans, R. J. (2005), *The Third Reich in Power, 1933-1939*, London: Allen Lane.

Evans, R. J. (2008), *The Third Reich at War, 1939-1945*, London: Allen Lane.

Fabiszak, M. (2007), *A Conceptual Metaphor Approach to war Discourse and its Implications*, Poznań: Adam Mickiewicz University Press.

Fabiszak, M. and P. Kaszubski (2005), 'A corpus based study of war metaphors', in P. Cap (ed.), *Pragmatics*, 301–19, Berne etc.: P. Lang.

Fairclough, N. (1995), *Critical Discourse Analysis. The Critical Study of Language*, London: Longman.

Fairclough, N. (2005), 'Critical discourse analysis in transdisciplinary research', in R. Wodak and P. Chilton (eds), *A New Agenda in (Critical) Discourse Analysis: Theory, Methodology and Interdisciplinarity*, 53–70, Amsterdam: Benjamins.

Fairclough, N. (2014), *Language and Power*, London: Longman.

Farkas, O. (2012), 'Conceptualisation of the state in Hungarian political discourse', in S. Kleinke, Z. Kövecses, A. Musolff and V. Szelid (eds), *Cognition and Culture*, 154–62, Budapest: ELTE University Press.

Farkas, O. (2014), 'The concept of the STATE in Hungarian political discourse: Variations reflected in the language of the constitutions', in F. Polzenhagen, Z. Kövecses, S. Vogelbacher and S. Kleinke (eds), *Cognitive Explorations into Metaphor and Metonymy,* 101–14, Frankfurt am Main: Peter Lang.

Farley, J. (1972), 'The spontaneous generation controversy (1700-1860): The origins of parasitic worms', *Journal of the History of Biology*, 5 (1): 95–125.

Fauconnier, G. (1994), *Mental spaces. Aspects of Meaning Construction in Natural Language*, Cambridge: Cambridge University Press.

Fauconnier, G. and M. Turner (1998), 'Conceptual integration networks', *Cognitive Science*, 22 (2): 133–87.

Fauconnier, G. and M. Turner (2002), *The Way We Think: Conceptual Blending and the Mind's Hidden Complexities*, New York: Basic Books.

Feldman, J. and S. Narayanan (2004), 'Embodiment in a neural theory of language', *Brain and Language*, 89: 385–92.

Figes, O. (1996), *A People's Tragedy. The Russian Revolution 1891-1924*, London: Pimlico.

Fillmore, C. J. (1975), 'An alternative to checklist theories of Meaning', *Proceedings of the Berkeley Linguistics Society*, 1: 123–31.

Fitzpatrick, S. (2006), 'Social parasites: How tramps, idle youth, and busy entrepreneurs impeded the soviet march to communism', *Cahiers du Monde russe,* 47 (1–2): 377–408.

Forceville, C. (1996), *Pictorial Metaphor in Advertising*, London: Routledge.

Forceville, C. (2009), 'Non-verbal and multimodal metaphor in a cognitivist framework: Agendas for research', in C. Forceville and E. Urios-Aparisi (eds), *Multimodal Metaphor*, 19–42, Berlin and New York: Mouton de Gruyter.

Forceville, C. and E. Urios-Aparisi (eds) (2009), *Multimodal Metaphor,* Berlin: Mouton de Gruyter.

Fortescue, Sir J. (1997), *On the Laws and Governance of England*, edited by S. Lockwood, Cambridge: Cambridge University Press.

Foucault, M. (1982), 'The order of discourse', in R. Young (ed.), *Untying the Text. A Post-Structuralist Reader*, 48–78, London: Routledge & Kegan Paul.

Foucault, M. (2002), *The Archaeology of Knowledge*, London: Routledge.

Frank, R. M. (2008), 'Introduction: Sociocultural situatedness', in R. M. Frank, R. Dirven, T. Ziemke and E. Bernárdez (eds), *Body, Language and Mind, Vol. 2: Sociocultural Situatedness*, 1–18, Berlin and New York: De Gruyter Mouton.

Frank, R. M. and N. Gontier (2011), 'On constructing a research model for historical cognitive linguistics (HCL): Some theoretical considerations', in M. E. Winters, H. Tissari and K. Allan (eds), *Historical Cognitive Linguistics*, 31–69, Berlin and New York: De Gruyter Mouton.

Friedländer, S. (1998), *Nazi Germany & the Jews*. vol. 1: *The Years of Persecution, 1933-1939*, London: Phoenix.

Friedländer, S. (2007), *Nazi Germany & the Jews*. vol. 2: *The Years of Extermination, 1939-1945*, New York: HarperCollins.

Gallese, V. and G. Lakoff (2005), 'The brain's concepts: The role of the sensory-motor system in conceptual knowledge', *Cognitive Neuropsychology*, 22: 455–79.

Gavriely-Nuri, D. (2010), 'If both opponents "extend hands in peace" – why don't they meet? – mythic metaphors and cultural codes in the Israeli peace discourse', *Journal of Language and Politics*, 9 (3): 449–68.

Gibbs, R. W. (1994), *The Poetics of Mind: Figurative Thought, Language, and Understanding*, Cambridge: Cambridge University Press.

Gibbs, R. W. (2005), *Embodiment and Cognitive Science*, Cambridge: Cambridge University Press.

Gibbs, R. W. Jr. (2011a), 'Are "deliberate" metaphors really deliberate? A question of human consciousness and action', *Metaphor and the Social World*, 1 (1): 26–52.

Gibbs, R. W. Jr. (2011b), 'Advancing the debate on deliberate metaphor', *Metaphor and the Social World*, 1 (1): 67–9.

Gibbs, R. W. and M. Tendahl (2006), 'Cognitive effort and effects in metaphor comprehension: Relevance theory and psycholinguistics', *Mind & Language*, 21 (3): 379–403.

Gibbs, R. W. and M. Tendahl (2011), 'Coupling of metaphoric cognition and communication: A reply to Deirdre Wilson', *Intercultural Pragmatics*, 8 (4): 601–9.

Giora, R. (2003), *On our Mind: Salience, Context, and Figurative Language*, New York: Oxford University Press.

Glucksberg, S. (2001), *Understanding Figurative Language. From Metaphors to Idioms*. With a contribution by M. S. McGlone, Oxford: Oxford University Press.

Glucksberg, S. (2008), 'How metaphors create categories – quickly', in R. W. Gibbs (ed.), *The Cambridge Handbook of Metaphor and Thought*, 67–83, Cambridge: Cambridge University Press.

Glucksberg, S. and B. Keysar (1993), 'How metaphors work', in A. Ortony (ed.), *Metaphor and Thought*, 2nd edn, 401–24, Cambridge: Cambridge University Press.

Goatly, A. (1997), *The Language of Metaphors*, London and New York: Routledge.

Goatly, A. (2007), *Washing the Brain. Metaphor and Hidden Ideology*, Amsterdam and Philadelphia: Benjamins.

Goebbels, J. (1934), *Signale der neuen Zeit. 25 ausgewählte Reden*, Munich Zentralverlag der NSDAP.

Goffman, E. (1959), *The Presentation of Self in Everyday Life*, Garden City, NY: Doubleday, Anchor Books.

Goffman, E. (1967), *Interaction Ritual: Essays on Face-to-Face Behaviour'*, Garden City, NY: Doubleday, Anchor Books.

Goffman, E. (1972), 'On face work: An analysis of ritual elements in social interaction', in J. Laver and S. Hutcheson (eds), *Communication in Face to Face Interaction*, 319–46, Harmondsworth: Penguin.

Goossens, L. (2003), 'Metaphtonymy: The interaction of metaphor and metonymy in expressions for linguistic action', in R. Dirven and R. Pörings (eds), *Metaphor and Metonymy in Comparison and Contrast*, 349–77, Berlin: Mouton de Gruyter.

Görlach, M. (1999), 'Regional and social variation', in R. Lass (ed.), *The Cambridge History of the English Language. Vol. III: 1476-1776*, 456–38, Cambridge: Cambridge University Press.

Gowland, D. and A. Turner (1999), *Reluctant Europeans: Britain and European Integration, 1945-96*, London: Longman.

Grady, J. and C. Johnson (2003), 'Converging evidence for the notions of *subscene* and *primary scene*', in R. Dirven and R. Pörings (eds), *Metaphor and Metonymy in Comparison and Contrast*, 533–54, Berlin and New York: Mouton De Gruyter.

Grady, J., T. Oakley and S. Coulson (1999), 'Blending and metaphor', in R. W. Gibbs and G. Steen (eds), *Metaphor in Cognitive Linguistics*, 101–24, Amsterdam and Philadelphia: John Benjamins.

Grotius, H. [1625] (2005), *The Rights of War and Peace*, edited by R. Tuck. 3 vols, Indianapolis: Liberty Fund.

Guilhaumou, J. (1989), *La langue politique et la Révolution Française*, Paris: Meridiens Klincksieck.

Guldin, R. (2000), *Körpermetaphern: Zum Verhältnis von Politik und Medizin*, Würzburg: Königshausen & Neumann.

Gullestad, A. (2012), 'Parasite', in *Political Concepts: a Critical Lexicon,* edited by The New School for Social Research, http://www.politicalconcepts.org/issue1/2012-parasite/ (last accessed 30 December 2013).

Hale, D. G. (1968), 'Intestine sedition: The fable of the belly', *Comparative Literature Studies*, 5: 377–88.

Hale, D. G. (1971), *The Body Politic. A Political Metaphor in Renaissance English Literature*, The Hague and Paris: Mouton.

Halliday, M. A. K. (1978), *Language as Social Semiotic: The Social Interpretation of Language and Meaning*, London: Edward Arnold.

Hamerton-Kelly, R. G. (1996), 'The king and the crowd: Divine right and popular sovereignty in the French revolution', *Contagion. Journal of Violence, Mimesis and Culture*, 3: 67–83.

Hamilton, T. (2012), 'Time to Blow taps on football as war metaphors', *The Washington Post*, 8 September 2012.

Hanne, M., W. D. Crano and J. S. Mio (eds) (2015), *Warring With Words. Narrative and Metaphor in Politics*, New York and London: Psychology Press.

Hansard (1991), *House of Commons Debate on the European Council in Maastricht 11 December 1991* (Hansard vol. 200, cc. 859-78), http://hansard.millbanksystems.com/commons/1991/dec/11/european-council-maastricht (accessed 1 June 2015).

Harris, J. G. (1998), *Foreign Bodies and the Body Politic. Discourses of Social Pathology in Early Modern England*, Cambridge: Cambridge University Press.

Harvey, A. D. (2007), *Body Politic. Political Metaphor and Political Violence*, Newcastle: Cambridge Scholars Publishing.

Hassl, A. (2005), 'Vom würdigen Gesellschafter der Götter zum servilen Hofnarren', *Wiener Klinische Wochenschrift*, 117 (Supplement 4): 2–5.

Hawkins, B. (2001), 'Ideology, metaphor and iconographic reference', in R. Dirven, R. Frank and C. Ilie (eds), *Language and Ideology, Vol. II: Descriptive Cognitive Approaches*, 27–50, Amsterdam: Benjamins.

Herrera-Soler, H. (2006), 'Conceptual metaphors in press headlines on globalisation', *Annual Review of Cognitive Linguistics*, 4: 1–20.

Herrera, H. and M. White (2000). 'Business is war or the language of takeovers', in M. Fornés, J. M. Molina and L. Pérez (eds), *Panorama Actual de la Linguistica Aplicada: Conocimientro, Procesamiento y uso del lenguaje*, 231–9, Rioja: University of Rioja Press.

Hickock, G. (2014), *The Myth of Mirror Neurons. The Real Neuroscience of Communication and Cognition*, New York: W. W. Norton & Company.

Hitler, A. (1933), *Mein Kampf*, 23rd edn, Munich: Franz Eher Nachfolger.

Hitler, A. (1992), *Mein Kampf*, translated by Ralph Manheim. With an introduction by D.C. Watt, London: Pimlico.

Hobbes, T. (1996), *Leviathan*, edited by Richard Tuck, revised ed, Cambridge: Cambridge University Press.

Hodges, A. (2011), *The 'War on Terror' Narrative. Discourse and Intertextuality in the Construction and Contestation of Sociopolitical Reality*, Oxford: Oxford University Press.

Hodges, A. (ed.) (2013), *Discourses of War and Peace*, Oxford: Oxford University Press.

Hoffman, B. (2004), 'The changing face of Al Qaeda and the global war on terrorism', *Studies in Conflict and Terrorism*, 27 (6): 549–60.

Holmes, J. and M. Meyerhoff (1999), 'The community of practice: Theories and methodologies', *Language in Society*, 28: 173–83.

Hönigsperger, A. (1991), '"Das Boot ist voll" – Zur Metapher in der Politik', *Folia Linguistica*, 25: 229–41.

Hornshøj-Møller, S. (1995), *Der ewige Jude. Quellenkritische Analyse eines antisemitischen Propagandafilms*. Beiträge zu zeitgeschichtlichen Filmquellen, Bd. 2, Göttingen: Institut für den Wissenschaftlichen Film.

Hornshøj-Møller, S. and D. Culbert (1992), '"Der ewige Jude" (1940). Joseph Goebbels' unequalled monument to anti-Semitism', *Historical Journal of Film, Radio and Television*, 12 (1): 41–67.

Huffington Post (2012), Ted Nugent: Obama Comments Were Metaphors, Not Threats, http://www.huffingtonpost.com/2012/04/19/ted-nugent-obama-comments-metaphors_n_1439009.html (accessed 1 June 2015).

Hufer, H. (2003), *Deutsche Kolonialpolitik in der Ära des Wilheminismus: Asien und der Boxeraufstand*. München: GRIN-Verlag.

Hughes, G. (1988), *Words in Time: A Social History of the English Vocabulary*, Oxford: Blackwell.

Hughes, G. (2006), *An encyclopedia of swearing: The social history of oaths, profanity, foul language, and ethnic slurs in the English-speaking world*, New York: M. E. Sharpe.

Hutton, C. M. (2001), 'Cultural and conceptual relativism, universalism and the politics of linguistics. Dilemmas of a would-be progressive linguistics', in R. Dirven, B. Hawkins and E. Sandikcioglu (eds), *Language and Ideology. Vol. I: Theoretical Cognitive Approaches*, 277–96, Amsterdam and Philadelphia: John Benjamins.

Hull, D. L. (1988), *Science as a Process: An Evolutionary Account of the Social and Conceptual Development of Science*, Chicago: University of Chicago Press.

Hull, D. L. (2000), 'Taking memetics seriously: Memetics will be what we make it', in R. Aunger (ed.), *Darwinizing Culture. The Status of Memetics as a Science*, 42–67, Oxford: Oxford University Press.

Hymes, D. H. (1968), 'The ethnography of speaking', in J. A. Fishman (ed.), *Readings in the Sociology of Language*, 99–138, The Hague and Paris: Mouton (First published 1962].

Inda, J. X. (2000), 'Foreign bodies: Migrants, parasites and the pathological nation', *Discourse*, 22 (3): 46–62.

Israel Ministry of Foreign Affairs (2015), *About Israel*, http://www.mfa.gov.il/mfa/aboutisrael/history/pages/israels%20war%20of%20independence%20-%20 1947%20-%201949.aspx (accessed 28 January 2015).

Jackendoff, R. and D. Aaron (1991), 'Review: *More than cool Reason: A field guide to poetic metaphor*', *Language*, 67 (2): 320–8.

Jagendorf, Z. (1990), 'Coriolanus: Body politic and private parts', *Shakespeare Quarterly*, 41 (4): 455–69.

Jakobson, R. (1960), 'Closing statement: Linguistics and poetics', in T. A. Sebeok (ed.), *Style in Language*, 350–77, Cambridge, MA: MIT Press.

Jia, W. (1997), 'Facework as a Chinese conflict-preventive mechanism: A cultural/ discourse analysis', *Intercultural Communication Studies*, 7 (1): 43–58.

John of Salisbury (1909), *Policraticus sive De nugis Curialium et vestigiis philosophorum*, edited by C. I. Webb. 2 vols, Oxford Clarendon Press (Reprint edition 1965, Frankfurt a. M.: Minerva).

John of Salisbury (1990), *Policraticus. Of the Frivolities of Courtiers and the Footprints of Philosophers*, edited by C. J. Nederman, Cambridge: Cambridge University Press.

Johnson, E. (2007), 'Patriarchal power in the Roman republic: Ideologies and realities of the paterfamilas', *Hirundo, The McGill Journal of Classical Studies*, 99–117.

Johnson, M. (1987), *The Body in the Mind. The Bodily Basis of Meaning, Imagination, and Reason*, Chicago: University of Chicago Press.

Jones, T. (2013), 'Rules for writing: Block that metaphor'!, *The Guardian*, 23 May 2013.

Jonson, B. (1966), *Volpone, or The Fox*, in *Volpone and Other Plays*, Harmondsworth: Penguin.

Jung, M., T. Niehr and K. Böke (2000), *Ausländer und Migranten im Spiegel der Presse. Ein diskurshistorisches Wörterbuch zur Einwanderung seit 1945*, Opladen: Westdeutscher Verlag.

Kallis, A. A. (2008), *Nazi Propaganda and the Second World War*, Basingstoke: Palgrave-Macmillan.

Kantorowicz, E. H. (1997), *The King's Two Bodies. A Study in Medieval Political Theology*, Princeton: Princeton University Press.

Karolewski, I. P. and A. M. Suszycki (2011), *The Nation and Nationalism in Europe: An Introduction*, Edinburgh: Edinburgh University Press.

Kellner, D. (2003), *From 9/11 to Terror War: Dangers of the Bush Legacy*, Boulder, CO: Rowman and Littlefield.

Kempshall, M. S. (1999), *The Common Good in Late Medieval Political Thought*, Oxford: Clarendon Press.

Kempson, R. M. (1977), *Semantic Theory*, Cambridge: Cambridge University Press.

KhosraviNik, M. (2010), 'The representation of refugees, asylum seekers and immigrants in British newspapers: A critical discourse analysis'. *Journal of Language and Politics*, 9 (1): 1–28.

KhosraviNik, M., M. Krzyżanowski and R. Wodak (2012), 'Dynamics of representations in discourse: Immigrants in the British Press', in M. Messer, R. Schroeder and R. Wodak (eds), *Migrations: Interdisciplinary Perspectives*, 283–95, Vienna: Springer.

Kipling, R. (1994), *The Works of Rudyard Kipling*, Ware: Wordsworth.

Kittay, E. F. (1987), *Metaphor. Its Cognitive Force and Linguistic Structure*, Oxford: Oxford University Press.

Koller, V. (2004), *Metaphor and Gender in Business Media: A Critical Cognitive Study*, Basingstoke: Palgrave-Macmillan.

Koschorke, A., S. Lüdemann, T. Frank, E. Matala de Mazza (2007), *Der fiktive Staat. Konstruktionen des politischen Körpers in der Geschichte Europas*, Frankfurt am Main: Fischer.

Kövecses, Z. (1986), *Metaphors of Anger, Pride, and Love. A Lexical Approach to the Structure of Concepts*, Amsterdam: John Benjamins.

Kövecses, Z. (1990), *Emotion Concepts*, New York: Springer.

Kövecses, Z. (1995), 'Anger: Its language, conceptualization, and physiology in the light of cross-cultural evidence', in J. R. Taylor and R. E. MacLaury (eds), *Language and the Cognitive Construal of the World*, 181–96, Berlin: de Gruyter.

Kövecses, Z. (2000), *Metaphor and Emotion: Language, Culture, and Body in Human Feeling*, Cambridge and New York: Cambridge University Press.

Kövecses, Z. (2002), *Metaphor: A Practical Introduction*, Oxford and New York: Oxford University Press.

Kövecses, Z. (2005), *Metaphor in Culture: Universality and Variation*, Cambridge and New York: Cambridge University Press.

Knowles, M. and R. Moon (2006), *Introducing Metaphor*, London: Routledge.

Kremer, T. (2004), *The Missing Heart of Europe: Does Britain Hold the Key to the Future of the Continent?* London: June Press.

Kulka, O. D. and E. Jäckel (eds) (2004), *Die Juden in den geheimen NS-Stimmungsberichten 1933-1945*, Düsseldorf: Droste.

Labov, W. (1972), *Sociolinguistic Patterns*, Philadelphia: University of Philadelphia Press.

Ladendorf, O. (1906), *Historisches Schlagwörterbuch*, Straßburg: Trübner.

Lakoff, G. (1987a), *Women, Fire, and Dangerous Things: What Categories Reveal about the Mind*, Chicago and London: University of Chicago Press.

Lakoff, G. (1987b), 'The death of dead metaphor', *Metaphor & Symbolic Activity*, 2 (2): 143–7.

Lakoff, G. (1990), 'The invariance principle: Is abstract reasoning based on image schemas?', *Cognitive Linguistics*, 1 (1): 39–74.

Lakoff, G. (1992), 'Metaphor and war. The metaphor system used to justify war in the Gulf', in M. Pütz (ed.), *Thirty Years of Linguistic Evolution. Studies in Honour of René Dirven*, 463–81, Amsterdam and Philadelphia: John Benjamins.

Lakoff, G. (1993). The contemporary theory of metaphor. In: A. Ortony (ed.). *Metaphor and Thought*. 2nd ed., 202-251. Cambridge: Cambridge University Press.

Lakoff, G. (1996), *Moral Politics: What Conservatives Know That Liberals Don't*, Chicago: University of Chicago Press (Revised version: 2002).

Lakoff, G. (2001), September 11, 2001. *Metaphorik.de*, 2001, http://www.metaphorik.de/aufsaetze/lakoff-september11.htm (accessed 2 November 2004).

Lakoff, G. (2003), *Metaphor and War, Again*, http://www.alternet.org/story.html?StoryID=15414 (accessed 2 November 2004).

Lakoff, G. (2004a), *Don't Think of an Elephant! Know Your Values and Frame the Debate. The Essential Guide for Progressives*, White River Junction, VT: Chelsea Green Publishing Company.

Lakoff, G. (2004b), Interview with D. Gilson: 'How to Talk like a Conservative (If You Must)'. http://www.motherjones.com/news/qa/2004/10/10_401.html (accessed 2 November 2004).

Lakoff, G. (2008), 'The neural theory of metaphor', in R. W. Gibbs (ed.), *The Cambridge Handbook of Metaphor and Thought*, 17–38, Cambridge: Cambridge University Press.

Lakoff, G. (2013), 'Obama Reframes Syria: Metaphor and war revisited', *The Huffington Post*, 6 September 2013, http://georgelakoff.com/2013/09/06/obama-reframes-syria-metaphor-and-war-revisited/ (accessed 28 April 2015).

Lakoff, G. and M. Turner (1989), *More than cool Reason: A Field Guide to Poetic Metaphor*, Chicago: University of Chicago Press.

Lakoff, G. and M. Johnson (1999), *Philosophy in the Flesh. The embodied Mind and its Challenge to Western Thought*, New York: Basic Books.

Lakoff, G. and M. Johnson (1980/2003), *Metaphors we live by*, Chicago: University of Chicago Press. [The main text of both editions is identical but the later edition contains a new 'Afterword', which is separately quoted below].

Lakoff, G. and M. Johnson (eds) (2003), 'Afterword', in *Metaphors we live by*, 243–76, Chicago: University of Chicago Press.

Lakoff, G. and Rockridge Institute (2006), *Thinking Points: Communicating Our American Values and Vision*, New York: Farrar, Strauss and Giroux.

Larson, B. M. H. (2008), 'Entangled biological, cultural and linguistic origins of the war on invasive species', in R. M. Frank, R. Dirven, T. Ziemke and E. Bernárdez (eds), *Body, Language and Mind*, Vol. 2: *Sociocultural Situatedness,* 169–95, Berlin and New York: Mouton de Gruyter.

Lenin, V. I. (ed.) (1989), 'The state and revolution [1917]', in *Collected Works*, vol. 25, 381–49, Moscow: Progress Publishers.

Lévy, B. -H. (2012), 'Construire l'Europe politique, ou mourir', *Le Point* 13 September 2012.

Lewis, C. T. and C. Short (1984), *A Latin Dictionary*, Oxford: Oxford University Press.

Libertad! online (2015), Dokument: Flugblätter der Kommune I zum Brüsseler Kaufhausbrand, http://www.info.libertad.de/blogs/7/568 (accessed 1 June 2015).

Liddell, H. G. and R. Scott (⁶1869), *A Greek-English Lexicon*, Oxford: Clarendon Press.

Liebeschütz, F. (1950), *Mediaeval Humanism in the Life and Writings of John of Salisbury*, London: The Warburg Institute.

Littlemore, J. (2015), *Metonymy: Hidden Shortcuts in Language, Thought and Communication*, Cambridge: Cambridge University Press.

Littlemore, J. and G. Low (2006), *Figurative Thinking and Figurative Language Learning*, Basingstoke: Palgrave Macmillan.

Littlemore, J., P. Chen, A. Koester and J. Barnden (2011), 'Difficulties in metaphor comprehension faced by international students whose first language is not English', *Applied Linguistics*, 32 (4): 408–29.

Livy (1998), *The Early History of Rome, Books I-II*, translated by B. O. Foster, Cambridge, MA: Harvard University Press (*Loeb Classical Library* 114, first published in 1919).

Low, G., Z. Todd, A. Deignan and L. Cameron (eds) (2010), *Researching and Applying Metaphor in the Real World*, Amsterdam and Philadelphia: Benjamins.

Lu, X. (1999), 'An ideological/cultural analysis of political slogans in communist China', *Discourse & Society*, 10 (4): 487–508.

Lukacs, J. (1990), *The Duel. Hitler vs. Churchill: 10 May – 31 July 1940*, Oxford: Oxford University Press.

Lynteris, C. (2013), *The Spirit of Selflessness in Maoist China: Socialist Medicine and the New Man*, Basingstoke: Palgrave Macmillan.

Lyons, J. (1977), *Semantics*, 2 vols, Cambridge: Cambridge University Press.

MacArthur, F. and J. Littlemore (2011), 'On the repetition of words with the potential for metaphoric extension in conversations between Native and Non-native Speakers of English', *Metaphor and the Social World*, 1 (2): 202–39.

MacDonogh, G. (2000). *The last Kaiser. William the Impetuous.* London: Weidenfeld & Nicolson.

McDonnel, M. (2006), *Roman Manliness: "Virtus" and the Roman Republic,* Cambridge: Cambridge University Press.

Maitland, F. W. (2003), *State, Trust and Corporation,* edited by D. Runciman and M. Ryan, Cambridge: Cambridge University Press.

Major, J. (2000), *The Autobiography,* London: HarperCollins.

Mannes, S. (1999), *Antisemitismus im nationalsozialistischen Propagandafilm. 'Jud Süß' und 'Der ewige Jude',* Cologne: Teiresias.

Marx, K. (1960), 'Der achtzehnte Brumaire des Louis Bonaparte', in K. Marx and F. Engels (eds), *Werke,* vol. 8, 149–58, Berlin/DDR: Dietz Verlag.

Masalha, N. (2003), *The Politics of Denial: Israel and the Palestinian Refugee Problem,* London: Pluto.

Matin, A. M. (1999), '"The Hun is at the Gate!": Historicizing Kipling's Militaristic Rhetoric, from the imperial periphery to the national center – Part 2, the French, Russian and German Threats to Great Britain', *Studies in the Novel,* 31 (4): 432–70.

Matthäus, J. (2004), 'Operation Barbarossa and the onset of the Holocaust, June-December 1941', in C. Browning (ed.), *The Origins of the Final Solution: The Evolution of Nazi Jewish Policy, September 1939 – March 1942,* 244–308, London: William Heinemann.

Matthes, A. (ed.) (1976), *Reden Kaiser Wilhelms II,* München: Rogner & Bernhard.

Matussek, M. (2010), 'Sarrazin-Debatte. Die Gegenwut', *Der Spiegel,* 6 September 2010.

Merton, R. K. (1948), 'The self-fulfilling prophecy', *The Antioch Review,* 8 (2): 193–210.

Messinger, G. S. (1992), *British Propaganda and the State in the First World War,* Manchester: Manchester University Press.

Mikalayeva, L. (2011), 'Negotiating ompliance: Discursive choices in a formalized setting of diplomatic communication', *International Journal of Communication,* 21 (2): 5–28.

Mitchell, P. (2012), *Contagious Metaphor,* London: Bloomsbury.

Morris, B. (2004), *The Birth of the Palestinian Refugee Problem Revisited,* Cambridge: Cambridge University Press.

Mouton, N. T. O. (2010), *On the Evolution of Social Scientific Metaphors. A Cognitive-historical Inquiry into the Divergent Trajectories of the Idea that Collective Entities – States and Societies, Cities and Corporations – are Biological Organisms.* PhD., Copenhagen: Department of International Culture and Communication Studies at Copenhagen Business School.

Muir, K. (1959), 'The background of *Coriolanus*', *Shakespeare Quarterly,* X: 137–46.

Müller, C. (2008). *Metaphors Dead and Alive, Sleeping and Waking: A Dynamic View,* Chicago, IL: University of Chicago Press.

Müller, C. (2011), 'Are "deliberate" metaphors really deliberate? A question of human consciousness and action', *Metaphor and the Social World,* 1 (1): 61–6.

Müller, C., A. Cienki, E. Fricke, S. Ladewig, D. McNeill, S. Teßendorf (eds) (2013), *Body – Language – Communication: An International Handbook on Multimodality in Human Interaction,* vol. 1, Berlin and New York: De Gruyter Mouton.

Müller, C., S. Ladewig, A. Cienki, E. Fricke, J. Bressem, D. McNeill (eds) (2014), *Body – Language – Communication Volume 2: An International Handbook on Multimodality in Human Interaction,* Berlin and New York: De Gruyter Mouton.

Musolff, A. (1996), *Krieg gegen die Öffentlichkeit. Terrorismus und politischer Sprachgebrauch*, Opladen: Westdeutscher Verlag.

Musolff, A. (2000a), *Mirror Images of Europe. Metaphors in the Public Debate about Europe in Britain and Germany*, Munich: iudicium.

Musolff, A. (2000b), 'Political imagery of Europe: A *house* without *exit doors?*', *Journal of Multilingual and Multicultural Development*, 21 (3): 216–29.

Musolff, A. (2001), 'Cross-language metaphors: *Parents* and *children, love, marriage* and *divorce* in the *European family*', in J. Cotterill and A. Ife (eds), *Language Across Boundaries*, 119–34, London: Continuum.

Musolff, A. (2004a), *Metaphor and Political Discourse. Analogical Reasoning in Debates about Europe*, Basingstoke: Palgrave-Macmillan.

Musolff, A. (2004b), 'The *Heart* of the European *Body Politic*. British and German Perspectives on Europe's Central *Organ*', *Journal of Multilingual & Multicultural Development*, 25 (5 and 6): 437–52.

Musolff, A. (2006), 'Metaphor scenarios in public discourse', *Metaphor and Symbol*, 2 (1): 23–38.

Musolff, A. (2009a), '*Love, Parenthood,* and *Gender* in the European *Family*: The British perspective', in A. -B. Renger and R. A. Ißler (eds), *Europa: Stier und Sternenkranz. Von der Union mit Zeus zum Staatenverbund*, 536–48, Göttingen: V&R unipress, Bonn University Press.

Musolff, A. (2009b), 'Metaphor in the history of ideas and discourses: How can we interpret a medieval version of the Body-State Analogy?', in A. Musolff and J. Zinken (eds), *Metaphor and Discourse*, 233–47, Basingstoke: Palgrave-Macmillan.

Musolff, A. (2010a), *Metaphor, Nation and the Holocaust. The Concept of the Body Politic*, London and New York: Routledge.

Musolff, A. (2010b), 'Political metaphor and bodies politic', in U. Okulska and P. Cap (eds), *Perspectives in Politics and Discourse*, 23–41, Amsterdam and Philadelphia: Benjamins.

Musolff, A. (2011), 'Metaphor in discourse history', in M. E. Winters, H. Tissari and K. Allan (eds), *Historical Cognitive Linguistics*, 70–90, Berlin and New York: De Gruyter Mouton.

Musolff, A. (2012), 'Immigrants and parasites: The history of a bio-social metaphor', in M. Messer, R. Schroeder and R. Wodak (eds), *Migrations: Interdisciplinary Perspectives*, 249–58, Vienna: Springer.

Musolff, A. (2013a), 'The reception of antisemitic imagery in Nazi Germany and popular opinion – lessons for today', in R. Wodak and J. Richardson (eds), *Analysing Fascist Discourse. European Fascism in Talk and Text*, 56–72, London and New York: Routledge.

Musolff, A. (2013b), 'The heart of Europe: Synchronic variation and historical trajectories of a Political Metaphor', in K. Fløttum (ed.), *Speaking of Europe: Approaches to Complexity in European Political Discourse*, 135–50, Amsterdam and Philadelphia: Benjamins.

Musolff, A. (2015), 'The role of holocaust memory in the Israeli-Palestinian conflict', in H. Starr and S. Dubinsky (eds), *The Israeli Conflict System. Analytic Approaches*, 168–81, London: Routledge.

Musolff, A., C. Good, R. Wittlinger and P. Points (eds) (2001), *Attitudes Towards Europe. Language in the Unification Process*, Aldershot: Ashgate.

Nacey, S. (2013), *Metaphors in Learner English*, Amsterdam and Philadelphia: Benjamins.

Neagu, M. and G. I. Colipcă-Ciobanu (2014), 'Metaphor and self/other representa-
   tions: A study on British and Romanian headlines on migration', in A. Musolff,
   F. MacArthur and G. Pagani (eds), *Metaphor and Intercultural Communication*,
   201–21, London: Bloomsbury.
Nederman, C. J. (1988), 'A duty to kill: John of Salisbury's theory of Tyrannicide',
   Review of Politics, 50: 365–89.
Nedermann, C. J. (ed.) (1992), *Medieval Political Thought – A Reader: The Quest
   for the Body Politic*, London: Routledge.
Nederman, C. J. (2004), 'Body politics: The diversification of organic metaphors in
   the later middle ages', *Pensiero Politico Medievale*, 2: 59–87.
Nederman, C. J. and K. Langdon Forhan (eds) (1993), *Readings in Medieval
   Political Theory 1100-1400*, Indianapolis and Cambridge: Hackett Publishing.
Nerlich, B. and N. Koteyko (2009), 'MRSA – Portrait of a Superbug: A media drama
   in three acts', in A. Musolff and J. Zinken (eds), *Metaphor and Discourse*,
   153–69, Basingstoke: Palgrave-Macmillan.
Nestle, W. (1927), 'Die Fabel des Menenius Agrippa', *Klio. Beiträge zur Alten
   Geschichte*, XXI: 350–60.
Netanyahu, B. (2011a), Statement before the United Nations Assembly, 66th session, 23 September 2011, http://www.aish.com/jw/me/Netanyahus_Speech_
   at_the_UN.html (accessed 19 January 2015).
Netanyahu, B. (2011b), Statement before the United Nations Assembly, 66th session, 23 September 2011, https://www.youtube.com/
   watch?v=ebOsg9CCj6c (accessed 19 January 2015).
Netanyahu, B. (2012), Statement before the United Nations Assembly,
   67th session, 27 September 2012, http://www.latinospost.com/
   articles/4677/20120927/netanyahu-un-general-assembly-2012-speech-
   transcript-video-iran-palestine-nuclear-obama.htm (accessed 19 January 2015).
Netanyahu, B. (2013), Statement before the United Nations Assembly, 68th
   session, 1 October 2013, http://www.haaretz.com/news/diplomacy-
   defense/1.550012 (accessed 19 January 2015).
Netanyahu, B. (2014), Statement before the United Nations Assembly, 69th
   session, 29 September 2014, available at (a) http://www.jpost.com/Arab-
   Israeli-Conflict/Full-text-of-Prime-Minister-Netanyahus-UN-speech-376626;
   (b) http://www.un.org/en/ga/69/meetings/gadebate/29sep/israel.shtml
   (accessed 19 January 2015).
Nevalainen, T. (1999), 'Early modern English lexis and semantics', in R. Lass (ed.),
   The Cambridge History of the English Language. Vol. III: 1476-1776, 332–458,
   Cambridge: Cambridge University Press.
New Oxford Bible (2001), *The New Oxford Annotated Bible*, 3rd edn, edited by
   M. D. Coogan, Oxford: Oxford University Press.
Niemeier, S. (2000), 'Straight from the heart – metonymic and metaphorical
   explorations', in A. Barcelona (ed.), *Metaphor and Metonymy at the Cross-
   roads. A Cognitive Perspective*, 195–213, Berlin and New York: W. De Gruyter.
Niven, W. (2002), *Facing the Nazi Past: United Germany and the Legacy of the
   Third Reich*, London and New York: Routledge.
Norris, S. (2011), *Identity in (Inter)action: Introducing Multimodal (Inter)action
   Analysis*, Berlin and New York: De Gruyter Mouton.
Opie, I. and P. Opie (1997), *The Oxford Dictionary of Nursery Rhymes*, Oxford:
   Oxford University Press.

Oxford English Dictionary on Historical Principles (1989), 2nd edn, edited by
  J. A. Simpson and E. S. C. Weiner, Oxford: Clarendon Press.

Pan, Y. (2000), *Politeness in Chinese Face-to-face Interaction*, Greenwich: Ablex.

Pan, Y. and Kádár, D. Z. (2012), *Politeness in Historical and Contemporary
  Chinese*, London: Bloomsbury.

Panther, K. -U. and G. Radden (eds) (1999), *Metonymy in Language and Thought*,
  Amsterdam: Benjamins.

Pappé, I. (2010), *The Ethnic Cleansing of Palestine*, Oxford: Oneworld.

Patterson, A. M. (1991), *Fables of Power: Aesopian Writing and Political History*,
  Durham, NC: Duke University Press.

Peil, D. (1985), *Der Streit der Glieder mit dem Magen. Studien zur Überlieferung
  und Deutungsgeschichte der Fabel des Menenius Agrippa von der Antike bis
  ins 20. Jahrhundert*, Berne: Lang.

Pelinka, A. (2001), 'Anti-Semitism and ethno-nationalism as determining factors
  for Austria's political culture at the Fin de Siècle', in H. Tewes and J. Wright
  (eds), *Liberalism, Anti-Semitism, and Democracy. Essays in Honour of Peter
  Pulzer*, 63–75, Oxford: Oxford University Press.

Pelinka, A. and R. Wodak (eds) (2002), *Dreck am Stecken. Politik der Ausgren-
  zung*, Vienna: Czernin.

Peltonen, M. (2009), 'Political rhetoric and citizenship in *Coriolanus*', in
  D. Armitage, C. Condren and A. Fitzmaurice (eds), *Shakespeare and Early
  Modern Political Thought*, 234–52, Cambridge: Cambridge University Press.

Pérez-Soba, M. and R. Maas (2015), 'Scenarios: Tools for coping with complex-
  ity and future uncertainty?', in A. J. Jordan and J. R. Turnpenny (eds), *The
  Tools of Policy Formulation: Actors, Capacities, Venues and Effects*, 52–75,
  Cheltenham: Edward Elgar.

Philip, G. (2010), '"Drugs, traffic, and many other dirty interests": Metaphor and
  the language learner', in G. Low, Z. Todd, A. Deignan and L. Cameron (eds),
  Researching and Applying Metaphor in the Real World, 63–80, Amsterdam
  and Philadelphia: Benjamins.

Philips, B. J. (2003), 'Understanding visual metaphor in advertising', in L. M. Scott
  and R. Batra (eds), *Persuasive Imagery: A Consumer Response Perspective*,
  297–310, Mahwah, NJ: Lawrence Erlbaum.

Piquer-Piriz, A. M. (2010), 'Can people be cold and warm? Developing understanding of figurative meanings of temperature terms in early EFL', in G. Low,
  Z. Todd, A. Deignan and L. Cameron (eds), *Researching and Applying Metaphor in the Real World*, 21–34, Amsterdam and Philadelphia: Benjamins.

Pinar Sanz, M. J. (2005), 'Ideological implications of the use of metaphors in
  the discourse of sports news', in J. L. Otal Campo, I. Navarro i Ferrando and
  B. Bellés Fortuño (eds), *Cognitive and Discourse Approaches to Metaphor and
  Metonymy*, 113–22, Castelló de la Plana. Publicacions de la Universitat Jaume I.

Pinker, S. (2007), *The Stuff of Thought: Language as a Window into Human
  Nature*, London: Allen Lane.

Plutarch (2001), *Plutarch's Lives:* Volume 1. The Dryden Edition, edited by
  A. H. Clough, New York: Random House.

Posch, C., M. Stopfner and M. Kienpointner (2013), 'German postwar discourse
  of the extreme and populist right', in R. Wodak and J. E. Richardson (eds),
  Analysing Fascist Discourse. European Fascism in Talk and Text, 97–121,
  London: Routledge.

Pragglejaz Group (2007), 'MIP: A method for identifying metaphorically used words in discourse', *Metaphor & Symbol*, 22: 1–40.

Press Complaints Commission (1996), *Annual Report*. http://www.pcc.org.uk/reports2/reports/1996/reviewyear.html (accessed 9 July 2014).

Rakova, M. (2002), 'The philosophy of embodied realism: A high price to pay?', *Cognitive Linguistics*, 13: 215–44.

Rash, F. (2005), 'Metaphor in Hitler's *Mein Kampf*', *metaphorik.de*, 9: 74–111.

Rash, F. (2006), *The Language of Violence. Adolf Hitler's Mein Kampf*, Berne: Peter Lang.

Rash, F. (2012), *German Images of the Self and the Other. Nationalist, Colonialist and Anti-Semitic Discourse, 1871-1918*, Basingstoke: Palgrave-Macmillan.

Reisfield, G. M. and G. A. Wilson (2004), 'Use of metaphor in the discourse on cancer', *Journal of Clinical Oncology*, 22 (19): 4024–7.

Reisigl, M. and R. Wodak (2009), 'The discourse-historical approach (DHA)', in R. Wodak and M. Meyer (eds), *Methods of Critical Discourse Analysis*, 87–121, London: Sage.

Renaud, A. (1995), 'Squelettiques métaphores politique', *Libération*, 21 March 1995.

Richardson, J. E. and M. Colombo (2013), 'Continuity and change in anti-immigrant discourse in Italy: An analysis of the visual propaganda of the Lega Nord', *Journal of Language and Politics*, Special Issue: 'Discourse and politics about migration in Italy', 12 (2): 180–202.

Rice, S. (2012), '"Our language is very literal": Figurative Expression in Dene Sųłiné, [Athapaskan]', in A. Idström and E. Piirainen (eds), *Endangered Metaphors*, 21–76, Amsterdam: John Benjamins.

Rigney, D. (2001), *The Metaphorical Society: An Invitation to Social Theory*, Lanham, MD: Rowman and Littlefield.

Robert, P. (1977), *Dictionnaire alphabétique & analogique de la langue française*, edited by A. Rey and J. Rey-Debove, Paris: Société du Nouveau Littré.

Röhl, J. C. G. (1988), *Kaiser, Hof und Staat: Wilhelm II. und die deutsche Politik*, Munich: Beck.

Rosenberg, A. (1936), *Der Mythus des 20. Jahrhunderts. Eine Wertung der seelisch-geistigen Gestaltenkämpfe unserer Zeit*, Munich: Hoheneichen Verlag.

Rote Armee Fraktion [Red Army Faction] (1987), 'Das Konzept Stadtguerilla', in W. Pohrt, K. Hartung, G. Göttle, J. Bruhn, K. H. Roth and K. Bittermann (eds), *Die alte Straßenverkehrsordnung. Dokumente der RAF*, 21–45, Berlin: tiamat (first published in 1971 as a pamphlet).

Rousseau, J. -J. (1990), *Du Contrat Social. Texte et Contextes*, edited by J. Médina, A. Senik, C. Morali and G. Chomienne, Paris: Magnard.

Rousseau, J. -J. (1994), 'The social contract or the principles of political right', in C. Betts (ed.), *The Social Contract*, 43–175, Oxford: Oxford University Press.

Rousseau, J. -J. (2002), *Discours sur l'économie politique: Texte et Commentaire*, Paris: Vrin.

Sarrazin, T. (2000), *Deutschland schafft sich ab. Wie wir unser Land aufs Spiel setzen*, Munich: Deutsche Verlags-Anstalt.

Sawday, J. (1995), *The Body Emblazoned: Dissection and the Human Body in Renaissance Culture*, London and New York: Routledge.

Schäffner, C. (1991), 'Der Zug zur deutschen Einheit', *Sprachreport*, 4/91: 1–3.

Schama, S. (1989), *Citizens. A Chronicle of the French Revolution*, New York: Vintage Books.

Schank, R. C. and R. P. Abelson (1977), *Scripts, Plans, Goals and Understanding: An Inquiry into Human Knowledge Structures*, Hillsdale, NJ: Lawrence Erlbaum.

Schmitt, C. (2002), *Der Begriff des Politischen*, Berlin: Duncker & Humblot.

Schmitz-Berning, C. (2000), *Vokabular des Nationalsozialismus*, Berlin and New York: de Gruyter.

Schneider, T. F. and H. Wagener (eds) (2007), *'Huns' vs. 'Corned beef': Representations of the other in American and German Literature and Film on World War I*, Göttingen: V&R unipress.

Schoenfeldt, M. (1997), 'Fables of the belly in early modern Europe', in D. Hillmann and C. Mazzio (eds), *The Body in Parts: Fantasies of Corporeality in Early Modern Europe*, 243–62, London and New York: Routledge.

Schwartz, P. and J. A. Ogilvy (1998), 'Plotting your scenarios', in L. Fahey and R. Randall (eds), *Learning from the Future,* 57–80, New York: Wiley.

Schwarz-Friesel, M. and J. -H. Kromminga (eds) (2014), *Metaphern der Gewalt. Konzeptualisierungen von Terrorismus in den Medien vor und nach 9/11*, Tübingen: Francke.

Scollon, R., S. Wong Scollon and R. H. Jones (2012), *Intercultural Communication: A Discourse Approach*, Oxford: Blackwell.

Scully, R. (2014), 'Europe and the European Union', in J. Fisher, D. Denver and J. Benyon (eds), *Central Debates in British Politics*, 119–34, London: Routledge.

Semino, E. (2008), *Metaphor in Discourse*, Cambridge: Cambridge University Press.

Serres, M. (2007), *The Parasite (Posthumanities)*, Minneapolis, MN: University of Minnesota Press.

Shachar, H. (2014), 'The Holocaust is not your metaphor to use in modern political debates', *The Guardian,* 27 January 2014.

Shakespeare, W. (1976), *Coriolanus*, edited by P. Brockbank, London: Methuen.

Shida, Z. (2002), *China and the US: A Unique Relationship,* http://www.china.org.cn/english/2002/Mar/29138.htm (accessed 18 May 2015).

Shogimen, T. (2008), 'Treating the body politic: The medical metaphor of political rule in late medieval Europe and Tokugawa Japan', *The Review of Politics*, 70: 77–104.

Shorter Oxford English Dictionary (2002), edited by W. R. Trumble and A. Stevenson, Oxford: Oxford University Press.

Shrimsley, R. (2014), 'David Cameron opts out to keep Britain at heart of Europe', *Financial Times,* 30 October 2014, http://www.ft.com/cms/s/0/89088d16-5e9f-11e4-b81d-00144feabdc0.html (accessed 17 June 2015).

Silberstein, S. (2002), *War of Words. Language, Politics and 9/11*, London and New York: Routledge.

Sieyès, E. (1989), *Qu'est-ce que le Tiers État? Précédé de L'Essai sur les Privilèges*, edited by E. Champion, Paris: Quadrige/Presses Universitaires de France.

Simons, M. (2015), 'What's with all the war metaphors? We have wars when politics fails', *The Guardian,* 16 February 2015.

Sinding, M. (2015), 'Governing spirits. Body politic scenarios and schemas in the French revolution debate', in M. Hanne, W. D. Crano and J. S. Mio (eds), *Warring With Words. Narrative and Metaphor in Politics*, 78–102, New York and London: Psychology Press.

Skinner, Q. (1978), *The Foundations of Modern Political Thought*, 2 vols, Cambridge: Cambridge University Press.

Sontag, S. (1978), *Illness as Metaphor*, New York: Vintage Books.

Sösemann, B. (1976), 'Die sog. Hunnenrede Kaiser Wilhelms II. Textkritische und interpretatorische Bemerkungen zur Ansprache des Kaisers in Bremerhaven vom 27 Juli 1900', *Historische Zeitschrift*, 222: 342–58.

Sperber, D. (1996), *Explaining Culture. A Naturalistic Approach*, Oxford: Blackwell.

Sperber, D. (2000), 'An objection to the memetic approach to culture', in R. Aunger (ed.), *Darwinizing Culture. The Status of Memetics as a Science*, 163–73, Oxford: Oxford University Press.

Sperber, D. and D. Wilson (1995), *Relevance: Communication and Cognition*, Oxford: Blackwell.

Sperber, D. and D. Wilson (2008), 'A deflationary account of metaphors', in R. W. Gibbs (ed.), *The Cambridge Handbook of Metaphor and Thought*, 84–104, Cambridge: Cambridge University Press.

Spurgeon, C. F. E. (1993), *Shakespeare's Imagery and what it Tells us*, Cambridge: Cambridge University Press.

Starr, H. and S. Dubinsky (2015), *The Israeli Conflict System. Analytic Approaches*, London and New York: Routledge.

State of Palestine – Ministry of Information (2009), *Years on: al-Nakba*, http://www.minfo.ps/English/index.php?pagess=main&id=224&butt=5 (accessed 28 January 2015).

Steen, G. (2007), *Finding Metaphor in Grammar and Usage*, Amsterdam and Philadelphia: Benjamins.

Steen, G. (2008), 'The paradox of metaphor: Why we need a three-dimensional model of metaphor', *Metaphor and Symbol*, 23 (4): 213–41.

Steen, G. (2011), 'What does "really deliberate" really mean? More thoughts on metaphor and consciousness and action', *Metaphor and the Social World*, 1 (1): 53–6.

Steen, G., E. Biernacka, A. G. Dorst, A. A. Kaal, I. López-Rodríguez and T. Pasma (2010), 'Pragglejaz in practice. Finding metaphorically used words in natural discourse', in G. Low, Z. Todd, A. Deignan and L. Cameron (eds), *Researching and Applying Metaphor in the Real World*, 165–84, Amsterdam and Philadelphia: Benjamins.

Stern, J. (2000), *Metaphor in Context*, Cambridge, MA: MIT Press.

Tagliamonte, S. A. (2012), *Variationist Sociolinguistics. Change, Observation, Interpretation*, Oxford: Wiley-Blackwell.

Tassinari, F. (2006), *Variable Geometries: Mapping Ideas, Institutions and Power in the Wider Europe*, Brussels: Centre for European Policy Studies.

Taylor, J. R. (1995), *Linguistic Categorization*, Oxford: Oxford University Press.

Taylor, P. M. (2003), *Munitions of the Mind. A History of Propaganda from the Ancient World to the Present Day*, Manchester: Manchester University Press.

Tegel, S. (2007), *Nazis and the Cinema*, London: Continuum.

Temkin, O. (1973), *Galenism: Rise and Decline of a Medical Philosophy*, Ithaca, NY: Cornell University Press.

Tendahl, M. (2009), *A Hybrid Theory of Metaphor: Relevance Theory and Cognitive Linguistics*, Basingstoke: Palgrave Macmillan.

Tendahl, M. and R. W. Gibbs (2008), 'Complementary perspectives on metaphor: Cognitive linguistic and relevance theory', *Journal of Pragmatics*, 40 (I): 1823–64.

Thacker, T. (2014), *British Culture and the First World War: Experience, Represen-tation and Memory*, London: Bloomsbury.

Tipler, C. and J. B. Ruscher (2014), 'Agency's role in Dehumanization: Non-human metaphors of out-groups', *Social and Personality Psychology Compass*, 8 (5): 214–28.

Trim, R. (2011a), *Metaphor and the Historical Evolution of Historical Mapping*, Basingstoke: Palgrave Macmillan.

Trim, R. (2011b), 'Conceptual networking theory in metaphor evolution: Diachronic variation in models of love', in M. E. Winters, H. Tissari and K. Allan (eds), *Historical Cognitive Linguistics*, 223–60, Berlin and New York: De Gruyter Mouton.

Trudgill, P. (2011), *Sociolinguistic Typology: Social Determinants of Linguistic Complexity*, Oxford: Oxford University Press.

Turner, M. (1990), 'Aspects of the invariance hypothesis', *Cognitive Linguistics*, 1: 247–55.

Turner, M. and G. Fauconnier (2003), 'Metaphor, metonymy, and binding', in R. Dirven and R. Pörings (eds), *Metaphor and Metonymy in Comparison and Contrast*, 469–87, Berlin and New York: De Gruyter.

Twardzisz, P. (2013), *The Language of Interstate Relations: In Search of Personification*, Basingstoke: Palgrave Macmillan.

United Nations (UN) General Assembly (2015), http://www.un.org/en/ga/ (accessed 15 January 2015).

van der Heijden, K. (2005), *Scenarios: The Art of Strategic Conversation*, 2nd edn, New York: Wiley.

van Dijk, T. (1998), *Ideology: A Multidisciplinary Approach*, London: Sage.

van Dijk, T. (2008), *Discourse and Context. A Sociocognitive Approach*, Cambridge: Cambridge University Press.

van Dijk, T. (2014), 'Discourse-cognition-society: Current state and prospects of the socio-cognitive approach to discourse', in C. Hart and P. Cap (eds), *Contemporary Critical Discourse Studies*, 121–47, London: Bloomsbury.

Vande Winkel, R. and D. Welch (eds) (2007), *Cinema and the Swastika. The Inter-national Expansion of Third Reich Cinema*, Basingstoke: Palgrave Macmillan.

Vandenberghe, J., P. Goethals and G. Jacobs (2014), '"Economic conquistadors conquer new worlds": Metaphor scenarios in English-language newspaper headlines on Spanish foreign direct investment', in A. Musolff, F. MacArthur and G. Pagani (eds), *Metaphor and Intercultural Communication*, 167–83, London: Bloomsbury.

Wales Online (2010), South Wales man called Jews parasites, *Walesonline*, 9 June 2010, http://www.walesonline.co.uk/news/wales-news/2010/06/09/south-wales-man-called-jews-parasites-91466-26622717 (accessed 31 December 2010).

Wang, C. and A. Dowker (2010), 'A cross-cultural study of metaphoric understand-ing', in G. Low, Z. Todd, A. Deignan and L. Cameron (eds), *Researching and Applying Metaphor in the Real World*, 105–22, Amsterdam and Philadelphia: Benjamins.

Watts, M. T. (2009), *Reading the Landscape of Europe*, Rochester, NY: Nature Study Guild Publishers.

Watts, R. J., S. Ide and K. Ehlich (eds) (2005a), *Politeness in Language. Studies in its History, Theory and Practice*, Berlin and New York: de Gruyter.

Watts, R. J., S. Ide and K. Ehlich (2005b), 'Introduction', in R. J. Watts, S. Ide and
K. Ehlich (eds), *Politeness in Language. Studies in its History, Theory and Practice*, 1–17, Berlin and New York: de Gruyter.

Watzlawick, P., J. H. Beavin and D. D. Jackson (1967), *Pragmatics of Human
Communication: A Study of Interactional Patterns, Pathologies, and
Paradoxes*, New York: Norton.

Welch, D. (2007), *Propaganda and the German Cinema 1933-1945*, London and
New York: I. B. Tauris.

Wengeler, M. (2005), 'Von den kaiserlichen ‚Hunnen' bis zu Schröders ‚unein-
geschränkter Solidarität'. Argumentative und lexikalische Kontinuitäten in
deutschen "Kriegsbotschaften" seit 1900', in D. Busse, T. Niehr and
M. Wengeler (eds), *Brisante Semantik, Neuere Konzepte und Forschungsergeb-
nisse einer kulturwissenschaftlichen Linguistik*, 209–32, Tübingen: Niemeyer.

Who ate all the goals? (2012), *Tabloid coverage of Euro '96*, http://www.
whoateallthegoals.com/2012/06/coverage-in-sun-and-daily-mirror-during.html
(accessed 9 July 2014).

Wierzbicka, A. (1986), 'Metaphors linguists live by: Lakoff and Johnson contra
Aristotle', *Papers in Linguistics*, 19 (2): 287–313.

Wilks, M. (1963), *The Problem of Sovereignty in the Later Middle Ages*,
Cambridge: Cambridge University Press.

Wilson, Deirdre (2000), 'Metarepresentation in linguistic communication', in
D. Sperber (ed.), *Metaprepresentations: A Multidisciplinary Perspective*,
411–48, Oxford: Oxford University Press.

Wilson, D. (2011), 'Parallels and Differences in the treatment of metaphor in
relevance theory and cognitive linguistics', *Intercultural Pragmatics*, 8 (2):
177–96.

Wilson, D. and R. Carston (2006), 'Metaphor, relevance and the "emergent
property" issue', *Mind & Language*, 21: 404–33.

Wilson, D. and D. Sperber (1992), 'On verbal irony', *Lingua*, 87: 53–76.

Wilson, D. and D. Sperber (eds) (2012), 'Explaining irony', in *Meaning and
Relevance*, 123–45, Cambridge: Cambridge University Press.

Wilson, T. (1979), 'Lord Bryce's investigation into alleged German atrocities in
Belgium, 1914-15', *Journal of Contemporary History*, 14 (3): 369–83.

Winters, M. E. (2011), 'Introduction: On the emergence of diachronic cognitive
linguistics', in M. E. Winters, H. Tissari and K. Allan (eds), *Historical Cognitive
Linguistics*, 3–30, Berlin and New York: De Gruyter Mouton.

Wodak, R. (2001a), 'What CDA is about – a summary of its history, important
concepts and its developments', in R. Wodak and M. Meyer (eds), *Methods of
Critical Discourse Analysis*, 1–14, London: Sage.

Wodak, R. (2001b), 'The discourse-historical approach', in R. Wodak and M.
Meyer (eds), *Methods of Critical Discourse Analysis*, 63–94, London: Sage.

Wodak, R. (2005), 'Discourse analysis (Foucault)', in D. Herman, M. Jahn and
M. -L. Ryan (eds), *Routledge Encyclopaedia of Narrative Theory*, 112–14,
London: Routledge.

Wodak, R. (2007), 'Critical discourse analysis', in C. Seale, G. Gobo, J. F. Gubrium
and D. Silverman (eds), *Qualitative Research Practice*, 185–201, London: Sage.

Wodak, R. (2013), '"Calculated Ambivalence" and Holocaust Denial in Austria', in
R. Wodak and J. E. Richardson (eds), *Analysing Fascist Discourse. European
Fascism in Talk and Text*, 73–96, London and New York: Routledge.

Wodak, R. and P. Chilton (eds) (2005), *A New Agenda in (Critical) Discourse Analysis. Theory, Methodology and Interdisciplinarity*, Amsterdam and Philadelphia: Benjamins.

Wraight, C. D. (2008), *Rousseau's The Social Contract: A Reader's Guide*, London: Continuum.

Wulf, J. (1966), *Theater und Film im Dritten Reich*, Frankfurt am Main, Vienna and Berlin: Ullstein.

Yu, N. (1998), *The Contemporary Theory of Metaphor: A Perspective from Chinese*, Amsterdam and Philadelphia: John Benjamins.

Yu, N. (2003), 'Metaphor, body and culture: The Chinese understanding of gall-bladder and courage', *Metaphor and Symbol*, 18: 13–31.

Yu, N. (2008), 'Metaphor from body and culture', in R. W. Gibbs (ed), *The Cambridge Handbook of Metaphor and Thought*, 247–61, Cambridge: Cambridge University Press.

Zimmer, C. (2011), *Parasite Rex: Inside the Bizarre World of Nature's Most Dangerous Creatures*, New York: Simon & Schuster.

Zinken, J. (2007), 'Discourse metaphors: The link between figurative language and habitual analogies', *Cognitive Linguistics*, 18 (3): 443–64.

Zinken, J., I. Hellsten and B. Nerlich (2008), 'Discourse metaphors', in R. M. Frank, R. Dirven, T. Ziemke and E. Bernárdez (eds), *Body, Language and Mind. Vol. 2: Sociocultural Situatedness*, 363–85, Berlin and New York: Mouton de Gruyter.

Zuckerman, L. (2004), *The Rape of Belgium. The Untold Story of World War I*, New York: New York University Press.

Zurek, M. B. and T. Henrichs (2007), 'Linking scenarios across scales in international environmental scenarios', *Technological Forecasting and Social Change*, 74: 1282–95.

Index